Letters to
POPE FRANCIS

Letters to POPE FRANCIS

The Pope Who Came
from the Ends of the Earth

Rodolfo deG. Ibañez, PhD, MD (hc-MMS)

LETTERS TO POPE FRANCIS
The Pope Who Came from the Ends of the Earth

Rodolfo deG. Ibañez, PhD, MD (hc-MMS)

Published in 2015 by

ST PAULS
7708 St. Paul Road, San Antonio Village
1203 Makati City, Philippines
Tel. (632) 8959701 to 04 • (632) 8966771
Fax. (632) 8907131
Website: www.stpauls.ph
E-mail for orders: wholesale@stpauls.ph

ISBN 978-971-004-234-0
Light Readings and Inspirationals

Printing Information:
Current Printing: first digit

1	2	3	4	5	6	7	8	9	10

Year of current printing: first year shown

2015	2016	2017	2018	2019	2020

ST PAULS is an apostolate of the priests and brothers of the **SOCIETY OF ST. PAUL**
who proclaim the Gospel through the media of social communication.

DEDICATION

Fr. Joseph Cremades
Minister of God, Servant of Man

TABLE OF CONTENTS

MESSAGE

For several years now, I have been blessed with the grace of accompanying pilgrimages to the Holy Land and to the shrines of our Blessed Mother Mary and saints in Europe. I never cease to be inspired and awed by the realization that every pilgrimage seems to be a new experience. We would visit the same places, read the pertinent scriptural passage and I would give the same commentary and reflection. And yet at the end of the pilgrimage I would invariably see something new in that one particular pilgrimage. Many a pilgrim would thank me, saying he has learned much during the pilgrimage. And I reply "I also thank you. You may not have realized that I also have learned much from you." From their prayers and sharing about their life's religious experience, the times and the ways that they have felt God's presence were grace-filled moments for new and deeper spiritual insights for me. It reminds me of our Lord praying "I give you praise, Father, Lord of heaven and earth, for although you have hidden these things from the wise and the learned you have revealed them to the childlike" (Lk 10:21).

Kuya Rudy is one of those pilgrims who have opened new horizons for me. I appreciate his skill in juxtaposing vignettes of our human existence with the Gospel stories of our Lord's life and teachings. Moreover, Kuya Rudy has the gift of finding for a story he narrates an appropriate authoritative resource from philosophy or apologetics or Mariology or theology or history—even humor!

Congratulations and thanks for this wonderful pilgrim companion. My prayers and blessings.

+Raul Q. Martirez, DD
Christ the King Church

AUTHOR'S NOTES

Even before we started on our pilgrimage, the idea that I should write about the experience, however that turned out, insinuated itself. I indulged the thought, allowing it to tantalize me with the promise of the challenge and, ultimately, the joy and fulfillment that come at the end of every chase. Already I imagined what it would demand of me: copious notes, research, interviews, conceptualizing, and planning the angle of approach—the whole *enchilada*. In other words—hard work and long hours—and lots of it. And, of course, the sheer pleasure of doing it and the deep satisfaction when it is done.

Initially, my intention was simply to share any meaningful event that might present itself any time during the religious journey, or even sketches of the more interesting members of the "Marian Pilgrims of Bishop Raul Martinez," as we felicitously called ourselves. We were, after all, visiting the very sites of Mama Mary's apparitions; some very remarkable things were bound to happen.

Before we left on the pilgrimage, I had an intimate talk with Fr. Joe, my spiritual advisor, on the possible effects on a person who visits the apparition sites of the Blessed Virgin Mary. He said, "Rudy, the unfavorable press heaped upon the Church has caused some followers to move to other Christian congregations, or reject any form of organized religion, or worse, question the existence of God.

"A personal spiritual encounter, which may include private revelation, is sometimes the best way to fortify oneself from the insidiousness of the attacks on the Church of Jesus Christ. The faithful who maintain an intimate relationship with the Lord are his Church. There seems to be a misconception that the doors, the windows, the pews, even the steeple on the roof, are the Church.

"Rudy, you and I are the Church of Christ. We have a Magisterium under the leadership of the Pope to guide our teachings.

Errors committed by the clergy in the interpretation of Church teachings are put aright by the Magisterium.

"It is unbelievable, Rudy—the number of people who have been set on the road to a more intense relationship with Jesus Christ through the Blessed Mother," Fr. Joe concluded.

I carried his words with me with guarded expectation of anything out of the ordinary.

A more awe-inspiring sight cannot be seen than the thousands upon thousands of people who gathered to receive the blessing of the Bishop of Rome, Pope Francis. It was not rare to hear from those who had been in the self-same place during the watch of other popes that…"there was never this large a multitude." The magnetism of Pope Francis was incredible as it was palpable. My son Jun blurted, "Dad, as Pope Francis passed, he looked directly at me. He smiled and he waved." I heard the same comment from the other pilgrims. Yes, the new pope did make you feel that in the anonymity of that humongous throng, the running dialogue was only between him and you.

We felt his love that day. And that day we fell in love with him.

High expectations are in the air with Pope Francis. Everyone is waiting to see how his papacy will be defined. If his initial action of embracing the poverty of St. Francis is any portent, the winds of change that will bring the people closer to the Church are here.

As our pilgrimage moved along, we discovered many things we never knew before, both positive and not so positive. All of Mama Mary's apparition sites teemed with thousands of pilgrims. But sadly, we saw the truth of the frequently repeated statement that the Church of Jesus Christ in Europe is dying. A perceptive lady in our group candidly remarked, "Churches here are museum for old people and holy saints." How true, especially the museum part.

For weeks, I relived our experiences in my mind, the good memories clashing with the not-so-good. What my dear friend John said kept interrupting my thoughts: *"Rudy, I no longer believe in any form of organized religion."*

A few months back we talked about his disappointments with the seeming ineptness of most priests assigned in his parish. He regrets that the so-called leaders in his parish have allowed God's wonderful Church to be irrelevant, humdrum, uninspiring. Worst—unspiritual, truly an antithesis of the Christian proclamation. John feels that the almost one hour spent hearing this kind of Mass did not help him with his very much anticipated connection with the living God. My departure on the pilgrimage put our lively discussion on hold, although I promised that I would get back to him upon my return.

An idea began to take shape in my head on how to intertwine John's disillusionment with our Marian experience on the pages of this book, taking care that everything is finally balanced with Christ's teaching. John's love for the Lord has never once faltered despite the emptiness that he finds in the homilies of the priests in his parish and his being witness to certain clerical practices which do not sit well with him.

I was excited. Thereafter my sleep became fitful. One night I had a dream: I am playing chess. Patterns and lines are converging on the chess table. I see the knights leaping, the pawns moving in formation, the bishops kneeling and praying as the white queen confronts the black king whose castles begin to crumble. All the black pieces are coming to the defense of their king. But the inevitable is here—the white Queen will mate in two… I woke up.

I make it a habit to open *Zenith.org* which brings readers up to speed with what is happening with the Pope. The news greeted me with an announcement of Pope Francis' "First Apostolic Exhortation, *Evangelii Gaudium* or Joy of the Gospel." Indeed, the inevitable is here. The Lord has sent us the answer. It is the bishop which the queen set up to mate the prince of darkness.

I felt the gentle push of the Holy Spirit. Actually, it was a shove.

As the letters unfurled in succession, I saw our book take a life of its own. One inescapable truth emerged: a new enemy confronts the Church. After Pope John Paul II consecrated Russia to the Immaculate Heart of Mama Mary, communism is history. The new enemy is secularism.

Secularism is indiscriminate in its attack. All religions, Christian, Jew, Buddhist, Taoist, Islam—any form of belief in one Supreme Being is fair game because secularism exorcises the holiness in people.

Secularism teaches that there is no heaven or hell, that people should live only in the present. It destroys the sanctity of marriage where the most vulnerable are the young.

In the pages of this book, it is the author's fondest hope that you will discern and feel—beyond the human experience of joy and laughter, sadness and pain—the soothing presence of *Kuya* Hesus through the intercession of Mama Mary.

In the words of St. Louis de Montfort, "She (Mama Mary) is an echo of God, speaking and repeating only God. If you say, 'Mary,' she says, 'God.' "

RODOLFO DEG. IBAÑEZ
March 16, 2014

$\mathcal{P}$REFACE

Letters to Pope Francis: A Review

I started the journey with Tito Rudy's book in September when I had just been through a personal loss of great magnitude. My father passed away in July of this year and in the months after his passing, I had become deeply unsettled, fearful, and angry.

I have to admit that any excitement I have had about being part of this book's journey was dampened by my personal doubts and fears. Even as I was afraid to disappoint Tito Rudy, who is the father of a very dear and longtime high school friend and *kumpare*, I could not summon the joy of words I used to have. Then, I had neither optimism nor hope with which to draw my inspirations; I was all grief.

But I have always tried to listen hard to the messages the Universe sends me and in the days that followed, I joined Tito Rudy vicariously on a virtual pilgrimage. As he wrote of his time in the baths of Lourdes, as he beheld the transfigured host in Luciano, as I listened to him speak of faith over and over to his friend John, I began to heal from inside out.

I write this from the perspective of one whose faith has been tested throughout most of her life. I know only too well the experience of a sleeping Catholic. If I write of disenfranchisement and disenchantment, it is because I know of it firsthand. As a parent of a young man with profound autism, I can honestly say that worship in the Catholic Church has not been the most welcoming of all our experiences. And yet, even as my family and I have often felt alienated from the Catholic institution and its community, our faith in God and our love for his Church—both individual and as a family—have never been stronger.

It's difficult to confess this "shame" to the whole world, to bare one's soul without fear of judgment or condemnation. I feel compelled, however, to declare this, if only to set the background from which I was coming from that day in September, the first time I read this book.

I sat down to reading this book by chapters in the order with which Tito Rudy had organized his thoughts. It was mechanical reading in the beginning, truth to tell, and it took a grudgingly long time to rid my mind of rut and dullness. I felt disappointed in myself, like I was purposely failing to grasp something important and that I needed to know.

The next time I set myself to reading, I sat down, closed my eyes, and in a whispered prayer, asked for divine guidance. I had all these questions that I wanted to ask, too, and like his friend John, I was wallowing in a quagmire of doubt and fear. I wanted to feel a deeper, more sincere connection with Tito Rudy's words. And as prayer drained my mind of all its disorganized, frenetic, angry energy, I began to understand that even as he writes to Pope Francis, he was writing to each of us—to me—as well.

Tito Rudy's book is not meant for light reading, though it is peppered with jovial humor and compelling anecdotes. He is a fascinating storyteller, weaving memories into absorbing narratives. You will find snippets of his life's journey liberally sprinkled here and there: the doting son to his *Nanay*, husband and equal partner to his wife, the father to his four children, and grandfather to their children. He allows us a virtual ride on the pilgrimage of faith he took with his family in 2013 and uses this as a jumping point for the questions he asks. As in his previous books, there are references to golf, clearly his favorite game, and takes it to task as a most useful analogy for life's challenges.

Beyond the personal, there are also passages on Church history and discussions of religious concepts which should challenge most readers but for its honest attempt to lay things in black and white. There are insightful commentaries on organized religion, its failings and successes, as well as its relevance in modern day life. All these will resonate with the common man and woman, as we strive to perfect our soul and our worship of God. As such, *Letters to Pope Francis* is meant for poring over, for a slow and deep perusal of one's faith and belief in relation to the world around us.

I started this journey angry and afraid, unable to come to terms with my father's passing. I grieved for my loss and this grief spilled into my life as a darkness that blotted any joy and hope. In page after page, however, I was embraced by the Lord's mercy and reassured constantly of his love. I felt the faithfulness God has promised of us.

Somewhere in those pages, too, in the words Tito Rudy used, I began to hear the voice of my father. My father was never a religious man. He was a man of this world—bigger than life, bold, successful in his own right, the very picture of a self-made man. Not even seven strokes and a ruptured aortic aneurysm could put him down; he always came out rebounding. In the last years of his life, before dementia chipped slowly and cruelly at his mind, he made his peace with God and all the enmities life had thrown at him. Here he was, in these pages, too, reminding me that Life can only be cherished more beautifully and more joyfully with God, that even in moments of deepest sorrow and affliction, Christ suffers with us and for us. It is this that gives me a sense of healing, after being wounded all these months.

Letters to Pope Francis must be read with an open heart, when we are ready to cast out our isolation and find a sense of belonging, and when we believe with conviction that the Church Jesus Christ founded on earth transcends our human weaknesses and shortcomings. It does not pretend to hold all the answers to our questions, but points us in the direction of faith in the quest for truth and justice.

"Consider it all joy, my brothers, when you encounter various trials, for you know that the testing of your faith produces perseverance. And let perseverance be perfect, so that you may be perfect and complete, lacking in nothing" (Jas 1:2-4).

It is a journey certainly worth taking.

JENNIFER ONG-CUAYCONG
October 15, 2014

Acknowledgment

Fr. Joe, my spiritual advisor, planted the seed of this book in my head when my family was about to leave for a Marian pilgrimage in celebration of our 50th wedding anniversary.

A tiny green leaf sprouted after I literally came to face Pope Francis. In the words of my son Jun, who wheeled me just a few feet from Pope Francis' canopy, "Dad, Pope Francis and I had eye contact and he waved at me. Feeling *ko, parang ako lang ang tinitingnan niya!* It's like he only had eyes for me!"

But the leaf had to be nurtured. It's like reading a mystery fiction. We are spellbound by the plot and couldn't wait to turn the page and find the answer to the question, "Who killed the Butler?"

How do you do that in a true-to-life story centered on the teaching of Jesus Christ? And so, I can only expressed my greatest joy when my friend, **Ruben Evangelista Reyes**, agreed to help write the book. I tell you, without him this book would not come to life. Thank you, Ben, I owe you one, again!

Yet, no matter how good the author is, he is bound to fail. My friend, **Long Perez,** from Unilab days, assured us, I will not. You will feel his touch in the pages of the book with his meticulous editing. I remember many times he came to me to say, "Rudy, do you really want to add this paragraph?" Thank you, Long, the second time around!

I met Pinky Cuaycong when I requested her to review this book. Pinky is the best friend of my son Jun and his wife Ondine. They said, "She is the best there is."

Let me lift a few lines: "My father was never a religious man. He was a man of this world-bigger than life, bold, successful in his own right, the very picture of a self-made man. Not even seven strokes and a ruptured aortic aneurysm could put him down; he always came out rebounding. In the last years of his life, before dementia chipped slowly and cruelly at his mind, he made his peace with God and all the enmities life had thrown at him. Here he was, in these pages, too, reminding me that life can only be cherished more beautifully and more joyfully with God, that even in moments of deepest sorrow and affliction, Christ suffers with us and for us. It is this that gives me a sense of healing, after being wounded all these months."

I told her, "Wow! The way you personalize the review, made the book even more authentic."

"*Salamat* Pinky, *sa uulitin.*"

What more can I say? "Mom, Clark Gable *na tayo,* the end *na*!"

Beginnings

Dear Pope Francis,

My name is Rudy. I recently completed the assignment which my diocese gave me as one of the extraordinary ministers of Holy Communion of the Church. To touch Christ's Body repeatedly was a reward I never deserved. My services to the Church do not by any means end here. You can be sure that I shall serve the Church in other ways.

A palpable aura of kindness and humility permeates the first actions of your papacy as you gently endeavor to change some of the hoary traditions of our faith to bring back into focus the fact that when Jesus Christ commanded Peter to build his Church, he wanted it to be a Church for the poor. Jesus had not meant to isolate the nobles and the rich from him but rather to emphasize that the poor, such as they are, are more in need of help and special care from the Church.

Some may misinterpret your love for the poor but the least kindness you can show them is greater than the greatest wrong you may do because you see in all its clarity—and pain—how the poor have never had the opportunity to partake of even the tiniest morsels that the rich and the nobles take for granted. Truly, kindness is one of the greatest gifts God gave us from the cross!

The Gospel is not lacking in parables expressing Jesus' preference for the poor. Could it be that the real lesson being preached is about *envy?* The pride and vanity that may well reign in the hearts of men clothed in richness and power can easily drive them to demand the same love that God professes for the poor. But the inflated egos of the privileged are just as easily pricked by the teaching of St. Paul the Apostle: *love is not envious*; and the exhortations of St. Augustine to avoid envy at

"Let us protect with love all that God has given us!"
Pope Francis' homily on the day of the inauguration of his Petrine ministry
March 2013

Photograph courtesy of
Catholic Church England and Wales
http://www.flickr.com/photos/catholicism/8561060993/

all cost, for in his words, *it is a monstrous vice*. Truly, God really is the perfect teacher, though he teaches in mysterious ways.

As you continue to read my letter, you will discern its purpose which at this point I shall leave unspecified.

Pope Francis, I borrowed from Wikipedia details of your teachings and battles to better the world with the hope that more people will welcome the phenomenon you are creating. In a very short period of time, you have changed the lackluster attitude of the dwindling number of Christ followers, who seemingly have forgotten his ultimate sacrifice to give the people the chance to once again be part of his kingdom. An upsurge in Mass attendance—including of lapsed Catholics—has not gone unnoticed. I know of no way I can make your sojourn on earth any more interesting than it already is but if through my letter I can attract a handful more to a critical appreciation of what you have set out to do, then I have done my bit.

Pope Francis, the People's Pope

I write this letter shortly after my family returned from a trip to Lanciano, Italy, where the miracle of the Eucharist happened on the 700th year of our Lord. I borrowed the narration of events from Google but focus only on the highlights to better comprehend the story.

The story goes that there was a priest plagued by a doubt as to whether the consecrated host was truly the Body of Christ, and the consecrated wine truly his Blood. He had difficulty believing in the mystery of the transubstantiation: the miraculous changing of the bread and wine into the Body and Blood of Christ.

One morning, as he was celebrating Mass, doubts and errors weighed upon him more heavily than ever. By a most singular and marvelous grace, he saw the bread changed into flesh and the wine into blood. Frightened and confused by such a great and stupendous miracle, he stood quite a while as if in a divine ecstasy; but eventually, his fear gave way to the spiritual happiness that filled his soul, and he turned his joyful yet tearful face to those around him, exclaiming, "… Behold the flesh and the blood of our Most Beloved Christ."

At those words, the bystanders ran to the altar and began, with tears, to cry for mercy. The faithful, who, having become witnesses themselves, spread the news throughout the entire city.

Pope Francis, we saw the host and the blood of Christ in Lanciano. Bishop Raul, the spiritual leader of our pilgrimage, presided the Mass for us. I felt a bit sad because as the Mass was being celebrated, tourists where moving up the altar looking at the host and the blood of Christ. They did not mind or cared less that Mass was ongoing right at the second tier of the altar.

I heard so much about the dwindling church attendance in Masses all over Europe. It doesn't take a theology professor to theorize why the Church is failing in this generation. My friend John and I usually would have lively discussions about what is going on. To be more precise, he said that the question to be asked should be, "Why is church attendance dwindling?"

Indeed, I found it intriguing but perhaps not surprising that we did not have any problem finding parking space in most of the churches we visited than in shopping malls. When we took a break and the bishop allowed us time to shop, we had to walk quite a way because parking spaces were not available near shopping malls, especially for tour buses. It was obvious: a clear sign that people with the means and leisure time find the malls more inviting. And to top it, most churches we visited had only old people in attendance other than tourists who were there to gawk at old paintings and statues preserved through the centuries.

One time, John related to me the story of the 20-peso (PHP20) and the 1,000-peso (PHP1,000) bills. Peso is the currency we use in our country.

> PHP20 and PHP1,000 met in a bank cashier's box. "Hi," greeted the P1,000 upon seeing P20. "My, you look worn out and crumpled." Very proudly, he boasted, "Look at me still crisp in my almost mint condition."
>
> Forlornly, PHP20 agreed. "*Oo nga*, you're right. Most probably I am bored from having been in practically the same places."
>
> PHP1,000 replied, "You should visit places where I have been to. I am a regular visitor at Rustan's, Marks and Spencer, Lacoste, Burberry, and similar upscale and exclusive outlets. What about you?"
>
> The photo on the PHP20 appeared to shift his gaze downwards glumly, answered quite tentatively, "I was able to find myself on different occasions in the collection boxes of the Santa Cruz Church, the Quiapo Church, Lourdes Church, the Sacred Heart Church, and other suburban churches. But never in the posh places that you visited!"

Pope Francis, today twelve centuries after the miraculous occurrence in Lanciano, the Body and Blood of Christ remain intact, a sustained miracle! Upon superficial examination, the Host of Flesh, which is still in one piece and has retained the dimensions of the original "large host," has a fibrous appearance and a brown color, which becomes light-reddish if a light is placed in the back of the Ostensorium. The blood, contained in the chalice, has an earth color, inclined toward the yellow of ocher, and consists of five coagulated globules. Each of the parts is uneven in shape and size, and when weighed together, the total weight is equal to that of each piece.

The Lanciano miracle appears to be the same phenomenon you are creating. In a very short period of time, you've changed the lackluster attitude of Jesus Christ's dwindling followers, who have forgotten his ultimate sacrifice to give his people the chance to once again be part of his kingdom, into an upsurge in Mass attendance, including lapsed Catholics. Hopefully, the interest they find in this particular sketch of your travels will give them the motivation to continue reading the letter I am writing you...

I will move to the time when you were subject of allegations regarding the kidnapping of two Jesuit priests (Yorio and Jalics) during Argentina's "Dirty War." A human rights lawyer filed a criminal complaint accusing you of involvement in the kidnapping of the two priests. Nothing was specific in the charges so the lawsuit was dismissed. Yorio said in an interview that you did nothing to free them, in fact just the opposite.

But the other priest Fr. Jalics, upon your election as Pope, issued a statement confirming the kidnapping and attributing the cause to a former lay colleague who became a guerrilla, was captured, and named Yorio and him (Jalics) when interrogated. The following week, Jalics issued a second, clarifying statement: "It is wrong to assert that our capture took place at the initiative of Fr. Bergoglio... the fact is, Orlando Yorio and I were not denounced by Fr. Bergoglio."

In your *Evangelii Gaudium*, one of the guidelines that will define your papacy is interfaith dialogue. You said, "Dialogue is born from an attitude of respect for the other person, from a conviction that the other person has something good to say. It assumes that there is room in the heart for the person's point of view, opinion, and proposal.

To dialogue entails a cordial reception, not a prior condemnation. In order to dialogue, it is necessary to know how to lower the defenses, open the doors of the house, and offer human warmth."

With your statement, leaders of the Islamic community in Buenos Aires welcomed your election as Pope, noting that you "always showed yourself as a friend of the Islamic community, and a person whose position is "pro-dialogue."

As bishop and Pope, you restated the Church's teaching that homosexual practice is intrinsically immoral, but that every homosexual person should be treated with respect and love because temptation is not in and of itself sinful.

Your position is clear on the subject of women. "As far as the ordination of women, the Church has already spoken out and the answer is no. John Paul II made the Church's stance definitive. The door is closed. But let me tell you something, Our Lady was more important than the apostles, bishops, deacons, and priests. Women play a role that's more important than that of bishops or priests. How? This is what we have to explain better publicly."

At a meeting of Latin American bishops in 2007, you said, "We live in the most unequal part of the world, which has grown the most, yet reduced misery the least" and that "the unjust distribution of goods persists, creating a situation of social sin that cries out to heaven and limits the possibilities of a fuller life for so many of our brothers."

We suffer the same economic anomalies. In the Philippines, a mere 10% of the population controls the nation's economy and wealth. Sixty percent (60%) are poor, while the balance constitutes the so-called middle class. We appreciate your decision to bring back the Church to the poor.

Pope Francis, let me regress a bit. In November 2013, the world was shocked when it woke up the next morning and found the provinces of Leyte, Samar, parts of Cebu, Iloilo, and Palawan in the Philippines devastated by super typhoon Yolanda with wind velocity of 325 to 375 km/hr. Meteorologists and weather forecasters were one in saying that this was the strongest typhoon that ever landed anywhere in the world—and it picked the Philippines. The world for the first time came together in unity to bring aid to a hapless people who took the brunt of the typhoon. There were many stories of courage and faith that came out in the world press but all were saying that they had never seen a people show an even stronger faith in the Lord. Those who wanted to create chaos by blaming a sinful people who brought this anger from God were shortly marginalized into silence because of their irrelevance and irreverence.

People say that God works in mysterious ways. Perhaps at no time was this more evident than in the face of the devastation in the Philippines when the world forgot its disagreements and came together with one intention—one nation, one world—to help a suffering people. There is still a long way to go but the resilience of the Filipino people is on the lips of everyone. Our nation knows in heartfelt gratitude that your prayers and exhortations to give aid to our suffering countrymen opened the floodgates of sympathy from the international community, resulting in lives saved and a faster road to recovery. Truly you brought the Church of Jesus Christ to the poor.

In a moment in time the world found peace. We, Filipinos, are grateful to God for choosing us to be the instrument of that peace.

Amidst all the challenges the Philippines and the world are trying to contain, *Time* magazine bestowed on you the highest tribute as **2013 *Time* Person of the Year.**

I will not dwell anymore on the circumstances of your choice; the title they gave you is enough. However, let me comment on a particular paragraph they said about you:

> But what makes this Pope so important is the speed with which he has captured the imaginations of millions who had given up on hoping for the church at all. People weary of the endless parsing of sexual ethics, the buck-passing infighting over lines of authority when all the while (to borrow from Milton), "the hungry sheep look up, and are not fed." In a matter of months, Francis has elevated the healing mission of the church—the church as servant and comforter of hurting people in an often harsh world—above the doctrinal police work so important to

his recent predecessors. St. John Paul II and Benedict XVI were professors of theology. Francis is a former janitor, nightclub bouncer, chemical technician, and literature teacher.

Pope Francis, the statement "St. John Paul II and Benedict XVI were professors of theology. Francis is a former janitor, nightclub bouncer, chemical technician, and literature teacher" is both belittling and uplifting. Jesus Christ could have been born in the arms of royalty but he chose to be born among the sheep, cows, birds and other animals because he wanted to be with the poor and the downtrodden.

As great as your beginnings, your move to greater things continues to surprise the world.

Definitely, your *Evangelii Gaudium* will define your papacy… let's take a glimpse of it.

Evangelii Gaudium

The beginning of your greatness as "the best pope the Church ever had" is written in your *Evangelii Gaudium*. I read it not once but many times over. I cannot help lingering on every word, on every nuance of your first Catholic exhortations by which your papacy shall be defined. Nor could I stop the tears from welling in my eyes; a few times I needed to brush them away because I actually had difficulty reading with my sight blurred. I ask myself, "Why did you come only now?" But I know it is not late, your *Joy of the Gospel* is written with kindness and humility and provokes argument with no one even as it invites everyone to be with us. Different beliefs shall not be a hindrance for us to come together, for we shall accord each other the respect our faiths deserve. Prayerfully, we hope that your timely arrival will start the reversal of the secularism that grips the world.

Pope Francis, I entered the Vatican website and was gifted with a summary of your exhortation. I am not given to too much convoluted thinking; I try to keep my reasoning as straightforward and uncomplicated as possible. In paraphrasing your writing, if you will permit me such an honor, I shall write only in a manner that I feel will bring about an easier understanding of what you, the Pope, has intended. If in any way, I may have misread your meaning, let the more knowledgeable among your followers help others reflect on your words more clearly.

Evangelii Gaudium
Pope Francis 1st Apostolic Exhortation,
November 26, 2013

The Joy of the Gospel is a 2013 exhortation of Pope Francis on "the Church's primary mission of evangelization in the world." It touches on the Christian's obligation to help the poor, and the duty to establish and maintain just economic, political, and legal orders. The Pope says, "The world can no longer trust in the unseen forces and invincible hand of the market." He calls for action beyond a simple welfare mentality that attacks the structural causes of inequality. It is not a news item when an elderly homeless person dies of exposure, but it is news when the stock market loses two points. The Pope is critical of the overcentralization of the Church bureaucracy, poor preaching, and excessive emphasis on doctrine. He exhorts a more pastoral creativity and openness, and a "pastoral conversion in papal ministry."

Pope Francis is concerned in the Church becoming more judgmental than merciful. He wants a Church with the outgoing spirit of the pilgrim, always willing to joyfully bring the gospel to the ends of the earth as opposed to a Church closed in itself, languishing in the dull ennui of institutional inertia as history passes it by. The Pope worries that some Catholics are too attracted to the external form of the faith, while their hearts have grown cold.

Within his treatment of these broader themes are numerous insights:

God's inexhaustible mercy—How good it is to come back to God whenever we are lost. God never tires of forgiving us; we are the ones who get tired of seeking his mercy. The Eucharist, although it is the fullness of sacramental life, is not a prize for the perfect but a powerful medicine and nourishment for the weak.

Genuine religion is incarnate—Genuine forms of popular religiosity are incarnate, since they are born of the incarnation of Christian faith in popular culture. For this reason, they entail a personal relationship, not with vague spiritual energies or powers, but with God, with Christ, with Mary, with the saints.

Faith is always a cross—Pope Francis reminds us that this powerfully echoes Galatians 2:19-20, where St. Paul tells us that he has been crucified with Christ so that now it is Christ who lives in him, and in Colossians 3:3 where he applies this to us: "For you have died, and your life is hidden with Christ in God."

The way of beauty—Every form of catechesis would do well to attend to the *way of beauty*. Proclaiming Christ means showing that to believe and follow him is not only something right and true, but also something beautiful, capable of filling life with new splendor and profound joy, even in the midst of difficulties. Every expression of true beauty can thus be acknowledged as a path leading to the encounter with the Lord Jesus.

The revolution of tenderness—There is emphasis on our divine call to live in community with others… a message sorely needed in a time when so many are drawn on what could be described as the *inactive solitude* of virtual communities. The fact that we have been created in the image of the Trinity—the perfect divine communion—reminds us that we are meant to live with others and that no one is saved alone.

THE JOY OF THE GOSPEL
EVANGELII GAUDIUM

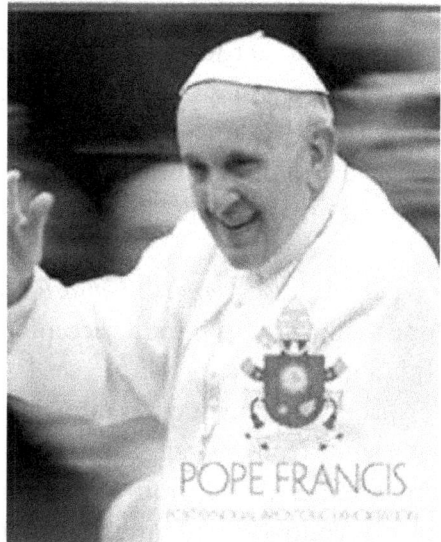

POPE FRANCIS

True faith in the incarnate Son of God is inseparable from self-giving, from membership in the community, from service, from reconciliation with others. The Son of God, by becoming flesh, summoned us to the revolution of tenderness.

Humility before Scripture—Whenever we attempt to discern the meaning of a text, Pope Francis says that we are practicing *reverence to the truth*, which he defines as *humility of heart which recognizes that we are not its masters or owners, but its guardians, heralds, and servants.*

The most vulnerable—the unborn—Among the vulnerable for whom the Church wishes to care with particular love and concern are unborn children, the most defenseless and innocent among us; human beings are ends in themselves and never a means of resolving other problems. Precisely because it involves the internal consistency of our message about the value of the human person, the Church cannot be expected to change her position on this question… This is not subject to alleged reforms or modernizations. It is not progressive to try to resolve problems by eliminating a human life.

The wounds of Christ—Sometimes we are tempted to be that kind of Christian who keeps the Lord's wounds at arm's length. Yet Jesus wants us to touch human misery, to touch the suffering flesh of others. He hopes that we will stop looking for those personal or communal niches which shelter us from the maelstrom of human misfortune and instead enter into the reality of other people's lives and know the power of tenderness.

Doubtless, *Evangelii Gaudium* will change the perspective of love, one that ushers us into the acceptance of who we are, whatever we are. It is a gift of love.

The gift of love comes in many forms. The pure laughter of a child or a smile from a stranger promises the greatness of an unfolding day. An unexpected call from my children abroad or the sudden embrace of my youngest daughter Nikki fills me with strange warmth only a parent can know, as does the sight of older daughter Leah and her mother interacting as only they could and having a magnificent time. Whatever doubt remains that my day would not be full of grace, vanishes. Can it get any better than this? Yet the "Good night, Love" of my wife completes my day and leaves a comforting feeling that our repose would be peaceful—her goodnight farewell is a perfect ending to a good beginning.

And as the night moves in perfect unison with the waning of the moon to meet the dawn, I awake refreshed to murmur, "Good morning, Lord," and pray once more for a perfect day, a day of new beginnings.

I have seen life and helped shaped lives in the last 34 years in a company where I launched my dreams of beginnings; for me, the same beginning is now an ending. Thirty-four years irretrievably gone, like a breeze passing, a song's fading refrain, the sad note of a bugle bidding goodbye to a fallen comrade-in-arms.

It is the cycle of life.

Pope Francis, please allow me to bring you into the fold of my family. The other night, the family celebrated my 76th birthday ("*pa lang*" we love to add, which, loosely translated, means "still young, no big deal"). As in the past, I was the recipient of many nice gifts, although truth to tell, I am not really one who, in that sense, hungers for gifts, least of all, of the expensive type. It is enough to simply enjoy the presence of my children, grandchildren, nephews and nieces, a few friends, and, of course, my wife, all who unfailingly and lovingly share their time to wish me their best for yet another milestone, especially as obviously there are fewer and fewer of them still left for me in this world.

On this particular night, a surging feeling enveloped me, a kind of adrenaline rush that fueled my energy, my wit, and my humor and kept the family tantalized to hear my discourse and response to all the gifts I received.

I have always had the idea that gifts from loved ones are decided upon only after a certain amount of deliberation on the part of the giver. In my particular case as the prospective recipient, I imagine a degree of difficulty in the decision process at arriving at what is proper and fitting for someone who apparently has everything he could wish for: a loving family, a home built in an atmosphere of love, replete with all the practical amenities to take away the drudgery of retirement where everything seems to play out in slow motion, the exact opposite of the fast-paced, energy-driven kind of world he had been accustomed to as a corporate man.

From this perspective, every gift is a treasure.

But the gifts from my grandson Diego and my only granddaughter Martina stood out from the rest; they were different. They were not expensive—in fact did not cost a centavo—nor required any extra effort to acquire; but they were not unlike precious gems and generated in me feelings I had not *known or felt* before.

Diego had written a short story rendered in the enchanting style of an Aesop fable. It was his gift to his grandfather. I read it to my captured audience with all the diction, commentaries, gestures, and humor to bring the story to life. It was a tale with unexpected insights and wisdom I had not expected to come from an 18-year-old. His story made me realize that Diego has matured with a kind of sensitivity rarely found in youngsters his age. I proudly announced to the group, "We have the beginnings of a new multi-award winning writer."

But there was yet a bigger surprise for the evening!

I opened another gift, this one from Martina. It was a framed collage of several pictures of Martina, her grandma Maleth, and me, with a poem ensconced within. I read with suspended disbelief the words she cobbled together in perfect arrangement that delivered a simple but heartfelt message of love. Was I reading a young Elizabeth Barrett Browning? I was less impressed with the way she chiseled her words—which, for me, bore all the earmarks of an emerging wordsmith that all young aspiring poets can hope to be—but I'm touched with the way her lines were singing with love, admiration, and such other sentiments that utterly melt any grandfather's heart. Here Pope Francis, read it with me and savor her words.

MOMENTS WITH YOU

You were there for me since day one,
I can't imagine my life with you gone.
Thanks for the good times we shared.
You're someone who really cares.

Spending time with you
is something I look forward to,
you stick by me and I stick by you
and never thinking twice about helping me, too
is something I really love about you.

You taught me things I never knew,
like one, two, three and red, green, blue.
It's not just me who is amazed by you,
other people see your greatness, too.
Even if you're a busy bee,
thank you for making time for me.

This is a little token from my heart.
These are my words unspoken.
—Marti (14 years old) December 11, 2013

And so, Pope Francis, I am now in a new beginning of life.

Leth and I in a cartoonist rendition in Universal Studios.

Aiming for the Diamond

*P*ope Francis, my wife and I are well into our years and for people our age, it is a struggle to keep awake past regular bedtime. I must have drifted off last night while watching History Channel recounts the struggles you endured for the people of Jesus Christ. You mentioned a number of things while carrying the battle for us, and even in my semi-conscious state, one of the statements you made etched itself deeply in my mind: "Jesus does not want us to look for him; Jesus goes out to greet his people."

I bolted upright in my chair upon hearing your words, words that brought memories accumulated in half a century of blissful marriage. I smiled in remembrance of the times that *Kuya Hesus* "greeted" us. Since my youth, Jesus Christ has always been an elder brother to me. I have always felt his hovering presence—when times were good and especially during those moments when my life hanged in the balance.

All our days have been graced with his presence—which I know with a certainty. He was in the sparkle I saw in the laughing eyes of Leth as she walked to the altar and stood at my side; when she gazed at me tenderly, squeezed my hand, and said, "I do." He was there that morning when relatives and friends gathered before the altar in prayer as Carlo, my firstborn, was freed from the clutches of the sin of Adam and Eve. As the purifying water of baptism was poured on his forehead, I heard the Father's voice, "This is my son of whom I am well pleased."

Kuya Hesus was there in the delivery room when the doctor carefully handed a glistening, wet bundle, my daughter Leah, for a tiny human person's first warm embrace from her mother.

No less was he there as my wife watched anxiously as our son Jun, all of seven years old, eased himself into a go-kart to compete in a race among all the seven-year-olds in our village. Nor, too, could anyone deny his presence when our precious Nikki, squealed with glee as I held her in my arms playing "Who's the girl Daddy loves the most?".

Pope Francis, Kuya Hesus greeted us more times than I can count. It all comes back now in an unbidden flood: the memory of Leth and me, Nikki in tow, as we flew to the States to catch the pinkish glow on the face of our first grandson Nicco. Then there was that morning when Leah put Christian on my lap, an abandoned baby plucked from orphanage, and said, "Dad, here is your new grandson."

And here we are mounting yet another snapshot in our album of life, aiming for the diamond with the first short story written by Diego, Leah's eldest, who is perhaps not even aware that he is helping us create more memories:

The Sound of the Forest

There was a little native boy who was bright and curious. Because he was such, he went against the tribe's advice and ventured into the world. He knew that he was still young and had many things to learn and so he decided that he needed a teacher who could guide him with care through life. This boy was truly smart.

He came by the tundra and saw something moved in the corner of his eye. Although he was scared and shivering from the frost, he yelled out, "Who's there?"

No answer came. Instead, the sound of rustling leaves answered; something moved again. He stomped his feet and shouted, "Who's there, show yourself!" And against the snowy white background stepped out a red dot. As the red figure came closer, he saw that it was a fox.

He heard stories from his tribe about how the fox was a wise and cunning creature and so he asked him whether he was willing to be the boy's teacher. The fox was quiet and slowly went closer to the boy; the fox was inspecting him.

After a while, the fox spoke and said, "You are a brave boy. Most people would have run away but you stayed and sought me out. I could have been a wolf but your bravery made you stay. Tell me, can you run fast?" The fox was curious.

The boy said that he could and so the fox tested him. The fox asked him to grab his tail and if he could, he would be the boy's teacher. After trying twice, he could not grab the fox's tail and while the fox was at the foot of the hill, the fox said "You're too slow, boy. I would not want a slow pupil who could not keep up with my wisdom. Perhaps the water buffalo can teach you." And so the fox ran away to his hole.

The boy decided that he would seek out the water buffalo in hopes that he would be his teacher. After his long journey, he reached the savannah where there was a water hole. Only one animal was there and the boy guessed that it was because of the animal's ferocious temper that no one dared enter the water hole.

The boy crept to the edge of the water hole and called out the water buffalo. The water buffalo raised its head and huffed at the boy. The boy once again asked for the water buffalo to step out so that they could talk. To no avail; he was ignored again.

A third time, growing impatient, the boy threw a rock near the water buffalo to catch its attention and this time the water buffalo spoke, saying, "Can you not see that I am busy bathing? The only time I will come out is to feed and if the water runs out. But I have all the water I need. Would you like me to come out and eat you?"

The boy answered no. He left the water buffalo alone, thinking that a teacher who was greedy and lazy was not a good teacher; anyway, he did not want to learn the traits of greediness and laziness.

The boy left again and wandered around the foot of the mountain. He found himself thinking about quitting his quest for a teacher but he was determined to learn from a wise teacher. And so he stood up and climbed the mountain.

He was halfway up when he stopped at a plateau and heard a shriek in the sky. He looked up and squinted as the sun was too bright for little eyes. He saw a majestic eagle soaring in the sky, flaunting its mighty wings. The boy opened his eyes and dropped his jaw from sheer delight. He watched the eagle soar and swoop in a dazzling dance in the sky. After a while, the eagle came down and settled beside him.

The boy offered the eagle some water because he thought that the eagle would be thirsty from all his aerial acrobatics. The eagle took a sip and thanked him. The boy told the eagle how amazing he was in the sky and the eagle thanked him modestly.

After conversing a while, the boy knew that he had to ask him whether he would be the boy's teacher. Thinking that he had softened the eagle's heart by praising him, he asked the question. The eagle looked at him and told him, "Young boy, I am terribly sorry but I cannot be your teacher."

The boy was disheartened and so he asked the majestic eagle why he could not be his teacher. The eagle answered, "Young boy, we are different from each other. I have wings, you have none. You have feet, I have none. What am I to teach that could be of value? The most I could be is your friend, but never your teacher."

The boy understood what the eagle was saying and so he climbed down the mountain, sad for not having found a teacher. He walked away from the mountain, past the water hole, and beyond the tundra. After walking for days, he found himself in a forest. He was so tired and so he went to sleep beside a tree stump.

Early in the morning, he woke up to whispers. He wanted to look for the man whispering and tell him to be quiet because he was sad and still sleepy. He went around the trees and found no one, still he heard the whispers. He looked farther and the whispers grew louder and louder. He reached the middle of the forest, yet there was no one around; but the voice was persistent and he could hear it clearly.

The voice told him to sit down, and somehow, he saw the stump next to which he'd had fallen asleep. Funny, but he remembered moving far away from the stump when he went searching for the whispers. Yet, here he was as if he had not moved at all. As he sat down, the voice spoke and said, "I am Grandfather Forest. What is worrying you?"

The boy answered, "I have been looking for a teacher who could guide me carefully through life but the totems I met have all turned me down. I don't think I will ever find a teacher."

Grandfather Forest laughed heartily and said to him, "Silly boy you are! I have watched you in this quest for a wise teacher. Is that all you seek?"

He said yes and both remained quiet. He could feel the wind as it blew through his hair.

The boy was at his wits' end in finding a teacher. So, shyly, he asked if Grandfather Forest could be his teacher. There was no sound, not even a whisper, from Grandfather Forest. The boy grew nervous waiting for an answer. He waited and waited, and finally Grandfather Forest spoke.

"The spirit of my wisdom courses through you. I have always been your teacher even before you began your quest. All you need to do now is notice the teachings and learn from them—for the pupil with shut eyes and shut ears will never learn even if the wisest teachers teach him!"

The boy understood and smiled as he left the forest. He grew up to be a strong man like the trunk of the trees. He was amenable like the wind. And he knew how to listen to the silence of the forest. He now hears the singing of the crickets, the steps of ants bringing food to their queen, the crawl of the centipede and saw the loving embrace of the trees as the winds help them hug each other.

He came back many years later, holding the hand of a little boy who was very much like him when he first made his quest as a young boy. He entered the forest and sat for a while on the stump which he had sat on many years ago. Although the forest did not speak, he heard the sound of the forest in the wind, the grass, the song of the insects crawling in unison to greet him. The young boy let go of his hands and held on to a tree branch and said, "*Tatay*, do you hear that?"

As the father and son walked away from the forest, the young boy, still holding on to his father's hand, was smiling and laughing. The father asked, "Why do you laugh?"

The son replied, "I can hear the sound of the forest."

The son curiously asked, "Tatay, who was that old man speaking?"

The two boys smiled.

Pope Francis, I believe with all my heart that the love Leth and I have for each other is gilded with kindness and patience. To be honest, we have had our disagreements. A few times we came to the brink of a chasm that might have been difficult if not impossible to bridge. How easily we could have squirmed out of the sheltering embrace of Kuya Hesus! We may forget that he nourishes marital love as a farmer nurtures his plants. At that point we caught ourselves, ashamed and contrite, reaching for each other's hands and long before we knew it, we were hugging each other.

We remember the first rule of encounter in marriage, "Before you fight, hold each other's hands." And if you still want to fight, follow rule two, "Hug each other tight."

Leth is an A-1 personality. She is quite the achiever. But her fuse is short. As years rolled by, I learned how to come up with creative "gimmicks" that could quickly defuse her. She is the type that gets stressed with every little thing not to her liking. I remember how difficult it is to drive in America. When you missed a turn to get out of the freeway, you'd have to travel long miles to turn around and get back to your intended egress. So there we were in the land of the eternal PX goods. I was driving and Leth was doing the navigating. But we kept missing the off-ramp to exit the freeway. Finally, she exploded and blurted, "*Marunong ka bang mag*-drive? (Do you know how to drive?)"

I said to myself, uh-uh, here it comes. I turned at her with an angry face, as angry as I could make myself look and growled at her like a tiger. She gaped open-mouthed at me and then burst into laughter, "*Ang pangit mo!* (You're so ugly!)" And we both broke up laughing.

We were still laughing when we saw the exit sign. With a shout, Leth said, "*Ayun na,* Dad! (There it is, Dad!)"

And so we ended up kissing with only the vaguest notion of why we wanted to fight in the first place. We kept the patience of the Lord, recalling the letter to the Hebrews 10:36-38:

> You need endurance to do the will of God and receive what he has promised. "For, after just a brief moment, he who is to come shall come; he shall not delay. But my just one shall live by faith, and if he draws back I take no pleasure in him."

Pope Francis, we never drew back. We have stayed together this long because we know how to talk to each other. Years back, on the very first time I brought Leth home from our church wedding, I promised her that she would be my love forever. Words spoken at her in anger would never pass my lips. I would never meet her angry words with similar angry words. There would be peace between us always: that was my pledge.

We realized, too, that beauty is only skin deep. Even as we were falling in love, we were drawn to each other physically. But we matured into the knowledge that if our marriage were to last, we needed something of transcendental value when the physical attraction faded.

While our tastes differ, we never intended to change each other. We love each other the way we are and we want to preserve that. The day never ends without a hug, or a kiss, or a word that touches each other's heart; we are generous with "I love you, Love!"

And then, of course, our children are the bond that cements us into one because we have consecrated them to God and we are always seeking the help of our Mother.

One night while lying in bed, letting what was on television to lull us to sleep, Leth sat up and asked, "Dad, what's your plan for our golden anniversary, *anong plano mo?*" nudging me gently on the shoulder.

"*Ikaw, anong gusto mo?* What do you have in mind?" I replied in my usual cautious way to be sure that I did not throw a monkey wrench in the works.

"I don't want a grand wedding celebration, Dad. We already had that on our 40th. This time, perhaps something more intimate, just you and I and the children."

I sat up in bed, this time anxious, "Have you planned anything yet?"

"Leah and I were talking. She saw Bishop Raul in their regular CFM meeting and the good bishop invited her—actually our family—to join him in a Marian pilgrimage. What do you think, are you well enough to make the trip? It could be quite taxing."

She caught me unawares. I sat silent, not saying anything for some moment. I was afraid. I wondered: could I do it?

I knew that I was fit enough for routine activities. I had been doing a lot of researching and writing but that was purely mental, requiring little physical effort. I spent two times a week with my students, again easy for me because after every lecture I'd stop and rest. My service to the Lord took place on Sundays and I have all my grandkids as my *alalays* or assistants. But on the move nonstop 12 hours a day for two weeks—was I up to it?

I answered her with a question, "*Anong palagay mo, kaya ko ba?* (Do you think I am well enough to handle it?)"

"I Am a Pagan"

$\mathcal{P}$ope Francis, let me be honest. I had mixed feelings coming to this pilgrimage. My issues were mostly about my health so you can understand why that could be a problem.

In the last three years, I have been working hard to recover from a chronic obstructive pulmonary disease (COPD). A pulmonologist (the greatest in the world, I swear!) has successfully helped me stay the deleterious effects of COPD. It took a lot of discipline but I was determined to stick to a daily regimen of breathing exercises combined with flexing and stretching to loosen my muscles, especially in the chest area.

Throughout this ordeal, I learned more about COPD. I found out that we are born with 300 million alveoli or air sacs, but illness, pollution, asthma, and stress deplete them. The worse is pneumonia which wipes them out in one fell swoop—and I have had two bouts of it in a span of one year. The doctor said that my alveoli have been destroyed and that I had to develop surrogate lungs made up basically of muscles and joints to compensate for the loss. My surrogate lungs would be the additional pathways to allow me to inhale oxygen and exhale carbon dioxide—in other words, to breathe. It was something I never gave any deliberate thought to until I was diagnosed with COPD.

Today, taking long walks does not reward me with the relaxation and peace that it used to, but fills me with fear and anxiety. I imagine myself gasping for air instead of enjoying the clean, sharp exchange of oxygen that walking brings. And what unknown allergens may be riding on the breeze just waiting to pounce on me? My trigger does not necessarily have to be noxious gases or obnoxious smells; even the faint aroma of cologne or the scent of women and babies can cause me to gasp for air and make me afraid for my life.

I liken this fear to a feeling of terror and hopelessness in a world away from God. I dread most the day when my fear shall possess me totally and I will blame God for my condition. Family and friends will not fare any better, for I will defiantly slap away their helping hand and words of compassion, seeing in their gesture only pity for what I have become.

At night as I lay down to examine the details of my day, I felt the human fear gnawing at my heart turn into the fear of the Lord. As if assisted by unseen hands, I found myself beginning on a path toward God. The Lord's response was immediate. I was rewarded with the strength to vanquish fear, and the fortitude not to give in to despair, no matter how insistent it was to break down my resolve. Any doubts I harbored because I thought my Kuya Hesus had abandoned me, fell away, dispelled by a new resolution to fight any and all adversity.

I drifted off to sleep, praying the Rosary to Mama Mary.

I knew that I had to make the trip.

The planned pilgrimage was chock-full with meaning and significance for my wife and me as it coincided with the marking of our 50th wedding anniversary. Leth thought that it would be wonderful to bring along our four children and their spouses. "*Huwag na muna ang mga apo,*" she said. "No grandchildren this time; they will have their chance."

To reassure me, my son Jun promised to fetch along a wheelchair. The thought of a motorized wheelchair to drive and maneuver was instantly appealing. But my wife said, "NO!" As you might already know, we have rules in the house that we follow with no room for compromise. Rule number one—Mom is always right. Rule number two—If Mom is wrong, follow rule number one.

So that settled it and ended my daydream of an electric wheelchair. I was stuck with a muscle-powered model. Mom thought that I might

I am enjoying my wheelchair with my family. At the background is the church of St. Jerome in Lisbon.

get too comfortable on a self-propelled one that I would stop walking entirely; she might just be right.

So I went to Rome, not really whizzing along but seated on a wheelchair slowly being pushed by one of my children. But to my joy, the wheelchair turned out to be a magic wand. At the airport, my wheels got me preferred check-in status and as well at the lines at immigration and boarding—with my entire family in tow. What better way to start this trip than being first?

As registered pilgrims, we had tickets for an audience with you, Pope Francis. But if one wanted to sit near you, he'd have to line up as early as four o'clock in the morning.

That day, we left the hotel at almost 8:00 in the morning. No one seemed to want to wake up at 3:00 a.m., groggy as we were from jet lag after the long flight. We decided to take our chances. After all, you were scheduled to appear not earlier than midmorning. And with the warm weather that day, our decision to sleep late was preordained.

Yet as if wonders never end, here my wheelchair was coming to the rescue again!

We were moved from the long line of pilgrims from all over the world and quickly whisked to just a few meters where you would stand. We were with two other pilgrims from our delegation: Ma'am Remy who was likewise on a wheelchair and her daughter Chinee who trundled her mother's wheelchair; my son Jun provided the manpower behind mine.

None of us expected you to ride in your open vehicle and be driven right by where we were seated. But you just passed in front of us! We couldn't believe it! My son Jun said, "Dad, Pope Francis and I had eye contact and he waved at me. Feeling *ko, parang ako lang ang tinitingnan niya!* It's like he only had eyes for me!"

I whispered to Jun, "Thank the wheelchair." I had the feeling that God had more miracles planned for us pilgrims.

That afternoon we drove to San Giovanni Rotondo to "meet" St. Padre Pio, the other saint whom the Church acknowledges as having stigmata; the other one is St. Francis of Assisi.

Jun said, "Dad, *siguro ako puwede rin maging santo.* (Dad, I think I, too, can be a saint)."

"Huh, *bakit?* Why do you say so?"

"Because I am also astigmatic."

"Har, har, har, *ang mais mo.* You're corny!" My son Jun is the funny one. Even when he was growing up, he and I would exchange jokes for hours. He is the life of the family and his brother and sisters—even their *barkada* or crowd—always want him around. Jun has a way with people, and even strangers he meets for the first time gravitate to him. Our pilgrim group felt the same about him; and as the bus carried us to our next destination, you could hear his infectious laughter.

It was a five-hour ride to the Church of St. Padre Pio. Brother Millard, our administrative guide, certainly knew how to make good use of the time. He announced a "getting to know you" session, as a way of breaking the ice and making the pilgrims comfortable with their fellow travelers. It was fun, proving once more that "people are funny," as Art Linkletter, a well-known TV host of the '70s, used to say.

A lady made her way to the front of the bus and literally grabbed the microphone from Bro. Millard. She introduced herself by saying,

"I am Linda and I am a pagan. Frankly, I don't know what I am doing in this pilgrimage."

Her introduction broke up the bus. I have listened to many speeches in my life but I have to admit that this, by far the best intro I have ever heard, more so as it was unleashed on pilgrims, who were presumably doing the trip to strengthen their bonds with the Lord!

A pagan in our midst! Incredible!

Linda was good and going, and warming up, she went on, "You know, the last two days I have never been in so many churches in such a short time and for me, churches are museums for old people and holy saints!"

More laughter and shouting erupted and just wouldn't stop. When it quieted a bit, she delivered her *coup de grace:* "You know we are leaving Rome and I have not done any shopping yet? How can you do this to me? Rome is Gucci!"

I couldn't control myself, I was laughing and hooting and my wife who herself was laughing hard, had to caution me, "Dad, easy *ka lang, ang* asthma *mo* (Take it easy, remember your asthma)."

For those who don't know, an asthmatic episode can be precipitated by too much laughing; I could have easily landed in the hospital. I would have billed Linda for it, just in case that happened. Hehe!

The bus stopped for a bathroom break, a good thing. With Linda's smashing talk, the next speaker would definitely have big shoes to fill. As we climbed back on the bus, I got to do some serious thinking about what she said.

People go on religious pilgrimages in search of spiritual renewal. So to hear what the lady said was quite a shocker. Did Linda really mean it? Or was it just a way to cover stage fright?

We were this time in Lourdes, the place where Mama Mary appeared to the visionary, St. Bernadette. I got the chance to walk with Linda as we headed towards the shrine of our Lady. By way of making conversation, I said, "I know you are familiar with the story of the Good Samaritan, but do you know the origin of the word pagan?"

She was silent.

I continued, "In the Old Testament, and even during the time of Jesus Christ, anyone who was not a Jew or Greek was labeled a pagan. Children of God, that's what the Jews and Greeks considered themselves, for even the latter had their own gods." And anyone else was excluded and therefore a pagan.

For her to truly appreciate the word "pagan," I relayed to her the story of the Good Samaritan:

> There was a scholar of the law who stood up to test [Jesus] and said, "Teacher, what must I do to inherit eternal life?" Jesus said to him, "What is written in the law? How do you read it?" He said in reply, "You shall love the Lord, your God, with all your heart, with all your being, with all your strength, and with all your mind, and your neighbor as yourself." He replied to him, "You have answered correctly; do this and you will live."
>
> But because he wished to justify himself, he said to Jesus, "And who is my neighbor?" Jesus replied, "A man fell victim to robbers as he went down from Jerusalem to Jericho. They stripped and beat him and went off leaving him half-dead. A priest happened to be going down that road, but when he saw him, he passed by on the opposite side. Likewise a Levite came to the place, and when he saw him, he passed by on the opposite side. But a Samaritan traveler who came upon him was moved with compassion at the sight. He approached the victim, poured oil and wine over his wounds and bandaged them. Then he lifted them up on his own animal, took him to an inn and cared for him. The next day he took out two silver coins and gave them to the innkeeper with instruction. 'Take care of him. If you spend more than what I have given you, I shall pay you on my way back.' Which of these three in your opinion was neighbor to the robbers' victim?" He answered, "The one who treated him with mercy." Jesus said to him, "Go and do likewise" (Lk 10:25-37).

I looked at Linda. She was nodding her head but her eyes remained noncommittal. "Linda, with your indulgence, may I share with you a few of my thoughts?"

She smiled at me. I began, "In the parable of the Good Samaritan, the lawyer asked, 'Who is my neighbor?' In answer, Jesus told the story of the Good Samaritan. But the lawyer's question raises another question, one that proceeds logically from the first: *Am I a good neighbor?*"

I continued, "Powerful worship of God always gives us the sensation of loving and caring with a kind of love that is full of sacrifices and self-denial. In the time of Jesus, people who were non-Jew, like the Samaritans, were despised for being impure ethnically and for the way they practiced their religion. The Mosaic Law of the time dictated that if the man waylaid by the robbers died, he who helped him would face defilement. Despite that danger to him, the Samaritan still stopped and gave succor to the injured man."

Linda was listening intently. I pressed on, "A measure of our love is how we serve those who are different from us. Many times we only come to the rescue of people who are known to us—our family and our friends. But have we reached out to those different from us?"

"I heard you say, '*I am a pagan.*' Are you really here solely to enjoy the trip and do some shopping?"

Bishop Raul Martirez, "The Fisherman," with his flock

My Pilgrim Friends

"No, Rudy, I'm here to assist my long-time friend, Ester. She is a cancer survivor. Actually, our other *barkada*, Suan, is also with us. We love Ester and we want to support her as much as we can—as much as she needs us."

Linda did mention that she joined the pilgrimage upon the invitation of her very close friend Ester, a cancer survivor. Ester wanted Linda to be with her on the trip to support her. Linda granted her friend's request, not really knowing what a pilgrimage was all about or what to expect, having joined one, albeit only as an uncommitted chaperone. She did it simply because her friend Ester mattered to her.

I had to find out how far Linda would go to lend a hand even to those who are complete strangers to her. "If Ester were not your friend, would you have gone out of your way for her—perhaps in other ways?"

Without blinking an eye, Linda replied, "Yes. And I have done that a few times for people not known to me."

I said, "Linda, I know you know that you can identify with the Samaritan. Do you still consider yourself pagan? If so, I want to be a pagan like you. Anytime."

We parted when we finally arrived at the grotto of our Lady of Lourdes.

After that short encounter, I often caught Linda as if in deep thought; I also noticed she interacted well with the younger members of our group, including Wally, who is married to my youngest daughter Nikki.

As it turned out, Linda and Wally had a common bond: Linda's son was a classmate of Wally at the Ateneo. When she learned of their connection, she remarked, "*Lagot na ako*! Oh no, I'm done for!"

Whether her mood change was due to the fact that her son might come to learn of what she said to us on the bus, or of her apparently genuine questioning of her faith, I had no way of knowing. After all, one's faith is between her and the Lord and the strength of this faith in times of difficulties and challenges is hers alone to measure and to say.

But I quite believe that Linda was honestly having questions about her faith. All of us, at one time or another asked ourselves why we are Christians; Christ's apostles themselves did.

At one time, Jesus was in a boat with his disciples and while he slept, strong winds buffeted the frail craft.

> [The disciples] came and woke [Jesus], saying, "Lord, save us! We are perishing!" He said to them, "Why are you terrified, O you of little faith?" then he got up, rebuked the winds and the sea, and there was great calm. The men were amazed and said, "What sort of man is this, whom even the winds and the sea obey?" (Mt 8:25-27).

As our trip moved on, my wife, our children, and I were stretched to our limit keeping up with the schedules, the same as the other pilgrims. Despite the physical demands, we strove with our entire beings to make the link with the Lord, often imploring the intercession of Mama Mary to pray for our triumphal search. It was an exhausting pilgrimage, physically and emotionally, but spiritually fulfilling.

Time flew and before we knew it, it was time to say goodbye.

I overheard Linda say to Bishop Martirez, "Bishop Raul, at the beginning of this pilgrimage, I was a pagan. Thanks to you, I am now a Christian."

I was not surprised. "It was the Holy Spirit and the smile of Mama Mary that made us all true children of Jesus."

Of the many impressions I had of Linda, it was the scene at the Manila International Airport that lingered in my mind.

I imagined her as a great motivational speaker with an introduction that quickly got my attention and made me interested in what more she had to say. The substance of the talk glued me to my chair; I could have heard a pin drop as the audience listened in awe and then at the end, the crowd stood up shouting, "More! More!"

That was the image of her that Linda left me at the winding of the pilgrimage. It is something I will remember for a long time. Her exact words may soon slip into the dim recesses of memory but the lessons that came with it, I will forever keep to heart.

At the airport, Mom, Nikki, and Wally clustered around my "savior" wheelchair before we proceeded to the immigration counter. Linda walked up to us to say goodbye. I watched her as she chatted with Mom and the kids. As she was about to leave, she leaned forward a bit and gave me a peck on the cheek, as if to say, "We are friends."

What an ending to a wonderful trip!

And now let me share one final lesson.

In the first apparition of our Lady of Fatima to Lucia, Francisco, and Jacinta, our Mother brought the children to a vision of hell to show why she wanted them to pray and make sacrifices for the conversion of sinners.

What did our Lady mean when she asked for prayers and sacrifices? What sacrifices are worthy of her request?

During the pilgrimage, I bought the book, *Fatima in Lucia's Own Words*. I borrowed a few lines to show what sacrifices can be pleasing to the Lord:

> That day when we reached the pasture, Jacinta sat thoughtfully on a rock.
> "Jacinta, come and play."
> "I don't want to play today."
> "Why not?"
> "Because I'm thinking, that Lady taught us to say the Rosary and to make sacrifices for the conversion of sinners, so from now on, when we say the Rosary, we must say the whole *Hail Mary*

and the whole *Our Father*! And the sacrifices—how are we going to make them?"

(I remember what Sr. Cecilia, our guide in Fatima, told us. The children wanted to finish their prayers right away so they could return to their games. They repeated the Rosary, mumbling through it continuously just like one continuous mantra... Hail Mary, Hail Mary... etc. Jacinta wanted to be sure they prayed the Rosary properly.)

Right away, Francisco thought of a good sacrifice:

"Let's give our lunch to the sheep, and make the sacrifice of doing without it."

In a couple of minutes, the contents of our lunch bags had been divided among the sheep. So that day, we fasted as strictly as the most austere Carthusian!

As I finish writing, I look at the time. It is 4:30 a.m. I usually take biscuit and tea before going back to bed. Today, I did not.

I pray that my little sacrifice would convert a sinner.

"Hail Mary, full of grace..."

Good morning, pilgrims!!

Pope Francis, Linda read this story in my blog. I had a pleasant surprise at her comments:

Yes, this PAGAN never dreamed to be among pilgrims!

With my eyeglasses, I read the bold prints—ITALY, FRANCE, SPAIN, PORTUGAL and instantly was packing my bags with my two friends—Ester and Suan. All I brought was my passion for adventure, no noble intentions and no miracle expectations.

But FATHER KNOWS BEST!

Whose prayers, among the 42 pilgrims, have to be near perfect in layman's eyes for God to listen to save a "pagan"? I got Bishop Raul Martirez as my prayer partner.

And whose prayers God has difficulty listening to since its short, free-flow, need-to-say-basis out of the blues? Yup, from a non-conformed pilgrim!

Jover, my pick-up as a prayer partner, since he didn't have one, was so significant. For Bishop Martirez, Jover is his right-hand; Jover packs his clothes, pushes his wheelchair and pulls up his luggage trolleys at all hotels and airports. Without Jover, "D" Bishop cannot function. So I bet "D" Bishop prays for Jover more than he can say Mass in a single day. My prayers were just "whispers" to his ears. The relationships among the three of us were more like whose glass needs to be filled the most. In destiny, everything falls in its place.

Rome for me was also F... Ferragamo, but I got F... FRANCIS, the Pope. ITALY has Spanish Steps but I got to "Holy Steps." My body did not complain since this pilgrimage was good for my soul. Destiny led me to meet you and your lovely family, Rudy, and my newfound "pilgrim-friends."

That was a complete and uplifting experience for me, Pope Francis. For the first time I was guided by the Holy Spirit to reach out to a sleeping Catholic. All the entire pilgrim group had to do was to pray for her to rekindle her faith… and she took care of the rest. With the whole darn bus cheering!

I know your lessons shall bear fruit because they are perfectly attuned to *God's inexhaustible mercy*… "How good to come back to him whenever we are lost, God never tires of forgiving us, we are the ones who get tired of seeking his mercy. The Eucharist, although it is the fullness of sacramental life, is not a prize for the perfect, but a powerful medicine and nourishment for the weak."

Loon, Bohol, Philippines

The earthquake destruction in Bohol, Philippines made even stronger the belief of the people of the Philippines in the Church. Photo above was taken by Marcos Caratao and RayNaReyn

Seismic Shift

*P*ope Francis, the month of December 2013 served up three important dates in my life. On December 8, on the solemnity of the Immaculate Conception of the Blessed Virgin Mary, you gifted the world with your *Evangelii Gaudium,* (The Joy of the Gospel). On December 11, I marked my 76th year in life's continuing journey. As my wife used to say, "We cannot be 18-year-olds forever, it's OK to age, *huwag lang paurong* (One should not grow more stupid with age)."

Of course, the other date is December 25, the third, and most important and most wonderful event, the birth of our Savior, the infant Emmanuel.

The homily of the priest who celebrated the vigil Mass essayed a lesson in our personal relationship with the Lord. He spoke of a group of atheists—proponents of "vague spiritual energies or powers"—who, in their desire to show how ridiculous it was to believe in God, mounted an interactive video-ad in the middle of Times Square in New York. The ad strongly proposed that during the holiday season, the word "Christ" should not be used when people greeted each other. As the video rolled, the word "Christ" in Christmas was erased and in its place was inserted the capital letter "X," so people read it as "X'mas." To complete the season's greeting, the ad encouraged the viewers to shout at each other, "Merry X'mas!"

The video went viral over the internet and raised a howl among Christians from all over the world. They demanded that the ad be taken down. The authorities, succumbing to the pressure, ultimately did so.

The homily gave me pause. If anything, it lent currency to a personal sense of a shifting attitude in people, certain receptiveness in them to the subliminal messages of those who are out to invalidate or overturn the teachings of Jesus Christ. Has his supreme sacrifice to save the world become an exercise in futility for a growing number of people? Wherefore, the plea of Abraham to save Sodom and Gomorrah from the wrath of God, and God's willingness to relent if there were people worthy to be saved has no more value?

A priest once commented that if the 80 million Catholics went to Mass on Sunday in all our churches, the most that could be accommodated would be about 65 million with all the 5,000 priests in the Philippines celebrating Mass every hour for 24 hours the entire Sunday. As it is, even with the diminishing number of Mass-goers, some of the celebrants' homilies tend to be repetitive, lackluster if not downright boring perhaps because there is not enough time to prepare due to sheer schedule overload. This could be one of the reasons why those standing at the back, especially men, need no further justification to walk out in the middle of the "sermon" to grab a smoke or chat with each other.

Christianity had a very troubled beginning.

It began as a mere outgrowth of Judaism. In the early centuries, most of its converts came from the lower echelon of Roman society—men and women who were considered third-class citizens, commoners and slaves. Into this shaky situation came Jesus Christ to establish the New Covenant to bring God's work to completion and fulfillment. It is easy to imagine what a great surprise, even shock, it was for the people of the Old Covenant to be presented with a very human Jesus, the son of an ordinary carpenter. "Is this truly the much-awaited Messiah?" they must have asked themselves. They had expected a divine or mystical messenger in the manner of an angel.

Jesus soon established his "Church" in the apostle Peter whom he called the "Rock." In Matthew 16:18, we read: "And so I say to you, you are Peter, and upon this rock I will build my church, and the gates of the netherworld shall not prevail against it."

After more than 2,000 years, the mission and ministry of Jesus march on. For the Church, "struggle" may be more aptly descriptive. And it has been so through the ages since Jesus handpicked his leaders and pioneers, who were mostly from the ranks of weak and sinful men.

Pope Francis, Jesus, during his three-year ministry, frequently resorted to the use of parables to effectively put across his divine messages; also, as claimed by some religious authorities, to throw the "secret marshals" of Pilate off the scent. Christians were suspected to be a secret society that regularly met on Sundays to "eat the body and blood of a man." The Roman government was certain that Christians were enemies of the state, atheists who refused to worship Roman gods or pay homage to the Roman emperor. Spies mingled with Jesus' audience with the single purpose of catching Jesus utter remarks that might be considered subversive.

I realize the weight of my letter. I thought that I might give you respite. After all, there are at least 37 references to laughter in the Bible, one among which is found in chapter 3 of Ecclesiastes: "There is an appointed time for everything,... A time to weep, and a time to laugh (vv. 1a, 4a).

I personally believe that God created humor to bring smiles, even laughter, to a troubled human being, not to debase or put down people who may feel to be at the center of a joke.

Today, some preachers effectively use humor to bring attention to God. A parson from the 19th century once commented, "A person without a sense of humor is like a wagon without springs, jolted by every pebble in the road."

Humor can be an effective tool when used as God intended it. It can heal certain ailments, physically and emotionally, as science has proven recently. Remember the old *Reader's Digest* section "Laughter is the Best Medicine"?

A man walking through the woods stumbled upon a preacher baptizing his flock in the river. The guy proceeded to walk into the water and subsequently bumped into the preacher.

The preacher turned around and asked the man, "Are you ready to find Jesus?" He answered, "Yes, I am."

So the preacher grabbed him and dunked him in the water. He pulled the guy up and asked loudly, "Brother have you found Jesus?" The man, spitting and sputtering, replied, "No, I haven't found Jesus."

The preacher, shocked at the answer, dunked him into the water again for a little longer this time. He again pulled the man out of the water. And, again asked, "Have you found Jesus, my brother?"

"The guy again answered, 'No, I haven't found Jesus!'

By this time the preacher was at his wits' end, but he decided to dunk the man in the water one last time. The preacher held the man for about 30 seconds and when the man began wildly kicking his arms and legs, the preacher hauled him up. The preacher again asked the fellow, "For the love of God, have you found Jesus?"

The guy, staggering in the water, gasped for breath as he wiped his eyes. Then he grabbed the preacher's shirt and asked, "Are you (gasp) sure (gasp) this is where (gasp) he fell in?"

We seem trapped in this warp: a world losing faith in God. Many search for him in other faiths. Others dismiss the concept of God entirely and live a hedonistic existence whose guiding principle is "eat, drink, and be merry."

Reading up on the matter of religiosity, I found the data revealing. It is probably old hat for many, but for the uninitiated, it is enlightening.

The "Eurobarometer Poll 2010" conducted among member-nations of the European Union (EU) is a survey on the religiosity of the people in most of Europe. Subjects were asked to find themselves under any of the three categories in the poll: (1) I believe there is God. (2) I believe there is some sort of spirit-god or life force. (3) I don't believe in God.

I tried to analyze the rather lengthy report with an attempt to get behind the numbers to arrive at some conclusion based on the result of the poll. The data below focus on countries which were considered the seat of Catholicism before Luther changed the configuration of religion. The bold numbers as heading correspond to the three aforementioned categories:

Country	1	2	3
Italy	74%	20%	6%
Spain	59	20	19
Germany	44	25	27
France	27	27	40
Portugal	70	15	12
United Kingdom	37	33	25

Adding together the number of respondents who no longer believe in God and those who believe in some sort of spirit-god or life force, we find less than one-third of the people in France still believing in God, followed in a diminishing degree by the UK and Germany. Considering the historical perspective of these countries, the finding could be quite alarming.

Recently, Prince Charles of England declared his concern over the apparently geometrical increase in the Islamic population in his country. He asked in strong words that the government and the people reverse the trend. It might just be too late for the country that counts itself among those that vigorously supported population control measures. Today in the UK, 58% no longer believe in God and an unidentified 5% are more than likely Muslims whose agenda is to control countries in Europe without firing a shot by simply populating them with their people who do not practice birth control.

In another study, theism was measured over a period of 20 years. Included here are countries known for their strong Catholic beliefs that reach back centuries in the past.

Theism

Country	1981	1999
Italy	84.1%	87.8
Denmark	57.8	62.1
Spain	86.8	81.1
Ireland	94.8	93.7
Sweden	51.9	46.6
France	61.8	56.1
Netherlands	65.3	58.0

Italy, Denmark, and Ireland are holding on tight to their faith in God. Spain, which brought Christianity to the Philippines, is losing ground. It leads one to think that our national hero Rizal was correct after all that Spain's purpose was really economics and that evangelization was only a by-product of their true intent.

In the US, Christianity on the whole is shrinking. Reports show that the percentage of adherents has gone down from 78.4% in 2000 to 73.80% of the total population in 2010, even as the number of Catholics grew from 23.9% to 25.0% over the same period.

Latin America continues to be the bastion of Christianity in the world, accounting for 90% of its population; and most of the believers are Catholics.

The Catholic religion, despite reported reduced church attendance, reflected steady growth rates in Italy, Denmark, Ireland, the US, and Latin America.

But there is more to this data than meets the eye. Let me begin with the thoughts of Richard Osting who owns a blog in Patheos.com.

"A seismic shift in religion worldwide," I've been seeing a seismic shift in religion worldwide. It manifests differently for different religions and different countries. This includes a struggle for the soul of Islam, the secularization of Europe, struggles in Protestant groups, etc. ...I'd love to see you try to make some sense of where we're headed at the "forest" level rather than looking at the "trees..."

The authoritative "forest" data on all faiths, nation by nation, come from the Center for the Study of Global Christianity at Gordon-Conwell Theological Seminary in Massachusetts. The center projects that trends in 2025 will basically continue the following patterns in religions' shares of the worldwide population in 1900 as compared with 2000.

> During the century, Christians of all denominations slipped somewhat, from 34.5 percent to 33 percent.
>
> All Muslims (including groups spurned by orthodox Sunnis) expanded from 12 percent to nearly 20 percent. (A spectacular growth for Islam—Author)
>
> The non-religious population scored even bigger gains, from negligible numbers to 12.7 percent, more due to Communist tyranny than voluntary secularization.
>
> (The downfall of Communism may be attributed to St. John Paul II having dedicated Russia to the Immaculate Heart of the Blessed Virgin Mother in 2005. However, secularism shortly reared its head and is now considered the primary enemy of the Christian religion.—Author)
>
> Hindus were up slightly, Buddhists down slightly.
>
> There were massive losses for ethnic and tribal traditions such as Chinese folk religions, animism, and shamanism, dropping collectively from 31 percent to just over 10 percent.
>
> The small Jewish population declined even more sharply.

Indeed, there's a major "struggle for the soul of Islam." It pits devout, relatively moderate traditionalists against politicized or violent salafis, jihadists, and binladenites with thin religious credentials but ample zeal and growing populist appeal...

Turning to "forestry" within the United States: Christianity suffers from self-inflicted wounds. Seemingly unending sexual molestation scandals have undercut the standing of Catholic leadership. The homosexual issue and other biblical disputes profoundly divide Protestantism between conservative evangelicals, often portrayed as obscurantist or bigots, and liberals, who seem adrift and uncertain about their heritage. Recent decades produced an unprecedented slide among relatively liberal churches and steady gains for the conservative Protestant congregations, which sometimes barely resemble the familiar churches of old as they strive to attract new members…

The analysis of Osting carries a lot of weight but it can be appreciated only in general terms, lacking as it is in supporting details. I did not want to leave the information hanging.

So I went one step further.

McDonaldization of the world

Additional readings from other sources showed alarming data to support Osting's claim, data that are valid and persuasive as they cover other disciplines and factors that contribute to the loss of belief in God. There are new terminologies or of play of words that came out to describe and give better understanding of what are causing the shift in religious beliefs. Two stick in mind:

Disenchantment of the world, because there is a change in culture that drives society to adapt secularization and shift society's close identification with religious values and institutions toward nonreligious (or irreligious) values and secular institutions. The secularization thesis refers to the belief that as society progresses, particularly through modernization and rationalization, religion loses its authority in all aspects of social life and governance.

Secularization is sometimes credited both to the cultural shifts in society following the emergence of rationality and the development of science as a substitute for superstition. Max Weber, a researcher on the subject of secularization, called this process the "disenchantment of the world"—and to the changes made by religious institutions to compensate. At the most basic stages, this begins with a slow transition from oral traditions to a writing culture that diffuses knowledge. This first reduces the authority of clerics as the custodians of revealed knowledge as the responsibility for education has moved from the family and community to the state.

In support of this culture change is the convergence of values that has been happening in tandem with development of science, which reduced people's dependence on the influence of superstitious beliefs traditionally dictating dependence on God as refuge to unexplained occurrences in their lives. As a result, sociologists invented a new term to describe this convergence of values.

McDonaldization of the world, or the globalization and converging of values during the past 30 years, has witnessed profound changes in political, economic, and social spheres, and increasingly rapid technological advances. This is often attributed to the phenomenon of *globalization. Capital markets* are today integrated around the globe, and movies and books circle the world in seconds. Hundreds of millions of people visit the same websites, watch the same TV channels, and laugh at the same jokes. These examples have contributed to the belief that globalization brings converging values, or a McDonaldization of the world.

Caricature of Pope Francis, acknowledged leader of the Catholic world

On the other hand, World Values Survey demonstrates that norms concerning *marriage, family, gender,* and sexual orientation show dramatic changes but virtually all advanced industrial societies have been moving in the same direction, at roughly similar speeds. This has brought a parallel movement, without convergence. Moreover, while economically advanced societies have been changing rather rapidly, countries that remained economically stagnant showed little value change. As a result, there has been a growing divergence between the prevailing values in low-income countries and high-income countries. These data support the Eurobarometer poll where countries in Europe considered as more advance societies are showing higher losses in belief in God in relation to North and South America.

Mr. Randy David, a respected sociologist, university professor, and newspaper columnist in our country, wrote an incisive analysis of the effect of this shift. The month of January is usually the celebration of the image of the Black Nazarene in our country. The tradition goes back hundreds of years. The legend goes that this particular icon was carried by a Spanish galleon from Mexico to the Philippines. Somewhere near the islands, pirates attacked and burned the sailing ship. The ship went down in fire. The only item that was saved was the statue of the Nazarene, now completely blackened because of the fire. The faithful saw this as a message from God. Henceforth, from the time it was installed in the Quiapo Church, a yearly procession takes place to celebrate the recovery of the icon and the countless miracles attributed to it through the years.

Last year (2014), the *Traslacion* or the bringing out and the return of the Black Nazarene to the Quiapo Church began with a Mass celebrated by our Luis Cardinal Tagle. Near the end of the Eucharistic celebration, a number of devotees rushed towards the Nazarene to take the statue and begin the procession. In the past, in mad rush which was more of a stampede, the "crown of thorns" fell from the head of the statue and disappeared. Fortunately, someone had picked up the crown and returned it, but only after the procession had been underway for some time.

The good Professor David believes that what motivated the person to return the crown was not fear of possible eternal bad luck but reverence for the image. He quoted the classic scholar, Paul Woodruff, "that views reverence as capacity for feelings and arising from a sense that is something larger than a human being, accompanied by the capacities for awe, respect and shame; it is often expressed in, and reinforced by, ceremony."

David is convinced that this virtue (of reverence) predates religion and exists independently of religious belief and as Woodruff wrote, "ritual and reverence in common life is so familiar that we scarcely notice them until they are gone... Home, above all, is the place where small rituals bring a family together, into a family where the respect they share is so common and familiar that they hardly recognize it as flowing from reverence."

Prof. David suggested, "Reverence is not mere respect for something; more than that, it is a feeling that impels us to do what is right."

"While we may often lose track of the idea and its importance, the virtue itself never disappears. Now and then we find ourselves groping for new forms of expression that can appease the nagging 'awareness of something missing,' " added Woodruff.

Woodruff's interpretation of reverence is limited to family values, a tradition that develops through the years but influenced by changing times. The change is not seen in material sense because it largely touches the sense of emotion or feeling. As a result, only an "awareness of something missing" is left for people to hang on. Many times the search for that sense of "awareness that something is missing" moves to the realm of the supernatural.

When family reverence is lost, reverence for the Almighty follows. Religiosity suffers and because of the need to replace the "awareness of something missing," people look for something easy to do where the "sense of guilt" no longer plays any role because people look at life only in the present.

This clearly supports the research of Euro-Monitor when it categorized people into those who believe in God, those who believe in some form of spirit-god or life forces, and those who do not believe in God.

This is the position I am taking in presenting to you the stories of my friends, those who are steadfast in their belief in the teaching of God, those who found relief in a different approach to the teachings of God, and those who still believe in God but no longer accept all forms of organized religion.

As we move on, Pope Francis, I carry with me your lesson, *"Genuine religion is incarnate...* Genuine forms of popular religiosity are incarnate, since they are born of the incarnation of Christian faith in popular culture. For this reason they entail a personal relationship, not with vague spiritual energies or powers, but with God, with Christ, with Mary, with the saints."

The Marian Pilgrims of Bishop Raul Martinez

Creeping Disenchantment

Dear Pope Francis,

Let me change the pacing of my letter and hopefully put in perspective many of the questions looking for answers during our dialogue in the tour bus. Bishop Raul did a capital job in clarifying many of them; but unfortunately, time did not allow us more detailed explanations of some of the intriguing issues that cropped up. Our country claims the unique distinction of being the only Christian country in the East; we adopted the faith of the early Christians, the Catholic faith, brought to our shores by colonizers. After the passing of a few generations, the faith is severely challenged; teachings that veer more than somewhat from what Jesus originally intended have sprung up like mushrooms after a thunderstorm. His sacraments seem to have become a bloody battlefield where people clash and part ways. The dogmas of our faith have come into stormy times, piling high tumultuously in our minds, a veritable Tower of Babel, especially for the younger generation, who seem to be looking for more "emotionality," in order to continue to accept the faith.

Unfortunately, many seem to see the grass greener on the other side of the fence even before they have watered their own garden. Already their eyes feast on the succulent hay in the pasture of the neighbor, forgetting that the barren ground under their feet is principally due to their own negligence and duplicity. This clamor for change is creeping on us slowly but surely, and will alter the rules and the very playing field where our children will do their own battle for eternal salvation.

I am writing you with utmost concern. Last night, I was fortunate to listen to the talk of Msgr. Sabino Vengco of the diocese of Malolos in central Philippines. The monsignor is a professor of theology.

In the many years of preaching, he has witnessed—and laments—the fast-growing number of Catholics lost to non-Catholic Christian charismatic movements. He says that the Church's enemy is no longer Communism after the dedication of Russia to the Immaculate Heart of Mary in 2005; the greatest enemy of the Church today is *secularism.*

Secularism, the monsignor says, takes away the belief that there is hell or heaven. It teaches that we should live only in the present; and to live in the now because time is now and there is no future for the soul to aspire to. His greatest regret is that this new teaching is what the young are seeking.

In the Philippines, we observe the same phenomenon of a younger generation drifting away from the faith of their fathers. This "shift" is immensely helped along by the fact that we have a lopsided ratio of only five thousand priests to 80 million Catholic faithful. Priests are grossly overloaded with so many clerical duties that they are often unable to even prepare a good homily for their parishioners, resulting in many of them moving away from the Church in disenchantment.

This is also the plaint of my friend John whose extreme disappointment in today's Church I am bringing up to you. John's disillusionment notwithstanding, it is heartening to note that comments and questions of the pilgrim group—who seem willing to listen and believe—serve as a counterpoint to John's very radical thoughts.

Before getting into that, let me emphasize that one of the purposes of this letter is to let the young know that we are interested in what they are saying, to give them hope that their elders are listening, to let them know God loves them, and that in them God reposes his hope. At the end of the day, it is they, the young, who will pick up needle and thread and continue sewing the word of God into the eternal mosaic that he has planned. Hopefully, we who have seen the ups and downs of life can help them and in the process benefit ourselves from the insights we continue to uncover and share along the way.

My grandson, an 11-year-old, who studies at the Ateneo, takes after my love for reading. In the house, we have a small collection of books. Often, he would scan the shelves for something to his liking. While there is the immense generation gap between us, he has a keen appreciation of the available titles which range from the easy-to-read paperbacks to the materials that are quite a bit of a challenge to tackle.

The *Lord of the Rings* while seemingly a novel to entertain, has many subplots, bordering on the realm of the spiritual; reading it left many blank spots in the mind of my grandson.

He came to me one day with a question. "Dadiruds (that's how he calls me), I enjoyed reading the book but I have difficulty understanding the 'power of the ring,' what's it about?"

I pushed my laptop aside and looked at him attentively while he awaited my answer.

"Luke, *baka kailangan,* perhaps it is best that you tell me first what you understand, then I can help expand on what you already know."

I have always made it a point not to spoon-feed my children and grandchildren. Reading is a learning process to enhance analysis and creativity and I believe in letting them work out the conflicts and resolutions that confront them on the written page. I wanted Luke to discover and internalize on his own the lessons which the book had to offer.

"Well, Dadiruds, there are several kingdoms in the story. They have leaders with good hearts as well as those with evil minds. Leaders of the kingdoms want power and strength. They have their respective rings which possess magical powers. But somehow, a ring was molded to possess all the powers of the different rings."

"The problem is," Luke added, "a person who puts on this all-powerful ring discovers an awesome overwhelming power making the wearer nearly invincible. Unfortunately, the goodness in them is overcome by evil of the ring." He paused to see if I was listening.

Then he continued, "The creator of the ring entrusted it to one of the Hobbits who had a clean heart. His mission was to throw this powerful ring into the pit of roaring flames to destroy it forever.

"The most ferocious leader of the different kingdoms coveted this ring so he could lord it over the rest. Only the destruction of the ring could stop his devilish scheme. I see in the story the unending fight between good and evil, where men with good hearts challenge the evil ones and bring lasting peace to the kingdoms," Luke concluded.

He sat keenly waiting for my reaction.

"Wow, Luke, you nailed that one perfectly on the head! For that, you deserve the complete set of the trilogy!"

No grandfather was happier than I.

And the visit we are making to the different apparitions sites of Our Mother is a gift I will love telling my friends, my *apos* and especially Luke.

One of the highlights of our pilgrimage that left an imprint in my mind was when we had a second session with Bishop Raul. It was entertaining and overflowing with lessons, to say the least. Pearls of wisdom from the bishop seem to be a commodity he never runs out of.

The many interesting comments I heard made me glad that I was part of the pilgrimage. Some were a bit difficult to comprehend, though:

"I am fortunate to enter a church—in Rome, to boot—after not doing so for a long time."

"Our children sent us on this pilgrimage."

"*Ayaw kong lumabo ang aking mata* (I do not want to lose my eyesight)."

"My children and I, are not close."

"Why do we worship Virgin Mary and the saints?"

"How come communities of other faiths are more vibrant than the Catholic Church?"

"The water is dry. Why did I not feel the cleansing spirit of the baths?"

"We have to share; it's the only option."

And there were more comments and questions which I can no longer recall. Those who had the courage and curiosity to ask were mostly from the younger members of our group—their questions on the whole centered on the absence of close interrelationships among parishioners in the Catholic Church, the ineptness of the priests in delivering their homilies, and the lack of a vibrant community. These could be some of the reasons that drove them to seek answers to their floundering faith in other church denominations.

The most frequently asked question of us Catholics is: "Why do you worship Mary?"

In our Mass at the shrine of Our Lady of Torreciudad in Spain, Bishop Raul shared a very nice story to illustrate the closeness of Mama Mary to her Son:

Bahala Ka!

There was a young boy who was afflicted with polio. Many times he would ask his mother why he had to suffer so much because of the disease. He asked, "Does Jesus love me?"

The mother, her heart rent by the boy's suffering, held him in her arms and replied, "Yes, darling, God loves you more than I love you and would do anything for you. Pray to Mama Mary—Jesus would never disappoint her mother."

When the boy's mother left, holding on to his bed for balance, he knelt and prayed, "Jesus, please have mercy on me, please heal me."

He listened for an answer, maybe a voice that would speak to him, or any sound. He heard nothing. So he spoke louder, "Jesus, please heal me."

Still no sound came. This time, with a threatening voice, he said, "If you don't help me, I will talk to your mother and tell her that you are ignoring me. You'll see. *Bahala ka!* It's your neck!"

Bishop Raul said that this demonstrates the abiding concern that Jesus has for children and the special place which Mama Mary holds in his heart. He cannot say no to her request no matter how impossible it may seem. The bishop reminded us that the Lord wants to hear us pray with the innocence of a child, and to stop rationalizing our relationship with him. Then he proceeded to the question often asked by non-Catholic Christians: "Why do you worship the Virgin Mary?"

The bishop explained, "We do not worship the Mother; we venerate her more than the saints to intercede for us. Other beliefs disregard her. They throw away her image. They say that God does not want us to pray to statues and images. And yet, in the Old Testament, God allowed Moses to put up a standard with the image of a snake, so when the Jews were bitten by a venomous serpent, all they had to do was look at the image and they were saved. Moses had pleaded for the people, "And the Lord said to Moses: Make a seraph and mount it on a pole, and everyone who has been bitten will look at it and recover. Accordingly Moses made a bronze serpent and mounted it on a pole, and whenever the serpent bit someone, the person looked at the bronze serpent and recovered" (Nm 21:8-9).

Bishop Raul paused. He looked at us fixedly, and asked in a stentorian voice, "When you hold the portrait of your mother, do you tear it to pieces and throw it away?"

"When you were young, in need of something, unable to help yourself, whom do you often call?"

"When you are hurt, don't you cry, 'Mama, please, my finger is bleeding, help me!'"

"Whom do you go to more than anybody else?"

My son Jun blurted, "It's Mommy." Then we heard somebody from the back say, "Mama," then another, "*Si Inay*," and on and on and on...

One of you asked me, "Why do we pray to the Virgin Mary?"

Bishop Raul was insightful. "When we pray to our Mother, we actually pray with her. The Virgin Mother constantly prays for us, whether we ask for her prayers or not, so when we finally find the courage to seek her intercession, when we pray for her help, she is actually already praying for us, all we are doing is praying with her to Jesus."

That engaging interaction happened in the cathedral of our Lady of Torreciudad; you will find this expression of love for the Virgin Mother so self-evident that it will leave you in awe. There is so much for the eyes to feast upon: the holy images, the architecture that captures the entire history of the Catholic faith, past and present, the solemn interior of the cathedral—even the way the pews are arranged...

Only one word describes what we saw: *class!*

This is the special way by which the members of the Opus Dei show their love for God and for our Mother.

The teaching of St. Josemaria Escriva can be summed up in these words: "Anyone can be a saint in the middle of the world. You do not have to be a religious because God believes you can bloom where you are placed."

Bishop Raul continued, "Opus Dei invites the leaders to come and join them. They have been accused of being elitist. But to incite change, you must invite leaders who are committed to change, guided by the Holy Spirit. What they have done to motivate leaders to join them is to form their priests very well and explain their position well. Their members go through intensive training. Anything they put up has a touch of class. They believe, to honor God, you have to give him only the best."

He stopped to allow his words to sink in, and then resumed, "In times of crisis, our Church always comes out with a person who gives an answer to the crisis. This was the role that St. Josemaria played. During the Spanish civil war, more than 2,000 priests and nuns were killed by the government. When the rebels led by Franco won, he had many people in government from Opus Dei which was then given the unsavory name of "Octopus Dei." But when you think about it, what Franco did was correct. He needed men of integrity who must penetrate every nook and corner of government and society.

In the personal prelature of Opus Dei, the work of God, he gave us universal call to holiness. You can be a saint while doing your work as janitor, or driver, or company executive, or teacher for as long as you do good work and offer it to God.

Pope Francis, this is the challenge—to hold the fort so Christ's disciples will stand fast, even as they ask questions to clarify their doubts. In that session with Bishop Raul, many concerns were raised but they seem trivial in comparison with the doubts of my friend John.

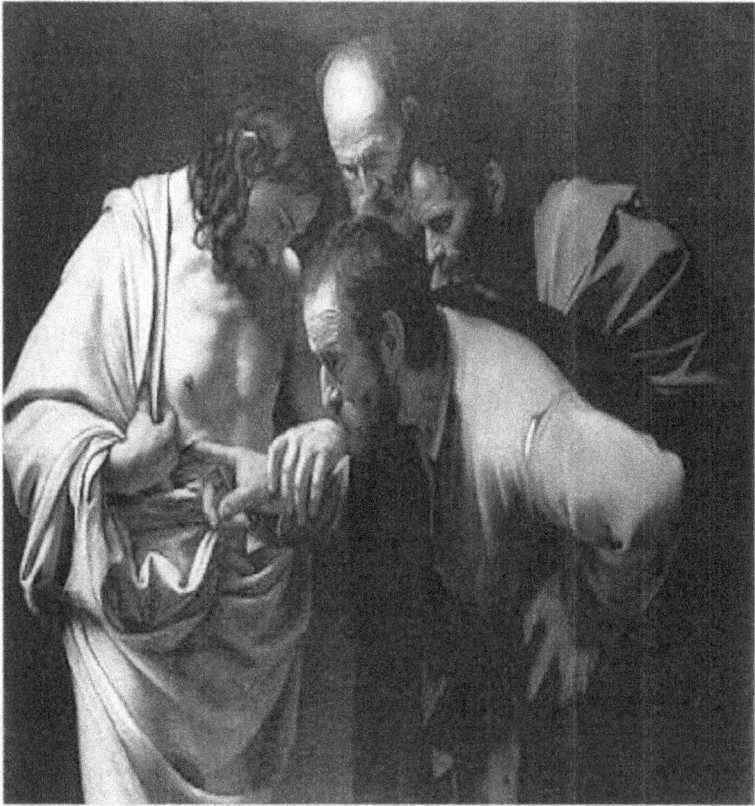

Doubting Thomas

Faith and Doubt

John is a friend from high school. The youth of today, seeing how they have their own reservations regarding their faith, would have no problem understanding where John is coming from and empathizing with him. He bristles with a laundry list of seemingly reasonable issues that beg for answers.

And what questions he asks.

Not a few times did my friend, John, share with me what I think were the most insightful perceptions of a number of Bible passages. In truth I have a long- standing invitation for him to join my Bible study group; our members will, no doubt, benefit from the fresh elements that John provides with remarkable ease and candidness.

He often poses to me challenging questions which some particular self-righteous persons may consider as bordering on the irreverent and heretical, blasphemous, even! However, I personally believe that those are his "searching" questions. Didn't Jesus himself admonish us to do this searching? He said, "Ask and it will be given to you; seek and you will find; knock and the door will be opened to you" (Mt 7:7).

Each time John pitches me those powerful questions, I would reel like a boxer hit at the solar plexus. I would break out in clammy sweat.

> "How come the Christian leaders, especially the Gospel writers, had not agreed on the exact birth date of Jesus?" "What about the other glaring inconsistencies in the accounts of the four evangelists?"

"How is it that the Holy Virgin Mary, Holy Mother of God, the most important female personality in the universe, was hardly mentioned in the most important book of the whole world—the Holy Bible? After the crucifixion, the Gospels have seemingly totally forgotten about her, where she resided, how long she lived."

John pressed his advantage, "If Jesus is the only Way to 'my Father's House,' what happens to the spiritual efforts of Buddhists, Muslims, Taoists, and believers in other faiths?"

"If God is a loving, omnipotent, and rational God, why did he create hell? Why did he give man free will when he already knew even before creation what the man would do with that gift?"

"How can anyone know about the Truth when it is humanly impossible to exhaustively try all the alternatives?"

John was a regular churchgoer. His *Nanay*, a single parent, was a fervent Roman Catholic. She made sure that he got his regular dose of *catesismo* whenever she was done with her chores as a store tender—a 12-hour job and sometimes even longer to accommodate late shoppers. His Nanay was an ardent devotee of the *Itim na Nazareno,* the Black Nazarene, and of *Ang Ina ng Laging Saklolo,* the Mother of Perpetual Help. Despite being perennially short in free time, John's Nanay very rarely missed the Friday Novena to the Black Nazarene in Quiapo, and the Wednesday Novena to Our Mother of Perpetual Help at the nearby Espiritu Santo Church along Avenida, Rizal. John always accompanied his mother in all her church forays and, of course, there was the never-to-be missed Sunday Mass. That, plus the short religious instructions conducted by a senior student of the secondary school affiliated with the Espiritu Santo Church, comprised the sum total of John's Catholic education.

John took pains detailing the specifics that drove him away from the church. Let me walk you to a few of them. There was a time when they were invited to lunch by the local parish priest on Good Friday. He expected a fare of fish and vegetables, in keeping with the Catholic tradition of abstinence from meat on this most solemn of days during Lent. But what greeted his eyes was a table groaning under the weight of *nilagang baka* (boiled beef), fried chicken, and a side dish of pork *chicharon* (cracklings).

Once, when John went to the church office to register and pay for the baptismal rites of a baby nephew for whom he would stand as principal sponsor, the parish official asked, "First class or ordinary, Sir?"

When John queried what the difference between the two might be, he was advised that the first class would have the ceremony performed in front of the central altar with all of the church lights ablaze. The officiating priest would be decked out in elaborate raiment. Ordinary would take place at the side altar and with none of the "extras."

John's uncle served as one of the respected elders of the parish community. He was also a church administrator of sorts. One Sunday, as the parish priest was about to begin the celebration of the Mass, a prominent local personage asked if his infant child could be baptized immediately before Mass got underway. The parents were in a hurry to know the answer. Whereupon John's uncle sidled up to the officiating priest and whispered the couple's request. The priest spoke as inconspicuously as possible, *"Magkano ang ibabayad?* (How much will they pay?)"

Apparently, John's uncle mentioned the correct figure because the priest commanded, *"Papasukin mo na* (let them in)."

A police officer, the brother of a business associate of John, had the most secure, risk-free police duty. His main qualification was "sealed lips." He was a bodyguard to the two children of a well-respected, high official in the Catholic priestly hierarchy!

A close personal friend of John was very much distressed. She tried to enroll her daughter in an exclusive all-girls Catholic school but was refused by the school officials. She was unable to present the school a marriage certificate. She is a single parent abandoned by the natural father of the child born out of wedlock; he is married.

Earlier, John had commented to me how unappealing the sermons of his parish priest were. He averred that this was true of the succession of priests assigned to his parish, wondering how these priests managed to hurdle their Homiletics. It seemed to John that the subject's "A" students were assigned to the bigger and "richer" churches where he had had a few occasion to hear Mass. "How I wish that *secret marshals* be assigned by the hierarchy to monitor the quality in terms of contents, relevance, and delivery of a priest's sermon."

John could only shake his head upon viewing the unruly mob at the Black Nazarene's long winding procession. One must be in his bare feet to join the procession, the better to feel the burning asphalt pavement underfoot or step on shards of glass and to bleed. Always there would be broken limbs among the "devotees" in the frenzy of their struggle to touch either the Nazarene's image or the towing rope that pulled the carriage where the statue stood. In a number of instances were cases of people who were trampled to death!

John finds it hard to believe that the parish churches do not frown on marrying couples with a retinue of sponsors in tow, sometimes as many as a dozen. The same is true during a child's baptism where it is not uncommon to count ten pairs of sponsors. John is often a witness, if not a participant, in this practice, having stood as a *Ninong* or godfather in several wedding and baptismal ceremonies. John has often observed how parents from the low-income sector of the populace would postpone the baptism of their infant because they were still saving the money to afford a big christening celebration to impress the *ninongs, ninangs*, relatives, and guests.

Widower John and his new wife were married in a civil ceremony. At the repeated advice of a friend, he asked to be married in a Catholic Church rite in his house. He requested the officiating parish priest to keep the ceremony as simple and as quiet as possible. His older children by his late first wife would stand as witnesses. "I am sorry, *hindi puwede ang* request *mo*. You have to follow church rules and protocol."

John, retorted, "OK *lang*, if those are the requirements." (He hoped he was able to conceal his utter frustration.) "Father, *puwede ba i*-bless *mo na lang itong mga* wedding rings *namin?* (Can you just bless our wedding rings?)"

"*Ah, hindi rin puwede.* No, that is not possible," the priest answered.

A much surprised John then asked, "If I place our rings on a plate together with some religious items, will you then bless them?" The priest could only shake his head!

John now understands why some people would rather avoid their priest: "Woe to you, scribes and Pharisees, you hypocrites. You lock the kingdom of heaven before human beings. You do not enter yourselves, nor do you allow entrance to those who are trying to enter. Blind guides, who strain out the gnat and swallow the camel!" (Mt 23:13, 24).

John rues that church leaders and congregation members have been enslaved more by religious protocol and folk religion than by the teachings of Jesus Christ! He is afraid that too much churchy protocol may discourage, even kill, the vibrancy of worshipping God.

One religious writer observed: "The church had lost its sparkle and dynamism, and had fallen into the trap of maintenance Christianity."

And now here comes John's knockout punch: "Rudy, my friend, I am sorry but I no longer subscribe to the practice of organized religion."

Pope Francis, I listened with the fullest attention and empathy to my friend, remembering well your admonition. I know there will be an opportune time when I can talk to him about your lesson, *The Revolution of Tenderness:* there is emphasis on our divine call to live in community with others… a message sorely needed in a time when so many are drawn on what could be described as the "inactive solitude" of virtual communities. The fact that we have been created in the image of the Trinity—the perfect divine communion—reminds us that we are meant to live with others that no one is saved alone. True faith in the incarnate Son of God is inseparable from self-giving, from membership in the community, from service, from reconciliation with others. The Son of God, by becoming flesh, summoned us to the revolution of tenderness.

"Do not worry too much about your children; your children have their own destiny and will find their own way." ... Inay... Author on the first row, extreme right

My Inay

Dear Pope Francis, let us leave the story of my friend John for a while. I sense an urgent nudging to balance my letter with anecdotes of love for the Lord, to lift the veil on the thought processes and emotions that make manifest the presence of God in our lives. As I compose this letter, I realize how propitious to write about our family, for the Sunday of the solemnity of the Holy Family is today.

The homily of the priest was inspired by the Holy Spirit. He spoke to us of the five languages of love. The little things we do, the smile we share, the nodding hello; opening the door for a lady, allowing someone to pass ahead, or keeping your peace even when someone jumps the line in front of you: these are gifts of love.

The opportunity to push the wheelchair of a loved one, to offer a glass of water to a person having a coughing fit, to drive your kids to school, or to accompany your wife when she does her marketing and carry the grocery she buys: these are acts of service that define your love.

And time, that precious commodity that seems always in short supply: I see the gleam in the eyes of Leth when I am home unexpectedly from my busy schedule and the joy in the welcoming shout of my children, "Daddy is here! Daddy is here!" Yes, so little time to meet all the demands on it, yet we do not know enough to spend more of it with our loved ones.

There are words that can either bring joy or sadness, especially to people who look up to us with respect; for them, anything we say is taken at face value. There is nothing in between—no gray—it's black or white, either words that soothe or words that cut and hurt.

How easy it is to bring joy with a simple, "Hi, how are you, are you well?" Or, the one phrase that we long to hear the most—the precious three words—yet hardly ever spoken, "I love you."

We are a hugging family, Pope Francis. The day does not end without each other feeling that touch of love. "Everything is OK with me. I am fine." Or, on the other hand, a lingering hug that signals something is wrong somewhere, "I need you, Dad, help me."

We held each other's hands tight while we sang, *"Ama Namin* (Our Father)," and when we wished each other the peace of Christ, we kissed and hugged. Pope Francis, there is no more ideal time or place to express true love in the family than during Mass. The Mass of the Holy Family is a gift from Baby Jesus, Mama Mary, and Papa Joe which deserves our utmost gratitude. As my friend John says, despite his growing ambivalence about his religion, "If we only thank God for the good he gives us, we would not have time for bad."

That particular morning in Lourdes, France, I woke up refreshed and unusually animated. My thoughts went caroming off in different directions although from somewhere scenes of long ago persisted in butting in on my consciousness. I looked forward to the day, filled with eager anticipation at its unfolding on such a storied land.

What lasting mark will Mama Mary leave on us today? It was natural, I suppose, that a pilgrimage to the Blessed Mother would rekindle in me recollections of my own mother who passed away years ago. I try not to think exactly when that was because that always tugged at my heart like it was just yesterday. But today in this quiet morning in France as I waited at my turn for a spiritual encounter with Mama Mary, thoughts of my late mother, *Inay,* came traipsing in on their own.

This morning, what played in my mind like a recurring theme were bits and pieces of "Oriental" wisdom that my mother would read or quote to me back when I was in high school. At that time, her words were a bird pecking nonstop at my ears, or the drone of a pesky mosquito about my head. Little did I know then that her words would eventually become the values which I would carry with me through life and pass on to my own children.

Nanay's random words, dimly recalled at first but slowly coming into sharper focus, arranged themselves into whole sentences like troops falling in formation, and then massed into paragraphs that carried complete thoughts.

I quieted my mind and bid it to resurrect the words of Inay that had lain forgotten in some remote backroads of the past. It took a little effort to remember exactly what those "gems" of wisdom were that Inay patiently taught in that gentle, sonorous voice of her; I hurriedly wrote them down in my ever loyal notebook where I scribble notes for future reference.

Some of you may have already encountered these words somewhere in your own lifetime—my apologies if somehow my version puts a different spin on the message or misses it entirely. Or worse, I might be conveying a lesson that is quite a departure from what my Nanay intended. Now that would be unacceptable. Already I beg for the understanding and forgiveness of my dear Inay.

> There are 1,000-year-old trees in the mountain but not many 100-year-old people because few people live that long. Think about it, it's a very lopsided ratio. It almost leads you to imagine facetiously that the stress of daily living is a natural weeding process so there will be more trees than people.
>
> Life is short; you don't have many years to live. Since you cannot take material things along with you when it is time to go, buy whatever things fancy you without being extravagant. But don't be miserly either. Spend the money that should be spent. Enjoy what should be enjoyed. Give to charity what you are able to donate. But don't leave all you have to your children—for you don't want them to become parasites. Don't worry about what will happen after you are gone, because when you return to dust, you are beyond praise or criticism.
>
> Do not worry too much about your children; your children have their own destiny and will find their own way. Your children, caring as they are, will be busy with their jobs, their commitments,

and the needs of their own families. Give allowances if sometimes they forget to visit because when they do come, they come with love ever flowing, like a rushing waterfall seen through the mist in the cool of the morning.

I don't know why the thoughts that occupied me that day were all about the past. It must be the place where I found myself standing that day. Maybe it was what Mama Mary wanted me to do in Lourdes—to remember the lessons which my own mother taught me when I was young.

Nanay loved her children with a unique kind of love, a love enough for us to feel that she would always be around when we needed her. Yet she kept a discreet distance between herself and us to make sure that we learned to figure out and solve problems by ourselves. She wanted us to grow up confident in our capabilities yet assured that her help was within hailing distance when we needed it.

In the twilight of her years, Nanay began "losing it." Her senior moments came with increasing frequency: small items or even money she couldn't remember where she placed, or whether she'd already put salt in whatever she was cooking, nor could she tell the difference—her taste buds had already betrayed her.

When we were younger, strange things happened which we could not explain. Were they a portent of things to come? I particularly remember the time when my *Kuya*, elder brother, had to force the lock of her *aparador*, an upright wooden cabinet, because we couldn't find her key no matter how much we tried. Nanay even offered a prize to the one who could find the errant item. Nine pairs of eyes searched high and low, moist at the thought of the prize—but none of us was successful.

Years later, her memory started playing tricks on Nanay, this time in earnest. We knew better this time, so we brought her to the doctor. She might have the beginnings of dementia, the doctor said. Funny thing about her condition, though, she could not remember things that just happened but she could clearly recall the details of events that took place years earlier. Many times, Nanay would ask me if

I had done what she asked me to do. My reply those days was pretty much the same—"*Huwag ka nang mag-alala, Inay, tapos na kahapon pa yun.* (Don't worry, Mom; I took care of it yesterday)." She would settle down, satisfied.

But after a while, when she saw me again, she would ask, "Rudy, *natapos mo na ba yung ipinapalinis ko sa iyo sa ibaba?* (Did you do the job downstairs as I asked you?)"

"*Opo, Inay.* (Yes, Mom)," I would answer cheerfully, pretending that she'd not asked me the same question just a few minutes ago. If you truly loved your mother, all her minor aberrations were easy to forgive. And I loved my Nanay.

Some say that age is a state of mind. But how might have that been explained to my mother who did not always comprehend the words you were saying? During those times, the only gentle recourse that gave her comfort was patience and a loving heart.

It is also during those times when the words of Khalil Gibran, the Lebanese poet whom everyone thought was a mystic, would calm me, "A mother is everything—she is our consolation in sorrow, our hope in misery, and our strength in weakness. She is the source of love, mercy, sympathy, and forgiveness. He who loses his mother loses a pure soul who blesses and guards him constantly…"

For a long time, I carried this particular stanza of his poem in my heart, especially the line: *She is the source of love, mercy, sympathy, and forgiveness.* It washed away some of the guilt feeling I had for not being able to be at the deathbed of my mother; it sounds so heartless and even cruel now to say it, but at that time, I let my job come first.

The sad truth is, even when I felt very close to Nanay, space and distance kept us apart. It was as if we were never really close after all. An anecdote from Mitch Albom's book *For One Day* will help explain the feelings I have about my relationship with my mother:

Times I did not stand for my mother

Take the shovel, the minister said. He said it with his eyes. I was to toss dirt onto my mother's coffin, which was half-lowered into the grave. My mother, the minister explained, had witnessed this custom at Jewish funerals and had requested it for her own. She felt it helped mourners accept that the body was gone and they should remember the spirit. I could hear my father chiding her, saying, "Posey, I swear, you make it up as you go along."

I took the shovel like a child being handed a rifle. I looked to my sister Roberta who wore a black veil over her face and was visibly trembling. I looked to my wife who was staring at her feet, tears streaming down her cheeks, her right hand rhythmically smoothing our daughter's hair. Only Maria looked at me. And her eyes seemed to say, "Don't do it, Dad, and give it back."

In baseball, a player can tell when he's holding his own bat and when he's holding someone else's. It did not belong to me. It belongs to a son who didn't lie to his mother. It belonged to a son whose last word to her is not said in anger. It belongs to a son who did not race off to satisfy the latest whim of a distant old man...

But that son was not around.

This son swallowed, and did what he was told. He shovelled dirt into the coffin. It landed with a messy spread, few gravelly pieces making noise against the polished wood. And even though it was her idea, I heard my mother's voice saying, "Oh Charley, how could you."

I can emotionally relate to Albom's story because I, too, did *not* stand for my mother.

We children loved her in our own special way. Mine was sort of a long distance love. Being the only one who decided to stick it out in our own country, I did not have the pleasure of physically being with her all the time. But I loved her no less. It was actually Inay who kept in touch almost every week with her letters.

Once I called her on the phone and said, "*Inay, hindi ka ba napapagod sa dami ng sulat mo sa akin?* (Mom don't you get tired of writing so many letters to me?)"

"Hindi naman, kasi pag hindi ako sumulat hindi ka naman susulat. (Not really, since if I don't write, you will not write)," she answered with just a hint of chiding in her voice.

"Pasensya ka na, Inay, heavy *masyado ang* load *ko sa trabaho.* (I'm sorry Mom, I'm just so overloaded with work)," I would say, although I knew I was just being defensive.

"What's wrong with your work anyway? Why not take a job that does not take you away from your family all the time?"

"I didn't want an ordinary job, Ma." I was this time beginning to feel that we were headed to the same conversation that I'd always have with my wife.

"What's ordinary, Rudy?" she persisted.

"You know, Mom, a job that doesn't make people think you don't exist, that you don't matter, that people will not miss you when you're gone." Did I explain it correctly? I wonder.

We had too many exchanges like this but at least it kept us talking to each other. "I write a lot because I want to hold our family together," Mother said.

While I failed her when she needed me most, I ask her to continue to be "the source of love, mercy, sympathy, and forgiveness" for a son who did not know any better. And if I may add, the saddest thing for a mother to say is, "My children and I, are not close." Those words from a mother sting deeply because then you know she is remembering the time when her children were so dependent on her, unable to do anything without her.

Time indeed catches up with us and puts us in place like a jigsaw puzzle falling together. When the energy of our youth has been expended and the beauty that once was ours begins to fade, and when the one possession we pray never to lose—the sharpness of our mind—is not there anymore, what is left but to cling to the love we gave our children, hoping that it is returned to us in kind?

Yet, we can only hope.

Pope Francis, my Inay, God, be kind to her soul, is here with me in Lourdes as I listen carefully to what Mama Mary's message for me is and hopefully, I will come to fully understand why she came the way she did and why she found herself in such a lonely place, when she could have come upon the nobles and the rich who surely would have received her in grandeur. It is a place where God leaves us a message, a message that is nothing other than that of the Gospel. *God comes to tell us that he loves us,—this is the heart of the message of Lourdes, and he loves us as we are with all our successes but also with all our wounds, our weaknesses, and our limitations* (Lourdes website).

Salamat po, Mama Mary

Pope Francis, Mama Mary, just like my Nanay, is always there for me. I came to Lourdes praying that she would help me with my breathing problems. I went up to her shrine with my son Jun pushing the wheelchair where I sat. It was a short climb, but steep. I requested to get off on the first landing. Jun was beginning to chase after his breath. The next climb, even shorter, was also steeper, maybe with 70- to 80-degree incline. With a mumbled prayer, I took the plunge or rather the climb, holding on to the railings for support. Simultaneously I did deep breathing exercise to force my lungs to expel the carbon dioxide beginning to be trapped (in my lungs).

I made it! Bishop Raul was there, "Rudy, believe *ako sa iyo, talagang mind over matter ang ginagawa mo.*" Bishop Raul and I both need wheelchairs when going up elevated areas, so perhaps my attempts to do things without the wheelchair was good enough reason for him to congratulate me. I smiled at him but at the back of my head, what was nagging me was that I was pushing myself; well, let's see how far Mama Mary would let me do what I wanted.

Everyone commented how lucky we were; our pilgrim group seemed to have the place all to ourselves. We were told that a big group just left the day before and another group of more than 17,000 people was coming in the next day. Talk about good fortune, we were nicely squeezed in-between which meant no lines at the *baths*. The baths were the one place that all of us wanted to visit. We ardently wished to dip in the ice-cold water and see what miracle, physical or spiritual,

Mama Mary would perform for us. The locals said that on regular days, the lines could take hours and the only pilgrims who were seriously physically challenged were given preferential treatment.

Pope Francis, my sons, Jun and Wally, and I went into the baths together.

There was a waiting room where I stripped naked down to my underwear. Solicitous volunteers attended to me. Before I stepped into the water, they wrapped me in a kind of terry cloth which I kept on even in the water.

Before I went into the main tub, I stood first on a step-down that was under water, most likely to acclimatize the pilgrim to the extremely low temperature. Immediately I could feel my feet starting to freeze in the ice-cold water. I gritted my teeth, trying to ignore the cold. I concentrated my focus on the crystal clear water.

When I looked up, before me was the image of Mama Mary. The volunteers requested that I pray with them. I have been praying the *Hail Mary* all my life. But now no words came to me. Then I had a chilly feeling entering my body, followed by a sense of heaviness that enveloped my entire being. I started to cry. I couldn't help myself.

People can spend a whole lifetime without giving any serious thought to the essence of life. Here I was face-to-face with the Mother of the Bringer of Life; and right then the notion that gripped me was that my own life unfolds every day with little real consequence because the essence of my life has been that, to be human. Yet, we know that a life which does not reflect the presence of the Lord does not amount too much, since we have narrowed our definition of it, as seeking and finding success in and of this world. We measure what we are by the kind of earthly achievement we credit ourselves, forgetting that the purpose of life is to prepare for the final meeting with the Lord.

Mama Mary eased my mind and pointed it to dwell on the pains suffered by her Son Jesus in giving his life for us. How unselfish of the Lady to put her Son always before, to the primacy of my Kuya Hesus.

At some point in our life, we pray for a good and peaceful death. So do I pray for that, now at 76 and counting? (In the Philippines, and I suppose elsewhere, it is a fairly common joke among the elderly

The drama of the relationship of Mother and Child is graphically interpreted with the Child's hand entombed in the hand of the Mother

to say, "I am now at *pre-departure*, just waiting for the final call for *boarding*.) My prayers to the Blessed Mother are prayers seeking her help; but she is not the one to grant me when and how my final hours will be. She is there to help me pray with her so my Kuya Hesus will remember me in all the years that I am still in my human form.

When I realized what the Mother wanted for me, I calmed myself. Then we started to pray together. I stepped into the bath, expecting the shock of the cold water again, but this time, I no longer felt it. It was neither cold nor warm. It was just perfect. I was told to go all the way under until my head was fully submerged. When they pulled me up, I felt dry. I requested for someone to pour water on my head. It felt wet but when I touched my hair, it was dry. In fact, my entire body was dry. I put my clothes back on as if I never went to the bath at all.

There was the feeling of lightness and of freshness that came over me that is difficult to explain. All I know is that I was touched by the Lord. I imagine that this was how I felt each time my Nanay bathed me as a child. Now I know why Nanay had been on my mind all morning.

After the bath, I went before Mama Mary's image at the Grotto and prayed the Rosary. The encounter and the thoughts I had in the bath kept coming back to me. I prayed even more intensely, savoring every word of the *Hail Mary*, as if looking for new meaning and insights in the prayer.

Jun and his wife, Ondine, recounted their own experience while praying to our Mother in the Grotto. As they glanced at her image, their eyes focused on her lovely face. Jun touched Ondine, "Look, Ondine, her eyes are following us, touching us with her words, 'I see you, I hear you, I love you.' "

For us who are strong believers, believing is enough. But we were also taught the need to understand our faith so we will not be blind followers because we did not know any better.

And then there was a gentle breeze. A voice whispered to me, "This is my beloved Son of whom I am well pleased."

I know those words. They were spoken at the river Jordan:

> Then Jesus came from Galilee to John at the Jordan to be baptized by him. John tried to prevent him, saying, "I need to be baptized by you, and yet you are coming to me?" Jesus said to him in reply, "Allow it now, for thus it is fitting for us to fulfill all righteousness." Then he allowed him.
>
> After Jesus was baptized, he came up from the water and behold, the heavens were opened [for him], and he saw the Spirit of God descending like a dove [and] coming upon him. And a voice came from the heavens, saying, "This is my beloved Son, with whom I am well pleased" (Mt 3:13-17).

Mama Mary says that she loves me. Is there any other explanation to this experience?

I do not know for sure.

I found an explanation in the last few pages of the book, *Fatima in Lucia's Own Words*, written by Joseph Cardinal Ratzinger, at that time Prefect of the Congregation for the Doctrine of the Faith;

we also know him as Pope Emeritus Benedict XVI. Let me precede his statement with the words of St. John Paul II:

> Throughout history there have been supernatural apparitions and signs which go to the heart of human events and which, to the surprise of believers and non-believers alike, play their part in the unfolding of history. These manifestations can never contradict the content of faith and must therefore have their focus in the core of Christ's proclamation: the Father's love which leads men and women to conversion and bestows the grace required in abandoning oneself to him with filial devotion.

Cardinal Ratzinger picks this up:

> Before undertaking an interpretation of the message of Fatima, we must still attempt to offer some clarification of their psychological character. In this field, theological anthropology distinguishes three forms of perceptions or "vision": vision with the senses and hence exterior bodily perception, interior perception, and spiritual vision…
>
> Interior vision does not mean fantasy, would be no more than an expression of the subjective imagination. It means rather that the soul is touched by something real, even if beyond the senses. It is rendered capable of seeing that which is beyond the senses, that which cannot be seen, seeing by means of the "interior senses"…
>
> Perhaps this explains why children tend to be the ones to receive these apparitions: their souls are yet little disturbed, their interior powers of perception are still not impaired. *"On the lips of children and of babes you have found praise,"* replies Jesus with a phrase of Psalm 8 (v. 3) to the criticism of the High Priest and the elders, who had judged the children's cries of *"hosanna"* inappropriate (Mt 21:16).

Perhaps at that precise moment when I looked at the image of Mama Mary, I became childlike once again in front of the Mother and wept. How could I not, when in her image, I also saw my Inay, whom I had not seen in a long, long time?

"Thank you, Mama Mary! *Salamat po, Inay!*"

Pope Francis, it was a morning to remember! We felt your teaching, *genuine religion is incarnate:* genuine forms of popular religiosity are incarnate, since they are born of the incarnation of Christian faith in popular culture. For this reason, they entail a personal relationship, not with vague spiritual energies or powers, but with God, with Christ, with Mary, and with the saints.

Experience and Faith

$\mathscr{P}$ope Francis, I continue my letter in relation to the sudden and totally disturbing outburst of my friend John that… "I no longer believe in any form of organized religion." In trying to discern why John is saying what he now says, I may have to cross the threshold separating the point of view of a layman struggling with the concepts—and yes, the mysteries—and practices of his faith into the rarefied realm of theology. I am fully aware that I am venturing into strange territory, the abstract subject being far from my comfort zone. On the other hand, my friendship with John goes back, and for me, it is unacceptable that it should be left at that, this gnawing idea he entertains of a Church that has done nothing but make things difficult for him.

I wanted to understand where John, in the popular colloquialism of today, "was coming from." I set aside some time for study, finally encountering what may be applicable "philosophy of thought" in the *Catholic Encyclopedia*. I read and re-read the meaning of *experience* as it influences faith in God. Needless to say, it was a stretch for me to fully understand every doctrine and theory put forth, but nonetheless, here is what I found:

Experience as tool for understanding is used often by Pragmatists. Professor F. S. Schiller, foremost English exponent of Pragmatism, thinks, "Pragmatism is in reality only the application of Humanism to the theory of knowledge." Humanism teaches that there is no absolute truth, but only truths, which are constantly being made true by the mind working on the data of experience.

In fairness to the Pragmatists, Schiller says, it must be recorded that when they claim to shift the center of philosophic inquiry from the theoretical to the practical, they explain that by "practical" they do not understand merely the "bread-and-butter" consequences but include practical consequences, such considerations as logical consistency, intellectual satisfaction, and harmony of mental content.

Knowledge begins with sense impressions which lead to percepts, concepts, or ideas. Incidentally, it may be remarked that the pragmatist fails to distinguish between a percept, which is particular and contingent, and an idea or concept, which is universal and necessary.

Let us take the word concept, and use it as a pragmatist does, without distinguishing its specific meaning. What is the value of the concept?

Concepts, we are told, are tools fashioned by the human mind for the manipulation of experience like the notions of one Time, one Space, or the distinction between thoughts and things. A concept, therefore, is true when we use it as a tool to manipulate or handle our experience, if the results—the practical results—are satisfactory. It is true if it functions well; in other words, if it "works."

Schiller expresses, concepts are "tools slowly fashioned by the practical intelligence for the mastery of experience"; they are not static but dynamic; their work is never done, for each new experience has to be subjected to the process of manipulation, and this process implies the readjustment of all past experiences.

Hence, as Schiller says, there are truths but there is no truth; experience is a stream out of which we can never step into; no item of experience can ever be verified definitely and irrevocably; it is verified provisionally now, but must be verified again tomorrow, when we acquire a new experience.

Therefore, the function of concept, of any concept or of all of them, goes on indefinitely. And if experience is in the shade of concepts even if the person experiencing it feels it real, his experience must continuously be verified again and again, for his experience may change as he lives to experience new things.

It stands to reason that the outburst of John resulted from experiences that dictated his position as far as organized religion is concerned.

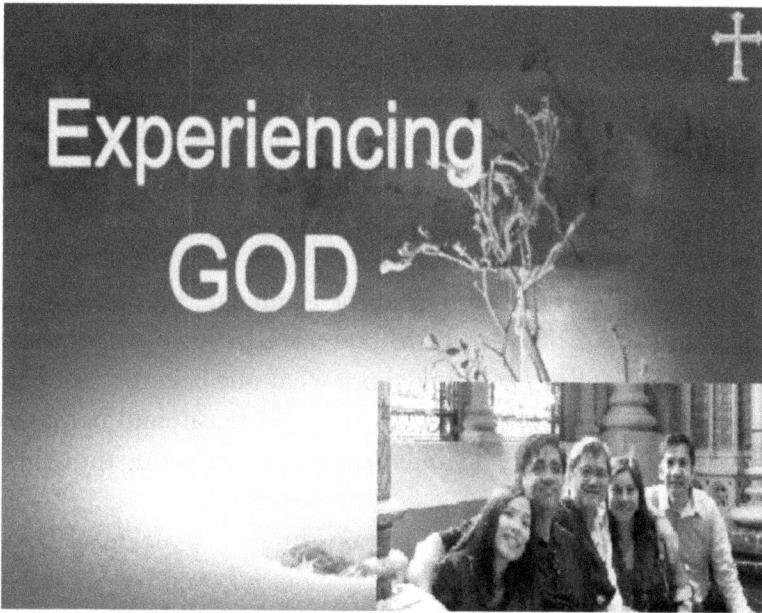

But Schiller also says that his unbelief in organized religion will be verified again and again by his mind as to its truthfulness and reality. New inputs that he perceives may change for the better or for the worse his current stand. His verification of that experience may lead him back to the fold as a Catholic or non-Catholic Christian which, as you yourself have said, our "conscience should respect."

John may go the other way. He may decide to be an agnostic—one, as you say, who is more "undecided" about his unbelief in God; or he make himself out as an atheist, one who is more "convinced" that there is no God.

Fr. Ranhillo Callangan Aquino, a theologian and the Dean of the San Beda College of Law, quotes Edward Schillebeckx: "Religion has something to do with interpretation of foundational, defining experiences. Experience which is narrated, is then retained in canonical writing, but that means that more fundamental than the writing or the scripture is the normative experience.

"But every experience," he continues, "is precisely experience only because it is interpreted. Without the concomitant interpretation, experience would not even be possible… therefore the lay person, who thinks about what he believes, and does so with some amount of systematicity, necessarily theologizes.

"Anselm the Benedictine intellectual put it best when he referred to the effort (of thinking about what he believes) as faith seeking understanding. Without faith, many things would be doubtful," he concludes.

Pope Francis, I have embraced the challenge that faces my friend John as my own, because I am convinced that only by seriously undertaking the effort to "think about what one believes" can I engage him intelligently regarding his growing skepticism and perhaps even bring about a satisfactory denouement to the competing thoughts now plaguing him.

While he was growing up, certain things happened to John that we would not wish on anyone, not even on our enemies. Giving it due consideration, John seems to have every right to ask, "Why are other communities more vibrant than the Catholic Church? Or putting it another way, what has the clergy done for Catholics?"

You have to understand that the '50s were a different decade. Those were uncomplicated years as far as our social and religious conventions were concerned. It was the practice then to visit relatives during Christmas, kiss the hands of your elders, and attend Mass in your Sunday's best. While in church proper, ladies covered their heads with *velos*, one hand clutching a Sunday Missal and the other furiously fanning themselves with scented *abanicos,* their way of adhering to proper dress code when coming to hear the word of God.

John's mother never went to Mass without that *velo* on her head. He remembers that his aunts wore the beautiful *barong-saya* with sleeves stiffened with *almirol* or starch.

During the Lenten season, families congregated in droves to visit the old Spanish churches during the *Visita Iglesia* ritual, timed after the Holy Eucharist was reverently brought out of the church, right after the Maundy Thursday evening prayers. The priest chose a location within the church compound so the people could symbolically be near the Lord; it was a tradition seen to strengthen the faithful's devotion.

A sight to behold it was—throngs of people visiting as many churches as they could, scurrying from one church to next, most of them afoot, for few had cars then.

When the moon was out, casting a silvery sheen on everything, pre-teen John and his friends were out, too, in full force, playing *patintero,* a local version of hopscotch, or *tumbang-preso* which entailed flipping an empty milk can in the air and making it stand as it lands; the one who could get the most somersaults from the can and land it upright, won.

In school, pre-pubescent boys of the '50s were having fun asking their classmates to sign autograph books, a not-too-subtle ruse to find out where the girl you had a crush on lived.

No McDonald's or Starbucks existed then. When hanging out with the *barkada,* your select crowd, the group used to go to *Aling Munding* for a steaming serving of *guinatan* or to *Kabisi's* bakery where for five centavos, you could enjoy *matsakaw,* a hard but crunchy biscuit that crackled satisfyingly when you bit into it.

My friend John grew up in a prayerful atmosphere that made him no less pious than his mother and the people around him. He never missed Sunday Mass, went to confession regularly, and received the Holy Eucharist almost daily. He believed strongly in the Lord, a child growing up in a world far removed from the pains and cares of life that is our inheritance, perhaps because his elders carefully shielded him from all that.

In John, no conflicting issues of faith clashed and caused in him any amount of discomfort or fretful anxiety. He went by what he saw and what he saw were his elders steeped in their piety and optimistic in their belief that closeness to the Lord and adherence to his teaching were the way—the only way—to material and spiritual salvation. John sensed how secure and unshakable their faith was, and even in his still-maturing mind, he knew that they deserved all the respect for such strength in what they believed; more than that, he saw that it was right that he patterned his life exactly in their mold.

What causes a heart so pure, so full of faith in its youth, to change as drastically as it ages?

"Should I keep the baby growing in my womb?"

13TH LETTER

I Grew in the Heart
of My Mom

John soon enough came to know that he was born out of wedlock. But the truth was broken to him in such a gentle manner that he accepted the fact with an open heart, even with a kind of secret pride that he was a "love-child." The loving aunt who told him the story of the circumstance of his birth made sure that trauma and confusion that are the common aftermaths of such a revelation would not find in John a victim.

John's parents had met in college, fell in love, and in an intimate moment, forgot themselves—and John was conceived; they were too young to marry. In those days, prominent families—the so-called *buenas familias*—like those to whom John's parents belonged, were very mindful of their image and took extra care that their reputation in society remained unsullied and always held in high esteem. What other people thought mattered greatly and an unwanted pregnancy had earthshaking repercussions in a "decent" household. One can easily imagine the scenario that would unfold when John's mother, trembling and with much hesitation, made the explosive announcement that she was carrying a child. It is a scenario that cannot be.

With the anticipated stigma looming like a malevolent cloud before her and her family, it was a tempting option to terminate the pregnancy. Having an abortion was a clandestine and illegal procedure, but then as now, there were people who would do it discreetly—for a hefty fee, of course. John's Nanay would have been freed of her predicament in a moment; all that she had to do was to learn to live with herself for the rest of her life.

But she was a devotee of the Blessed Virgin and for her there was only one option: she would keep John. No one and nothing could take him away. But no one and nothing!

"*Tiya* Vicky, you told me that my father left us when I was two years old. Why?"

"Your *Lolo*, our Papa," she patiently explained, "was very much opposed to your father who was then a mere law student. "Besides, he was *masyadong probinsyano* (too rural in his ways); Papa would derisively refer to him."

She added, "And the feeling was mutual. Your paternal grandfather didn't think well of your mother either. We heard him once ask, 'What woman would allow herself to be impregnated without the benefit of marriage?'"

Tears came unbidden to John's eyes. His Tiya Vicky pulled John close to her, wrapping him in a tight embrace. She whispered in his ears, "In the beginning after he learned of your birth, your father would every now and then visit you and your Nanay; we were then staying in an *accessoria* on Rizal Avenue Extension."

John's aunt stopped to compose herself, for she, too, perhaps overwhelmed by poignancy of the moment, was on the verge of tears. In a choked voice, she continued disconsolately, "Our place was less than 30 minutes away from UST where your father was studying law. He would drop by after class before proceeding to his boarding house somewhere near the La Salle College along Taft."

The woman released her nephew from her embrace to wipe her tears on the sleeve of her dress. Then she reached out again and draped her arm around his frail shoulder. "Your father wrote a note in his own hand where he asked your mother to take very good care of you." Then looking deeply into John's tear-filled eyes, she intoned solemnly, "Your father loved you very much, John. You must never forget that."

In quivering voice, she added, "Your Nanay, even today, treasures that note."

As it happened, just that morning in class, the preschool teacher, as part of the day's lesson, was showing the children the picture of a family. The children all noticed that the young girl in the picture had a different color hair from that of her brothers. One of John's classmates volunteered, "She must be an adopted child, look at her hair, and it's blonde and beautiful. Look at the hair of the others, they are dark like ours."

The boy sitting next to John leaned over and whispered to him, "I know all about adoption, I was also adopted."

"What does it mean to be adopted?" John asked out loud, looking expectantly at the teacher for an answer.

"It means," said the teacher, "the boy grew in the heart of his Mom unlike most of us, including myself, who grew in our Mom's tummy."

John asked his aunt, "Am I like an adopted child because I don't have a Dad?"

His Tiya Vicky smiled and nodded her head. John was at peace with himself. He knew that he grew both in his mother's tummy and in her heart. He concluded,: "God must really love me."

As much as he wanted to think that he was as normal as any child, events kept throwing him a left curve. When John was six years old, his mother took him for a visit to her uncle. *Lolo* Steve was an older brother of his maternal grandmother. They were seated at lunch when suddenly, the granduncle, who sat at the head of the table, blurted, "I don't know where that boy came from!" He was obviously referring to John, for he was staring at the direction of the child. It seemed that to some kinsmen John was a freak accident that should never be forgotten or accepted by the family.

That probably was the reason that he and his mother were staying with a half-brother. They lived on a two-bedroom apartment with hardly any space for anything else but to eat and sleep. Mother and son scrimped on everything: meals, water, and power consumption. Everybody was under strict instruction to turn off the lights before going to bed. It was a good thing that John had no problem falling asleep, an enviable ability he carries with him up to now. Most days his mother had to repeatedly call out his name to rouse him while preparing breakfast to make sure that he would be in time for school; John was ten years old then.

One particular morning, John woke up with a start and was surprised to feel numbness on his right side just below the rib cage. In a few minutes, the numbness progressed to intermittent pain, sharp and shooting, like a pointed stick jabbing at his insides. He had wakened up late and his mother had already gone off to work. The pain intensified and exhausted him; he couldn't make it to school today. And it won't be until several hours when Nanay arrived back from her work.

John crawled out of bed and plopped on a chair, thinking that it might be more comfortable there. He fidgeted and twisted in the chair, trying to find a position that would ease the pain; but it seemed only to grow more intense. He slid to the floor, laid flat on his back, and stretched out both his legs as far as they could go.

Sweet Mother of God, but it hurt! Strangely, John imagined that the pain had a color. And it was a searing streak of silvery blue that probed hot fingers into his side. Surely his mother would ask what he ate. It could be something that did not agree with his stomach. Stretched out on the floor, John looked with glazed eyes at the dirt-specked ceiling. The pain eased up a bit. He soon discovered that when he bent his right leg, the shooting pain went away and what remained was a dull ache that was more tolerable. He would remain in this position until his mother returned, John told himself; and he hoped that that would be soon.

When Nanay finally arrived after what seemed like a very long time, and accessed with alarm the situation of her son, she quickly funneled hot water into an empty vinegar bottle, wrapped a towel around makeshift hot water bottle, and pressed it on the spot of John's side that hurt. John shut his eyes and sighed in relief. The pain and discomfort abated somewhat. It was the healing warmth of the bottle; but John believed that it was the presence and touch of his mother.

However, at around four o'clock the following morning, the pain suddenly returned with a fierce vengeance. John gritted his teeth but that didn't prevent a wailing cry from escaping his lips. Tears rolled down his face in a copious stream. Nanay bundled him up, and hailed a passenger jeep to take them to North General Hospital (now Jose Reyes Medical Memorial Hospital), about an hour away by public transport.

John doubled up with pain in the passenger jeep even as his mother tried to soothe him. Minutes later, they alighted somewhere in Sta. Cruz district. John remembers them knocking at the house where a cousin of his father lived. There was hushed talk inside the house. John couldn't understand why they needed to stop in his uncle's house. His pain was becoming unbearable and he felt like throwing up. He saw his mother bid good-bye to an old woman. Just as they stepped out the door, John threw up.

"A few more minutes, John, we need to go to another house," Nanay said in a pleading voice.

John didn't say anything. The pain was more intense this time and he was trying his best to keep the gall from rising again in his throat. He needed to sit on the pavement because his legs felt like buckling under him. He had not taken anything the entire night before; hunger and the waves of nausea had sapped him of his strength. With a trembling hand, he made the sign of the cross just as his mother would when she needed something badly. He mumbled, "Make it go away. Please." When he looked up, there was a lady in front of them. Was this Mama Mary? John thought fleetingly.

The woman remarked in a worried tone, "*Ineng*, please, you need to bring the child to a hospital!"

Finally, after interminable hours it seemed, they arrived at the emergency room of North General. John was made to lie down on the examination table. Almost immediately, a number of people in white gowns, probably medical interns, came and began asking questions. John was writhing in pain and barely heard them. They turned to his mother instead. The resident on duty arrived, took a quick look and yelled, "Get Dr. Rotea, quick!"

Dr. Rotea did a rapid examination, looked at Nanay, and in an almost castigating tone exclaimed, "Why did you bring the child only now?"

Without waiting for reply, he turned to the supervisor and instructed, *"Sa* OR *na ito."* The good doctor knew an emergency case when he saw one; and he needed to operate right away.

Had the infected appendix not been removed on time, it would have resulted in *sepsis,* a usually fatal syndrome arising from the presence of microorganisms and their toxins in the tissues or bloodstream. John stayed in the hospital for almost a week. He required at least two weeks' bed rest to fully recuperate. His outlook was completely changed. The traumatic experience which he went through gave him another perspective. He realized that only he and nobody else could bring the change in his life as he promised.

While checking out of the hospital, John saw his mother handing over two pesos to the hospital concierge as a donation. It was all the money she had. Much later, he learned why they had to make all those stops on the way to the hospital. Nanay was literally begging for money for his medical treatment. For the first time in his life, he realized how poor they were.

John made a promise: he would bring his beloved Nanay out of the bondage of poverty. He would never let his Nanay beg for anything again—from anyone, especially not from his father's relatives.

"This I promise," John vowed, his hands clenched into fists. He raised them towards the heavens and with a fierce voice shouted, "Lord you have to help me… you owe it to me!"

Pope Francis, a young boy should never have to face hardships like this. The resulting trauma is too far-reaching and lasting. There must be a certain fundamental respect that elders must demonstrate when relating to the young.

Traits of courage, honesty, compassion and perseverance—these are virtues the young should be exposed to. We must also encourage them to discern the moral dimensions of stories and experiences which they encounter and adopt these as their own. When pride prevails, we tend to lose the innate goodness of our character which leads to a situation that the young get to experience the dark side of life. When this happens, what must they do?

Unlike courses in moral reasoning, the stories we must share with the young should open their eyes to the real and common world of shared ideals within a community of moral persons. Many times, whether consciously or not, we exhibit behavior that discourages the youth rather than motivates, deflates self-respect rather than builds confidence. We should show sincere love rather than fake a concern that children can actually see through quite easily, believe it or not.

Exposed to such a negative environment, where do you think would my friend John begin to learn about the sensibilities that would arm him for the battlefield we call life?

The things you want of us are sometimes difficult to comprehend, much less to do, even as we go on living. But as you said, time is now here, and we must wake up to change to make a better world and so we kiss... *The wounds of Christ...* "Sometimes we are tempted to be that kind of Christian who keeps the Lord's wounds at arm's length. Yet Jesus wants us to touch human misery, to touch the suffering flesh of others. He hopes we will stop looking for those personal or communal niches which shelter us from the maelstrom of human misfortune and instead enter into the reality of other people's lives and know the power of tenderness."

Pope Francis, I need your help to find an answer to my question, "Does experience really dictate our faith in God?"

Millions of devotees continue to survive the heat just to celebrate the feast of the Black Nazarene.

Black Nazarene

$\mathcal{D}$ear Pope Francis, Vatican II, as you well know, encouraged the Catholic Bishops' Conference of the Philippines to publish a version of the *Catechism of the Catholic Church* according to Filipino values and culture. Among others it teaches that Filipinos are family-oriented, meal-oriented, *kundiman*-oriented, *Bayani*-oriented, and spirit-oriented.

The *Catechism for Filipino Catholics* also affirms that one of the outstanding characteristics of our Church is we are a *pueblo amante de Maria*—a people in love with Mary. Marian devotion and piety seem conatural to us Filipinos… thus she is the center of family orientedness.

On the other hand, as *kundiman*-oriented, "Filipinos are naturally attracted to heroes sacrificing everything for love… Jesus as the suffering servant of the prophet Isaiah is portrayed through our favorite Filipino images of *Padre Nuestro Jesus Nazareno,* the *Santo Entierro,* or the Sacred Heart. Through these images, Jesus appears as one of 'the least of our brethren': the hungry and thirsty, the naked, the sick, the only stranger and the prisoner," (Mt 25:31-46) which truly describes the devotees of the *"Itim na Nazareno."*

A classmate of mine in college was an energetic disciple of the Black Nazarene. We both came from poor families; and were similarly driven by ambition to make something of ourselves. With the close proximity of our school to the famous Quiapo Church, it was inevitable that we absorbed some of the religiosity, or at least the external practices of it, that seemed to hang like permanent cloud over and around the area of the church. The classmate had been a devotee of the Black Nazarene since high school and every time we attended Mass in the Quiapo

Church, home of the much-revered icon, he would stay behind at length to pray before the darkened image.

> Once there was a religious man who spent much time at the feet of the Black Nazarene image praying and petitioning for favors. The Nazarene always granted the man what he asked for, often more than what he prayed for. So it went that every time the man needed something, he came and knelt before the Black Nazarene with his petition. His every wish and prayer were granted; hence he was seriously disinclined to engage in any productive activity, least of all if it required physical effort. One day found the man again at the feet of the Nazarene. With half-shut eyes, he murmured his wish beseechingly and repeatedly, begging that it be granted as all his wishes had been in the past. Suddenly, the Black Nazarene, in a loud booming voice that only the man could hear, said, *"Pag hindi ka umalis diyan, sisipain na kita* (If you don't move away from there, I will kick you!)"

We had a big laugh.

One feast day of the Black Nazarene, I joined my classmate— and a few hundreds of thousands others—in the annual procession. A jostling, pushing, sweaty multitude walked at a crawl fore and aft the *carroza* which carried the statue clad in purple robes and half-kneeling under a heavy cross. We were all barefoot, the unbelievable million or so who came to make good a *panata*, a personal pact, with God. "The greater the sacrifice, the more fulfilling the experience," my classmate explained. The heat of the asphalt pavement coming up through the soles of my feet was a reasonable sacrifice, the thought crossed my mind.

A UP professor in sociology, Randy David, who also writes a popular column, said, "I have been in pains to understand the core of beliefs behind this religious devotion. The Nazarene devotion seems to signify the continuing vitality of faith in the life of Filipinos. But, on the other hand, I cannot help wondering if this tremendous collective power can ever be harnessed as a positive force in the building of a prosperous nation and a decent society."

The sea of people moving in cadence as the *carroza* slowly snaked along the narrow roads of Quiapo district filled me with vague apprehension. Two long ropes attached to the right and left sides of the carriage were being pulled by the devotees. It seemed as if every one of the more than a million men wanted to put his hands on the rope and pull. But people were packed so tightly that it was virtually impossible to get into the line. It is no exaggeration to say that no space existed between bodies; mere breathing became a struggle. Those wanting to get their turn at the ropes walked alongside those already on the ropes, waiting for their chance to insinuate themselves in the tiniest break in the human wall. I was becoming desperate that I would never get to touch the all-precious rope. "Wait *ka lang, bubukas 'yan* (Just wait, it will open up)," my friend shouted hoarsely above the din. It was easy for him to say, for he was as thin as a reed.

Being an experienced "puller" of the rope, my classmate, as I guess, knew the routine; and it seemed, so did the rest. There was a prevailing spirit of oneness and sharing; every few minutes, someone already at the rope would signal the person walking next to him to get ready to take his place at the line. I stayed with a fortunate fellow and made eye contact with him. He nodded and said, *"Diyan ka lang, Bay, pasok ka pagsenyas ko* (Just hang in there, friend. I will signal you when to come in)."

I kept a close watch of the fellow. I wanted to be sure that I could synchronize my move perfectly to his stepping away; it would not be easy because scores of others probably had the same idea in mind. "And even as Filipinos carry their burden, individual and collective, they lend a helping hand to others with similar or greater burden. They pitch in and contribute whatever they can afford to give, aware they cannot be so poor as to have nothing to share. *Dahil ang kuwento ng Pilipino ay istorya din ng bayanihan, pagtutulungan, at pagbabahagi* (The story of the Filipino is the story of *bayanihan*, helping each other, and sharing with each other)," writes Gorgonio B. Elarmo Jr., whose mother is a devotee of the Black Nazarene.

In earlier years, up to about the time when my college classmate and I "worked" the ropes during the annual procession, the carroza was carried on the shoulders of men. The platform on which the image stood had the appearance of an oversized palanquin or litter, the preferred mode of transportation of royalty or gentlemen and ladies of substance in the olden times. Stout wooden poles, running parallel on opposite sides, were firmly attached to the high seat—for that was what it was, basically—and ferried on the shoulders of servants.

During the procession, able-bodied men took turns at the *pasan*, literally, the carrying. This probably was the most difficult, the most challenging—and the most coveted—place in which a devotee of the Nazarene wanted to position himself. The heavy weight of the carriage, the image and its accouterments pressed heavy on him from above, while a solid wall of humanity crushed on him from the sides. The air was hot and oppressive and not at all pleasant to breathe in. One could not stay too long under the load as the marshals would yank you out to make room for another clamoring devotee.

The crush of people around the carroza became a human stepping board for people to clamber upon to get onto the carriage. From there, they could launch a touch or one may kiss the image. In the melee, the crown has on occasion been knocked off the head of the image and its fingers broken. The less agile and daring simply hurled their handkerchief or towel at those who were already atop the carriage for the latter to wipe it on the image and throw it back at the owner. These items became priceless possessions and were claimed to be imbued with healing powers, which powers, however, were said to vanish after exactly one year; so people simply returned the following year, went through the same motions of pitch and catch, to gain back the attributes of the cloth.

Prof. David wrote of devotee Ramon Macaraig, a polio victim. "Despite his condition, he joins the annual procession without fail, hoping for a rare chance to climb up the platform bearing the statue and wrap his arms around it... in the meantime, his life dealt him another blow: leprosy, yet his faith is unshakeable... he believes Christ will one day make him walk and cure his affliction."

The devotees of *Padre Nuestro Jesus Nazareno* are exactly this: joyous and filled with hopeful anticipation.

The *Traslacion* lasted for hours even if the route it took only went around the Quiapo district. At the end of the procession, people tended to linger in the church, probably to thank the Lord for giving them another year to walk his *Via Crucis*. The veneration of people defied explanation. It could not be helped that the devotee saw the obvious parallelism between his tugging the rope or laboring under the pole upon which pressed the dead weight of the carriage, and Jesus' carrying the cross on the way to Calvary. In my case, I felt that I played the role of Simeon of Cyrene who had compassion for the struggling Christ and helped him carry his cross. It was a solemn, sobering feeling to imagine that for a moment I lightened the load of Jesus. The thoughts and sensations of those days linger with me, have become part of me, and will stay so till the last.

Pope Francis, I did some research on the devotion to the Black Nazarene and came across the paper of Msgr. Clem Ignacio of Quiapo Church. The study is lengthy and quite thorough and, more importantly, the gathered data perfectly dovetail into and enhance the concept Fr. Ignacio posits.

Archbishop Luis Antonio Tagle, DD, said, "To understand the devotee, you have to be a devotee. Only a devotee could best understand a devotee."

Fr. Catalino Arevalo, SJ, supported the Church leader's thinking and added, "Looking at how deep the devotion of the people is to the Black Nazarene, we can really say, it is real and the people's devotion is an authentic faith experience!"

The Traslacion of the Black Nazarene can be viewed as a "pilgrimage experience." Fr. Ignacio quoted Arnold Van Gennep who likened the Traslacion as a kind of rite of passage comprising three phases: separation, liminal phase, and aggregation.

The key is the point of liminality. This is the point where the pilgrims experience distance and release from mundane structures and institutions, where they are placed with their assigned roles and status in society. During the *limen,* they reach the threshold in and out of time. It is here that they receive "liberation," undergoing a direct experience of the sacred, either in the material aspect of miraculous healing or in the immaterial aspect of inward transformation of spirit and personality. This is the reason why pilgrims keep coming back. The cleansing, the bonding, the liberation, the experienced closeness with the divine, the "touching of heaven"—this is a kind of a personal "transfiguration." The paradigm underlying all Christian pilgrimages is really the Via Crucis. It is the Via Crucis, with all its purgatorial elements, which serves as the form of penance and prayer which initiates us to the paschal mystery of Christ.

At the liminal stage in the pilgrimage, heaven starts to open up; symbols become meaningful; awe, reverence, and silence manifest one's disposition to receive the imprint of the sacred in his/her life. "Bonding, cleansing, healing, and joy are the fruits of coming home to the life of the Trinity."

Cardinal Rosales suggested that in understanding more about the spirituality of the devotee, we should look at Mary who could help us look at Jesus. Mary was from Nazareth. Mary's poverty, simplicity, humility, patience, prayerfulness, compassion, love for children, her longing to be with Christ especially on the cross—these traits could be seen evident among the devotees of the Black Nazarene. A devotee of the Black Nazarene is poor, if not materially poor, at least one with the poor. Nazareth was a poor village. "What good can come out of Nazareth?" The *Anawims* or the poor of the Lord were the manifestation of God's providence and care for his people.

The devotion elicits compassion from people. Mary, the *Nazarena*, was very compassionate when she asked Jesus to help the couple at Cana. A lot of *bayanihan, pa-caridad*, volunteerism, is experienced in the Quiapo devotion. Even the practice of *pagpasan* is a very compassionate concept. Jesus always felt compassion for the crowd, the poor, the infirmed, and the children.

Mary carried the child Jesus in her arms. A very "incarnational spirituality" could be seen in this devotion as people touch, kiss, walk, bring cloths to wipe the face of Jesus. Touching was a very Galilean tradition. This bridging or connectivity with the object of one's devotion can be felt as if the image is very real.

In Nazareth, Jesus grew in age and wisdom in the sight of God and men. The Holy Family of Nazareth was the first school of faith. Devotees pass this devotion and tradition to their children and grandchildren. It is such a great consolation to see parents bringing their children to church and young people joining the procession of the Black Nazarene. There is hope for the Catholic Church in the Philippines.

We understand the apprehensions of our brothers in the ministry because we ourselves have not fully understood the depths of this devotion. And admittedly, when emotions run too high without reason, fanaticism sets in. However, first, we need to learn and understand about this devotion. We can learn more about it if we are willing to take off our shoes and kneel, to be touched and to bow. Only then will we see the beauty of the faith we have received from Christ viewed through the worshipful eyes of the *Anawims*.

Why do people appear to lose all their sense of propriety and balance in the mad scramble to pull the ropes of the Black Nazarene or better, to touch him? The very real possibility of injury or sometimes even death does not faze them; they plunge in, headlong in wild abandon, unmindful of the consequences. But the faith of the devotees is so strong that nothing but nothing will stop them from showing their love to Jesus. It is such a miniscule sacrifice; everyone is willing to give their lives to the Lord and to the Mother of our Lord.

There are ample opportunities for people devoted to the Blessed Virgin to be involved in her life in a deeper, more meaningful manner. As it is, a significant number of devotees feel that there is not enough reference to Mary after the ascension of the Lord to heaven. After the death of Christ, only John mentioned her in Revelation: "A great sign appeared in heaven: a woman clothe with the sun with the moon under her feet, and on her head a crown of twelve stars" (12:1). Paradoxically, there are also an equally significant number of people who are extremely troubled by the perception that the Blessed Mother is getting more veneration—even adoration—than her Son.

Does Kuya Hesus ever get jealous seeing his mother venerated by more devotees?

"Aba Ginoong Maria, napupuno ka ng grasya."

Mama Mary

Pope Francis, during our pilgrimage to Fatima, Portugal, I was one of those selected to lead the Holy Rosary prayer, as people from around the world joined the Marian procession in her shrine.

A process is followed where from among the thousands upon thousands of pilgrims visiting the shrine, representatives from ten nations are chosen. Each selected prayer-leader recites five beads of the Rosary in his own language. People who make up the entire congregation respond in their respective languages. I was paired with a Korean. However, for some reason, my prayer partner was not able to make it. I noticed the coordinator of the prayer sequence getting fidgety as the last decade of the Rosary, our assigned decade, was coming up, and the Korean was nowhere in sight. Finally, he approached me with an apology, "I am sorry, your prayer partner is not able to make it, can you please pray the complete decade?"

A thrill of excitement shot through me. Here was I, already euphoric to be one of the chosen few and this time being requested to pray the whole decade! I was not even aware of it but as I prayed, I was literally shouting. All I could hear was the sound of my voice reverberating over the entire ground. What gift the Mother had given me!

The spread of Marian devotions was preceded by St. Dominic's introduction of the Holy Rosary prayer among the people in need of an intercessor which was most needed during the Albigensian heresy. The people's faith is anchored on the belief that Jesus will never say no to his Mother. Petitions to her Son, especially those that are impossible, are favorably answered with the intercession of the Blessed Virgin.

The Holy Rosary of the Blessed Virgin Mary is a prayer that chronicles the life of Jesus Christ from his birth to the proclamation of God's kingdom, to his passion, death, and resurrection.

Non-Catholic Christians claim the prayer is boring, repetitive, and not based on the Bible. But if they look closely enough, they will realize that every decade of the Holy Rosary is drawn from passages in the New Testament.

The magnificence of the Rosary is found in the meditations that you do as you trace the life of Jesus. And so the oft-repeated comment that it is boring falls on its face because when you pray the Holy Rosary, you are literally reliving the Savior's life.

As we follow the life of Jesus Christ in the Holy Rosary, we realize that Mama Mary disappeared in the pages of the Gospels after the ascension. But John explains why. In Jn 21:24-25, "It is this disciple who testifies to these things and has written them, and we know that his testimony is true. There are also many other things that Jesus did, but if these were to be described individually, I do not think the whole world would contain the books that would be written."

And I dare say that if just a tenth of those books were written to give the world a chance to know more of the life of Christ, more than half of the stories would be about the Blessed Mother.

Even as I make this conclusion, our Mother came back to us many times in the form of apparitions and personal visits to mystics, to share her life after the ascension of the Lord.

Rev. Edward A. Ryan, SJ, in his foreword to the book of Raphael Brown, *The Life of Mary: As Seen by the Mystics* wrote: While some persons may, doubtless, wish that the readers of this book will remember at every page the prudent warning sounded in the introduction, that the work is to be read as a religious novel and not as a fifth Gospel, nevertheless many Catholics and non-Catholics, too, will be very thankful for this pleasing compilation of vivid narratives of the Blessed Virgin's life, "as seen by" four great mystics of the Church.

The Blessed Virgin, speaking of Pentecost, said to Venerable Mother Mary of Agreda: "My daughter, the children of the Church hold this blessing of Almighty God in small esteem and thankfulness.

The Divine Spirit, in coming for the first time upon the Apostles, intended it as a pledge and proof that he would confer the same favor on the rest of the children of the Church, and that he was ready to communicate his gifts to all who would dispose themselves to receive them. In our times, too, he comes to many just souls, although not so openly. Blessed is the soul who longs for his grace which enkindles, enlightens, and consumes all that is earthly and carnal and raises it up to a new union with God himself. As your true and loving Mother, I want you to have this happiness, and therefore I again urge you to prepare your heart by trying to maintain an unshatterable inner peace and calm, no matter what happens to you."

After the resurrection, there are stories of Christ meeting with the apostles. Bible scholars believed that his death caused the apostles to fear for their lives. The same Bible scholars and theologians concluded at the same time that only the presence of the Blessed Mother was the calming influence that sustained the apostles until the Lord sent the Holy Spirit, and gave them confidence to spread the Word.

During Mary's last years, The Blessed Virgin said to St. Bridget of Sweden: "After the ascension of my Son, I still lived a long time in the world. Such was the will of God, in order that by seeing my patience and my conduct, many more souls might be converted to him, and in order that the Apostles and other elects of God might be strengthened. Also the natural constitution of my being required that I would live longer and that thereby my crown might be increased.

"During all the time that I lived after my Son's ascension, I visited the places where he had suffered and where he had performed his miracles. Thus the memory of his passion became so imprinted on my heart that it ever remained quite fresh in my mind, whether I happened to be eating or working.

"My senses where so completely withdrawn from worldly things that I constantly alternated between new supernatural yearnings and sorrows, yet, I controlled my grief and my joy in such a way that I did not neglect any of my duties toward God. My way of life among people was such that aside from my scanty meals I paid no attention to what human beings thought of me or expected me to do."

During Mary's dormition, the Blessed Virgin said to Venerable Mother Mary of Agreda: "My daughter, I wish to inform thee of another privilege which was conceded to me in the hour of my glorious Transition. It was this: that all those devoted to me who shall call upon me at the hour of death, making me their Advocate in memory of my happy Transition and of my desiring to imitate my Son in death, shall be under my special protection in that hour and shall experience my intercession.

"And since death follows upon life and ordinarily corresponds with it, the surest pledge of a good death is a good life, a life in which the heart is freed and detached from earthly love."

Dormition is the time when the Blessed Mother went to sleep. Her soul separated from her body. Her body stayed on earth and after a short while, joined her in heaven. The Eastern Orthodox Church, which recognizes St. Andrew as its Vicar, holds that the body of our Mother is still on earth, uncorrupted, and will join her soul in heaven in the end days during the second coming. However, the Roman Catholic Church, in proclaiming the dogma of the assumption of the Blessed Virgin, stated that the Mother assumed into heaven body and soul. The Blessed Mother said the same thing to St. Bridget of Sweden.

In the assumption, the Blessed Virgin said to St. Bridget of Sweden: "One day while I was admiring the love of God in a spiritual ecstasy, my soul was filled with such joy that it could hardly contain itself and during that contemplation my soul departed from my body. You cannot perceive then and in what honor the Father, the Son, and the Holy Spirit welcomed it, and with what a multitude of angels it was carried upward."

"But those persons who were in my house with me when I gave up my spirit fully understood what divine mysteries I was then experiencing, because of the unusual light which they saw."

"Thereafter those friends of my Son who had been brought together by God buried my body in the valley of Josaphat. Countless angels accompanied them."

"My body lay entombed in the ground. Then it was taken up to heaven with infinite honor and rejoicing. There is no other human body in heaven except the glorious Body of my Son and my body."

"That my assumption was not known to many persons was the will of God, my Son, in order that faith in his Ascension might first of all be firmly established in the hearts of men, for they were not prepared to believe in his ascension, especially if my assumption had been announced in the beginning."

In book of Revelation, John, the apostle whom Jesus loved, described a figure applied to the Blessed Virgin Mary as Queen of heaven and earth. "A great sign appeared in the sky, a woman clothed with sun, with the moon under her feet, and on her head a crown of twelve stars. She was with child and wailed aloud in pain as she labored to give birth" (Rv 12:1-2).

The teaching of our faith is founded on Scripture and Tradition, carefully guarded by the Magisterium of the Church, and through which dogmas are proclaimed. Roman Catholic Marian dogmas have two functions: they present infallible Church teachings about Mary and her relation to Jesus Christ, and they praise Mary and, through Mary, God's deed on Mary. All Marian dogmas teach about her divine Son and highlight the divine nature of Jesus Christ.

There are four Marian dogmas among a large number of other teachings about the Blessed Virgin. There is now an ongoing discussion of a proposed fifth Marian dogma, the Blessed Virgin as Mediatrix and Co-redemptrix in the salvation of Christendom with Jesus Christ. Below are the existing dogmas about the Virgin Mary:

Name	First Magisterial definition	Dogma content
Perpetual virginity	Baptismal symbols since the third century	"Perpetual virginity of Mary" means that Mary was a virgin before, during, and after giving birth
Mother of God	Council of Ephesus (431)	Mary is truly the mother of God, because of her unity with Christ, the Son of God

Immaculate Conception	Pope Pius IX (1854)	Mary, at her conception, was preserved immaculate from original sin
Assumption into heaven	Pope Pius XII (1950)	Mary, having completed the course of her earthly life, was assumed body and soul into heavenly glory

Pope Francis, to properly place our devotion to the Black Nazarene and the Blessed Virgin Mary, the *Catechism for Filipino Catholics* explains the "doctrine" about the identity, meaning, suffering, commitment, and worldview of Filipino Catholics lived according to Christian morality, especially Christ's basic commandment of love... Christ's Spirit works from within to purify the warm piety of Filipino Catholic devotions from all superstitious practices and magical faith healers. Authentic Spirit-inspired Christian prayer helps direct these simple expressions of heartfelt love through Christ to the Father. Of particular importance are the traditional Filipino Marian devotions which draw on and express the deep yearnings of Filipino Catholics.

Our faith is basically captured by your teaching that... *genuine religion is incarnate...* Genuine forms of popular religiosity are incarnate, since they are born of the incarnation of Christian faith in popular culture. For this reason, they entail a personal relationship, not with vague spiritual energies or powers, but with God, with Christ, with Mary, and with the saints.

Our devotion to the Black Nazarene and to our Mother are beliefs ingrained in our hearts... they are here to stay because they are our ways of reaching the heart of God.

I Gave You Free Will

Pope Francis, I must admit that it took some doing—even a kind of moral courage—for John to throw down the gauntlet before the Lord. Courage is synonymous with bravery and of that Aristotle had this to say: "We become brave by doing brave acts."

Was it the same kind of courage whereof the great philosopher spoke? Or was it the rashness of a reckless person that bordered on stupidity, that drove John to fire his broadside against organized religion? Certainly, he was aware of the risks involved. At best, he could generate empathy or even a modest following, but it was more likely that his sudden turnaround would be an embarrassment to those who knew him.

There was, I could sense, a bit of the moth in John, flirting with the oil lamp to see how close he could get without searing his wings in the dancing flame. The dangerous flirtation notwithstanding, John felt safe; and his safety net came from no place else than his fundamental—and unshakable—belief in the Lord's teaching. Recall that John grew up in an environment of religiosity, although that by itself was no guarantee that he had learned the *true* teaching of the Lord. It is a fairly common situation and Bishop Raul bewails that fact that we Filipinos do not really know our faith. Our religious practices, are in the main, sacramental in approach. Our way of knowing God is ritualistic rather than one that comes out of conscious reflection. We are intimately acquainted with the sacraments but we are not evangelized. Along the way, the real teaching of God may have escaped us, raising the possibility that the Word of God is actually lost on us.

The "Dream Team" gifted with GOD'S FREE WILL.
Standing on the extreme left is the author, fourth is Veronica, and extreme right is John.

John in his youth believed that God was there at his beck and call. This is entirely plausible because in his particular situation, i.e., a love child with hostile relatives, he found much solace in God. Neither is it implausible to imagine that he carried the mind-set that God owed him into his adult life.

In his older years, John grew progressively unhappy with the disciples of St. Peter, a few of whom seemed not fully aligned with the teaching of Christ. Jesus teaches that his church is founded on good relationships. But often we allow pride to rule our lives, and pride, as we know, is the undoing of good relationships. Even the clergy, mortal as the members are, are not spared. Their superior knowledge of dogma and faith developed over years of intense study has given them the edge over us, "lesser mortals." Intellectual superiority is a heady brew and can easily be used as a bludgeon to hammer people into a flock of blind followers.

At this point, Pope Francis, we need to address his question, "If God is a loving, omnipotent, and rational God, why did he create hell? Why did he give man free will when he already knew even before creation what man will do with that gift?"

I simply want to put forward an explanation which I myself can understand. Free will is defined as the power of acting without constraint or fate; the ability to act at one's own discretion, to have self-determination and freedom of choice. This I can comprehend; and in my linear way of thinking, what I can understand can be understood by all:

If God knows our free will choices, do we still have free will?

I've always been puzzled by the notion held by some people that if God knows what we are going to choose in the future, then we don't really have free will. They say that if God knows we are going to make a certain "free will" choice, then when it is time for us to make that choice, because God knows what we are going to choose, we are not really free to make a different choice and God's foreknowledge means that we cannot have free will.

Quite honestly, I do not see this as being a problem at all. Let's work with the idea that we are free-will creatures and that God knows all things, even our future choices... Furthermore, let's define free will in the Open Theist sense as the ability to make equal choices between options, regardless of a person's sinful nature. Given these conditions, are God's omniscience and our free will incompatible as the Open Theists claim?

By analogy, knowing what will happen does not mean that we are preventing or causing that thing to happen. The sun will rise tomorrow. I am not causing it to rise nor am I preventing it from rising by knowing that it will happen. Likewise, if I put a bowl of icecream and a bowl of cauliflower in front of my child, I know for a fact which one is chosen—the icecream. My knowing it ahead of time does not restrict my child from making a free choice when the time comes. My child is free to make a choice and knowing the choice has no effect upon her when she makes it.

Logically, God knowing what we are going to do does not mean that we *can't* do something else. It means that God simply knows what we have *chosen* to do ahead of time. Our freedom is not restricted by God's foreknowledge; our freedom is simply realized ahead of time by God...

Part of the issue here is the nature of time. If the future exists for God even as the present does, then God is consistently in all places at all times and is not restricted by time. This would mean that time was not a part of his nature to which God is subject and that God is not a linear entity, that is, it would mean that God is not restricted to operating in our time realm and is not restricted to the present only.

If God is not restricted to existence in the present, our present, then the future is known by God because God dwells in the future as well as the present (and the past). This would mean that our future choices, as free as they are, are simply known by God.

Again, our ability to choose is not altered or lessened by God existing in the future and knowing what we freely choose. It just means that God can see what we will freely choose—because that is what we freely choose—and knows what it is.

Part of the problem in Open Theism is restricting God to the present only, his existence is defined in such a way as to imply that time is part of his nature and that he is restricted to it. The question is whether or not this is logical as well as biblical.

Scripturally, God inhabits eternity. Psalm 90:2 says, "Before the mountains were born, the earth and the world brought forth, from eternity to eternity you are God."

But this verse, and others, does not declare that God lives inside or outside of time. Rather, the Bible tells us that God is eternal. We can, however, note that the Bible teaches that God has no beginning or end… and that since the word "beginning" denotes a relationship to and in time, and since God has no beginning, that time is not applicable to God's nature.

In other words, God has no beginning and since "beginning" deals with an event in time, God is outside of time.

"To you in your bed there came thoughts about what should happen in the future, and he who reveals mysteries showed you what is to be" (Dn 2:29).

So, in relation to our free will and Gods predictive ability, there is no biblical reason to assert that God's foreknowledge negates our freedom.

There is no logical reason to claim that if God knows what choices we are going to make, it means we are not free. It still means that the free choices we will make are free—they are just known ahead of time by God.

If we choose something different, then that choice will have been eternally known by God. Furthermore, this knowledge by God does not alter our nature in that it does not change what we are—free to make choices.

God's knowledge is necessarily complete and exhaustive because that is his nature, to know all things. In fact, since he has eternally known what all our free choices will be, he has ordained history to come to the conclusion that he wishes to include and incorporate our choices into his divine plan: "Indeed they gathered in this city against your holy servant Jesus whom you anointed, Herod and Pontius Pilate, together with the Gentiles and the peoples of Israel, to do what your hand and [your] will had long ago planned to take place" (Acts 4:27-28).

Why? Because God always knows all things. In 1 John 3:20, "God is greater than our hearts and knows everything (cf. Matt Slick, *Christian Apologetics and Research Ministry*).

From the hospital, John and his mother went home to the same cramped apartment. If there was any improvement, Nanay provided him with a folding cot that was at least a step above in comfort from the hard plywood that used to be his bed. The cot was located under the stairwell and Nanay tacked old newspapers on the underside of the stairs to keep dust and dirt from drifting down on him as he lay on cot; as a "recovery room" it would have to do, although he thought that his mother should hang a curtain from the stairs to give him a sense that his was a real private room. But he decided that was too much to ask.

He needed to focus on the promise he made. Still, his Nanay very patiently stitched together a bedsheet for him from pieces of scrap cloth materials of various shape and size until she completed an entire spread done in a wonderfully motley, crazy-cut pattern.

There was no end to Nanay's caring love.

Each morning before she left for the store, she would leave on the chair beside him a glass of water, his medicines, and some loose coins. The coins were for his midday snack that the trusted *kasambahay* could step out and buy. In the evening when Nanay returned, she never failed to bring some *pasalubong*—John's favorite food or a book to read—to help him get quickly back on his feet.

The operation was taking time to heal. John was still weak and bound to his bed. One evening, voices aroused him from sleep; there were visitors in the house.

"*Kumusta ang bata* (How is the boy?)"

Pope Francis, John recognized the male voice. It belonged to his *Tiyo* Peter, Dr. Peter Ruiz, his father's older brother. John remembered meeting him in the past in an occasion which he could not recall although the sensation of the crisp twenty-peso bill that his uncle had pressed into his hand then suddenly came back to him. John opened his eyes. He saw that his uncle had come along with his wife, *Tiya* Minnie. Dr. Ruiz stood beside his cot, stooping slightly to avoid hitting his head against the stairs. The older man lifted the multicolored blanket and pulled up John's T-shirt to expose the bandage covering the incision. Then he peeled off the bandage. The look of grave concern on his uncle's face, although fleeting, did not escape John. The doctor carefully replaced the wound dressing.

"*Gagaling ka na* (You are going to get well soon)," he told John.

But the tone of his voice sounded as if he was saying it just for the benefit of the boy; something was bothering him. He turned to Nanay, and said, "*Mag-usap tayo*, Connie. Let's talk."

The three adults left John and walked the few steps to the living room. They began to talk in hushed tones that he could hardly hear. Then somebody started to sob. It was his Nanay. After a time, the three returned to his cot. Nanay's eyes were dry but they were swollen and red. Gently she said, "*May sasabihin sa iyo ang Tiyo Peter mo* (Your uncle Peter has something to tell you)."

"*Totoy, pumayag na ang Inang mo na sumama ka sa amin sa Bulacan. May mga* nurses *ako doon na mag-aalaga sa iyo. Matitingnan pa kita araw-araw* (Boy, your Mom has agreed for you to come with us in Bulacan where you will recuperate faster. We have nurses there who will take care of you and I will always see you and help in your recovery)."

His uncle owned a hospital in Hagonoy, a town on the plains of Central Luzon. Never having been there before, John could not imagine how far away the place was. His Nanay had not been asked to join him. He was only ten years old. So John tearfully cried out, "*Ayaw ko, po. Dito na lang po ako sa Nanay.*"

When John looked at her direction, Nanay was covering her face with a hand towel. But he could see her shoulders shaking. She was failing miserably in trying to keep her composure. Then she spoke. "Please John, go with them. They have nice hospital beds, the food is good, and I will visit you often."

Her last statement alarmed him. It had finally sunk in that it meant that he would be staying with them for a longer time than he could imagine. "*Papasyal tayong madalas dito sa Inang mo* (We will visit your mother as often as we can)," Tiyo Peter promised.

"*Nay, ayoko talaga* (I really don't want to go, Mom)!" John was adamant; he knew that he must be firm. He made a promise for his mother that he had to keep.

In a conniving tone that grown-ups use to inveigle children, Dr. Peter Ruiz said: "You will study in a private school. After high school, you will enroll in La Salle and we will live in my place just back of the school. Or maybe you want to go to UST? Your Mom said that you wanted to be a doctor, just like me. Come on, come with us, *hijo*."

Nanay was quiet. Despite his young age, John could sense how miserable all this had made his mother. "*Ayaw ko po talaga* (I really don't want to go)!" John repeated, his voice thick with all the stubbornness he was capable of. It was like he was being given up for adoption.

There was an audible sigh from Dr. Reyes. "Alright, I will not force you but please think about it. This is for your future and your mother's. If you change your mind, just let me know." Then to Nanay, he said. "Send me a telegram, Connie, and I will come for the boy."

Slipping Point

The years ahead were an arduous trek for John as he strove to fulfill the promise he made to his Nanay. The times changed him. The challenge he threw at God at his nadir became the beacon that guided his life. God was kind to him during the struggling years; but John did not think much of that. After all, the world owed him and it was only proper that he got his just dues.

When Nanay died, John was inconsolable. He could not comprehend that when he was at the threshold of fulfilling his vow to raise his mother from the clutches of poverty, God took her. It was a conspiracy and betrayal of the worst kind. The bitterness in him knew no limit. It was as if God gave him something and took something of infinitely more value in return. He realized this time that one has to pay for everything that he got. That feeling of numb acceptance never really went away as John plodded on to create a life of comfort for his family.

John surely realizes that his life is not unique. The world abounds with similar stories, mirror images but for small variations here and there. Environment exerts a great influence on how a child's future will turn out. John's mother always stood for him as much as other relations stood *away* from him. All his prayers were answered by God especially when he challenged the Lord to help him achieve a materially better life.

The turning point occurred on the way to the hospital. His Nanay had to beg to be able to pay for his operation. It hardened his heart such that ultimately he did not recognize anymore the verity that it was the Lord who was offering him what he needed

Your dream is limited only by your imagination

the most—a chance to study in a good school to prepare him for life's uncompromising challenges.

Before God answers prayers, he puts us in the crucible to test our worthiness and to be sure that we emerge purified as molten steel; we are tempered and honed, enough to cut our way through life's unending thickets.

In his adult years, John kept the bitterness of his youth buried deep within him. He delivered on his promise and did make something of himself. The road was difficult, uphill mostly. After high school, there was no money to support his college studies.

He once tried to seek the assistance of his father who was a judge this time. Surely he could spare a few pesos for his own son. But no help came. What he got was a lecture to live within his means. The incongruity of it all struck John with the subtlety of a rampaging bull: here he was in the gleaming mansion of his father being told to live only as he could afford. John turned his back and left.

But God was not giving up on him. The half-brother of his mother, his baptismal *Ninong*, who was a ranking executive of Columbian Rope Company, offered to take him in as a janitor-messenger. John grabbed at the chance. "This will be my first stepping stone to the beckoning future," John told himself, although for the life of him, he couldn't understand why the American comptroller had to interview him for such a minor position. Well, maybe the *Kano* just wanted to make sure that his Ninong had not recommended a deadwood for the job.

His pay, though meager, enabled John to enroll in college. Working during the day and studying at night became his routine. With his challenge to God driving his ambition to succeed, John showed remarkable industry and trustworthiness at what he was doing; and soon he was given the additional function of mail clerk, working directly under the executive secretary of the comptroller.

There were five female employees at Columbian. Two were so-so in the beauty department but the three others were the very picture of Filipina pulchritude that set many a Lothario's heart racing. There was Naty, the secretary to the wine group (the company also imported spirits), Winnie of the wine import group (who later married an NCAA basketball player), and Sally, John's immediate boss. The ladies were known as the *tres Marias*. They were always a threesome, probably because they were such lookers; you know like… "Birds of the same feathers…"

Every time Sally completed her day's delivery instruction to John, she followed it with, *"Ingat ka* (Please be careful)."

John did not give those parting words much thought, although they did have a nice ring to them. Sort of a *"Vaya con Dios.* Go with God." Probably just her way of motivating him to do his job well. Whatever. He was, after all, just about at the bottom rung of the company hierarchy; and things didn't usually happen that way.

It was not too long when John was promoted to microfilmer and copyflex operator. It was a sensitive job because the report he was filing went directly to the company's New York office; the comptroller just initialed the report. At one time John stumbled upon a high stack of round canisters containing exposed films. An investigation ensued and it turned out that those films contained vital data that were overdue at the home office for more than a year. Heads rolled and more important positions opened up. In 1958, just a year after he joined the company John was appointed assistant claims clerk, shipping department, working directly under his Ninong. His main job was to review relevant terms printed on the back of the bills of lading.

In not a few occasions was the company able to save money by disallowing erroneous claims uncovered by John's meticulous scrutiny of documents under his review. He moved up faster in the company after that.

One day, John got a pleasant surprise when Sally invited him to their town fiesta. By the time they arrived at the town, John admitted to himself that he had truly fallen in love with her. It was not spur of the moment; it had been two years since he first laid eyes on her. Since then, it was building up in him, but he pushed it away, this growing attraction he felt for the lady, who never failed to send him off with an *"Ingat ka"* and a gentle smile. But this time in the hour-long bus ride to the town fiesta, Sally sat next to him and the warm feel of their arms rubbing with every bump on the highway sent electric shivers through his entire being. They were trying to make small conversation above the din of the road but John heard nothing, only the wild thumping of his heart. He occasionally caught the faint scent of the perfume she wore, sweet and light as a breeze and... did she hear him sigh?

John was tongue-tied during the entire fiesta affair, except for the perfunctory greetings and meaningless chatter; he was in a daze, overwhelmed by his self-declaration that Sally had stolen his heart, totally and completely. But he didn't tell her, afraid that he might have just been presumptuous in thinking that the caring gestures of the object of his affection meant anything more. If Sally smacked him down with a cold brush-off, why that would be the very death of him!

He decided instead to write her a letter, the last recourse of the lovestruck whose tongues the cat ran off with. The words poured out, smooth-flowing and brilliant, for the language of love comes clothed in unrestrained eloquence, welling up as it does from the bottom of the heart.

John carefully drew a flowery "J" on the upper right hand corner of the page. He did not draw a heart impaled with Cupid's arrow on the opposite corner although he thought about it but mercifully decided that it would have been the height of corn. He had his friend deliver the letter, crossed himself, and hoped that the missive would land on fertile soil.

That same afternoon, John asked Sally if he could escort her home, which offer the lady quickly accepted. While waiting for their jeepney ride, John fidgeted, hemmed and hawed, and finally, mustering all his courage, he took a deep breath and in a quaking voice, asked, *"Nakuha mo ba ang sulat?* (Did you get my letter?)"

Sally, seemingly amused at the young man's nervousness, said, *"Oo, diniliver kanina ng alalay mo* (Yes, it was delivered by your friend earlier)."

Then she rewarded him with the sweetest smile that John had ever seen. It was as if heaven's door opened and John was as happy as any man could ever hope to be.

Pope Francis, Sally brought John to the crossroad of his life. But the obvious question to ask is: does God really have a plan for John's life?

Someone once told me, "I don't believe in God." I said, "That's unfortunate, because God believes in you." Before you were even born, before God began to fashion and form you, before he began to knit you together in your mother's womb, he had a dream for you and a plan for your life. He had a holy calling for you to fulfill. Paul told Timothy that it was God who saved us and called us to a holy life, not according to our works but according to his own design and the grace bestowed on us in Christ Jesus before time began" (2 Tm 1:9).

So, I said to my friend John, you might have been written off by everyone else. You might think that your life is far too flawed to be ever something beautiful. But our God is the master artist! He sees "an angel" in the shapeless rock of your life, and he wants to set it free. Throughout your life, no matter where you go or what you do, whenever God looks at you, he sees inside of you the potential he placed within you, and he is always calling to that potential as he called Lazarus out of the grave, "Come out!" God wants to take your life from the junkyard of the devil and turn it into a masterpiece, a trophy of his amazing grace and mercy.

In time John proposed marriage to Sally. The couple planned their big day carefully. Sally did not want a grand wedding and John was pleased, for his finances could only pay the cost of a simple celebration. His Ninong and Sally's parents offered to sponsor a bigger reception as befitted the occasion.

On the day of the wedding, there was another couple ahead of them. The church was richly decorated with an abundance of flowers and silken ribbons. As the bride walked to the altar, gingerly stepping on the lush red carpet and trailing a long train of lace, "Ohs!" and "Ahs" filled the air; it was a grand wedding by any standard.

John thought how lucky Sally was to be married in a church already decked out in splendid array. This must surely be a gift from God made available to them on the proverbial silver platter. What good fortune!

Some long minutes passed. John began to wonder why it was taking too long for them to be called to start the procession to the altar. When the church doors opened again, John knew the reason: all the decorations, which he had hoped to inherit so to speak, had been taken down.

He did not have Judas' thirty pieces of silver to pay the priest, supposedly one of St. Peter's disciples.

Pope Francis, there was no earthly reason for the priest or his subalterns to remove the wedding adornments from the ceremony that preceded John's and his bride's, other than church protocol, with total disregard for the possible humiliation it might cause. As you ascended the throne of Peter, your first word was to bring the Church to the poor. I will never hesitate to borrow your teachings about why our Church is the Church of the poor: the true Christian exudes great joy, for keeping this joy to ourselves serve for naught; happiness can only be real when it is shared.

The Christian sings with joy, carrying it with him wherever he may pass, a joy that easily translates to love of neighbor. Joy cannot be held captive: it must be let go. Joy is a pilgrim virtue. It is a gift given to those who choose to walk with Jesus: preaching, proclaiming joy, proclaiming Jesus along the ever-lengthening and widening path.

Some of you may yet be unsure about what you will do with your lives. Ask the Lord, and he will show you the way. The young Samuel kept hearing the voice of the Lord calling him, but he did not understand or know what to say. In the end, with the help of the priest Eli, he answered, "Speak, Lord, for I am listening" (1 Sm 3:1-10). You, too, can ask the Lord, "What do you want me to do? What path am I to follow?"

Pope Francis, you also teach us to be vigilant over ourselves. Let us not forget that hatred, envy, and pride defile our lives! (How diminished the priest in John's wedding has become in my eyes; but forgive me if I judge him without really knowing him.) Let me pause and explain myself a bit with this anecdote:

A Desire to Help

One mother was jogging through the park, pushing two toddlers in a stroller. As they approached a hill, she said, "OK, now I need you to help me." And they did! As she started up the hill, they each said, "I think I can, I think I can, I think I can…"

Sometimes it just takes the desire to help and you can find a way. One person known for his desire to help was Fiorello LaGuardia. LaGuardia was mayor of New York City during the worst days of the Great Depression and all of WWII.

He was adored by many New Yorkers who took to calling him the "Little Flower," because of his name and the fact that he was so short and always wore a carnation in his lapel. In many ways, LaGuardia was bigger than life—he rode the New York City fire trucks, raided city "speakeasies" with the police department, took entire orphanages to baseball games and, when the New York newspapers went on strike, he got on the radio and read the Sunday funnies to the kids.

One bitterly cold night in January of 1935, the mayor turned up at a night court that served the poorest ward of the city.

LaGuardia dismissed the judge for the evening and took over the bench himself. Within a few minutes, a tattered old woman was brought before him, charged with stealing a loaf of bread.

She told LaGuardia that her daughter's husband had deserted her, her daughter was sick, and her two grandchildren were starving. But the shopkeeper, from whom the bread was stolen, refused to drop the charges. "It's a real bad neighborhood, Your Honor," the man told the mayor. "She's got to be punished to teach other people around here a lesson."

LaGuardia sighed. He turned to the woman and said, "I've got to punish you. The law makes no exceptions, ten dollars or ten days in jail."

But even as he pronounced the sentence, the mayor was already reaching into his pocket. He extracted a bill and tossed it into his famous hat, saying, "Here is the ten-dollar fine which I now remit; and furthermore, I am going to fine everyone in this courtroom fifty cents for living in a town where a person has to steal bread so that her grandchildren can eat. Mr. Bailiff, collect the fines and give them to the defendant."

The following day, New York City newspapers reported that $47.50 was turned over to a bewildered woman who had stolen a loaf of bread to feed her starving grandchildren. Fifty cents of that amount was contributed by the grocery store owner himself, while some seventy petty criminals, people with traffic violations, and New York City policemen, each of whom had just paid fifty cents for the privilege of doing so, gave the mayor a standing ovation.

Sometimes it just takes the desire to help and you can find a way. Someone beautifully said, "Sympathy sees and says, 'I'm sorry.' Compassion sees and says, 'I'll help.'" When we learn the difference, we will make a difference (Steve Goodier).

I have to help John understand that organized religion is needed to fully comprehend what Jesus wants of us. Peter became the first vicar of his church, even after he denied him three times—because he asked the forgiveness of the Lord.

Please help me help John accept your teaching of *God's inexhaustible mercy*... "How good to come back to him whenever we are lost, God never tires of forgiving us, we are the ones who get tired of seeking his mercy. The Eucharist, although it is the fullness of sacramental life, is not a prize for the perfect but a powerful medicine and nourishment for the weak."

In High School, we called ourselves the "Lucky 7 Gang," in search of our dreams of who we shall become.
Standing at the extreme left is John and at the extreme right is the author.

Which One Are You?

Dear Pope Francis,

Please indulge me as I continue to trace the circumstances that sealed the decision of John.

Somewhere in my letter I wrote about Christianity having a very troubled beginning. It began as a mere offshoot of Judaism. In the earlier centuries, most of its converts came from the lower levels of Roman society, including its third-class citizens, the women, and other common people, including slaves. That was how Jesus intended it. He wanted to be with the poor. Jesus Christ would establish the New Covenant that brought God's work to completion and fulfillment. It greatly surprised the people of the Old Covenant to be presented with a very human Jesus, the son of a mere carpenter, as the much-awaited Messiah; they had expected a divine or more mystical messenger like an angel.

Jesus soon established his Church in the apostle Peter whom he called "Rock." In Matthew 16:18, "And so I say to you, you are Peter, and upon this rock I will build my church, and the gates of the netherworld shall not prevail against it."

The mission and ministry of Jesus continued on, struggled on may be the more descriptive term, as the Church marched forward on uncharted paths fraught with pitfalls and assorted obstacles. The chosen leaders to pioneer his teaching, the apostles, were weak, sinful men. It is a monumental puzzle—nay, paradox—why Jesus insisted on weak, sinful human beings, counting among them priests, bishops, even popes, to carry out his divine mission. Matthew, a tax collector, was considered by the Jews as a traitor and a renegade. Simon, a Zealot, was a fanatical nationalist who was sworn to eliminate the enemies of the state, traitors most of all. Matthew and Simon were two poles apart but under the auspices of Jesus, they labored as one. It was nothing short of a miracle, the handiwork of God, examples of which we continue to see even today.

Divergence in a Christian community is commonplace in our midst. We have read of priests who prey on children and those who willfully break their celibacy vows. John was witness to a "man of the cloth" who turned his assigned parish church into a sort of business enterprise for his own selfish ends! The history of the Church is replete with incidents and episodes that expose the weaknesses of a human organization despite its divine mission. But the Church is a dynamic body, continually embroiled in the process of freeing itself of sin and other human frailties. Its ultimate objective is to configure itself as the perfect image of Jesus Christ, the Head of the Church. I can hardly blame John and those of like mind to be tempted to give up on the Church or organized religion, as they call it.

My advice to my friend and his ilk is to hold fast to their Christian faith and not to prematurely pass judgment on the Church and organized religion but to love it as its Founder does. Who of the members of God's Church is without sin? In spite and because of our sins, Jesus willingly made the supreme sacrifice to free us from the bondage of evil.

Pope Francis, let's take a break from the heavy stuff and share a few light moments. These are, one-liner or two-, common among stand-up comedians:

> The parish priest was giving his Sunday sermon. He droned on in his monotone. Finally, someone seated at the back, yelled, "Please speak louder and clearer, Father. We can't hear you."
>
> The preacher raised his voice but soon lapsed back into his usual monotone. Again, the voice yelled, "Louder, Father, louder. We can't hear you!"
>
> A voice from the front row came back, "Stop complaining back there! Just shut up and thank God... or I'll change places with you."

As he was going out of the church, one Sunday, one man commented as he shook hands with the priest, "Your sermon, Father, was simply wonderful—so invigorating and inspiring and refreshing." The priest, of course, broke out into a big smile, only to hear the man say, "Why I felt like a new man when I woke up!"

A bus driver and a priest died at the same time. Although the driver was sent directly to heaven, the priest's case was apparently harder to decide. "I don't mind that you sent a bus driver to heaven," the priest was heard complaining. "But after all, I was a priest. So why should I be kept waiting?"

He was answered from on high, "Father, when you're preaching, everyone was falling asleep. But when the bus driver was driving, everyone was praying."

Were that all men of the cloth fill us with laughter even as they go about the very serious business of salvation of souls!

John strongly believes in our faith. For well does he remember that along the arching trajectory of his life, the Lord was always present, talking with him and cheering him on whether he was in the pits or at the top of his game. No matter what, Jesus ever picks a particular time or place to show his love and concern for us: he was there for John all of the time, a burning beacon to light the way.

John had a talk with me on the eve of his son's entering college. He thought that with my experience working in a big company and later in the academe, I would be able to help them decide which university was the most ideal.

The private schools that Kim—that's the name of John's son—was considering were all premier institutions. I told him that he could not go wrong with any of schools he had in mind but I ventured that UP, the University of the Philippines, was still the foremost institute of learning in our country. UP standards are high and students are trained to be self-reliant, resourceful, and extra diligent in their studies and in doing research for study materials. I added, "The academic achievements of the university rank it among the best in the world. It is a class by itself. It is the only educational institution that refuses accreditation from government educational audit bodies and rather lets its graduates speak for the school."

Father and son made the right choice.

One evening found John in the UP parking lot waiting for Kim who wouldn't get off from his Philosophy class until seven. He had just begun the semester in "Fine Arts—Visual Communications Course 101."

Kim had a good head on him. In high school, his teacher let on that he would graduate as class valedictorian. But Kim and his parents were met with a big disappointment. The teacher's hint was like a curved ball thrown by the pitcher; the man at bat thinks that the ball is coming straight at him, takes a swing, only to hear the ball impact the catcher's glove. But the umpire calls it foul—ball instead of a strike.

Kim made it to first honorable mention. The daughter of a teacher in the school was announced as the salutatorian; the valedictorian was the son of an active member of the parents-teachers association! John saw history repeating. It seemed that the gods from Olympus conspired against him. Again!

Once, while we were waiting to be served in a restaurant, John brought up again his disappointment with priests in his parish. A few days earlier he had e-mailed me regarding his troubling sense of unease. "Why it is that religion serves well my children and their families (here he hesitates with a few dashes in his letter and then continues), especially you who are foremost among those whom God has blessed with a good life. Why didn't religion take tight hold and held me captive?" John asked.

He felt somewhat guilty for allowing such thoughts to take root and thrive, knowing that God had provided him with all the opportunities to make good his challenge. He deserved more, much more, John thought. Nanay was nothing less than a *Manang*, in the most positive sense of the appellation. Today to be called a Manang conjures a frowsy, squat woman, past middle age, garbed in a shapeless brown dress, with a scapular hanging from her neck, who has nothing better to do than to hang around church premises, waiting to do the bidding of the parish priest. But the real Manang is one who attends daily Mass, observes all the holy days of the Church, fasts and abstains on the days when such are required. Such a one was John's dear Nanay; and he wondered why her piety did not rub off on him. "Why?" Could he be like the seed that fell among the rocks and did not grow?

I asked, "John, do you, in all honesty, admit that you are attracted to Christ, and that you seek his spirit to meet the challenges of life? You say that you subscribe to basic Christian truths but you also say that you cannot in all conscience, *sign on the dotted line*. And your reason is that there are certain theological ideas which some sectors of the Church dogmatize.

"If you answer *yes* to my question, it is obvious where the dichotomy lies. A Christian agnostic, as you call yourself, is but another bird of the same feather known as a *practicing atheist*. You said that your hesitancy to accept Christ's teaching is due to some actions of the Church where certain truths were twisted and dogmatized. What do you mean?"

John gave me a puzzled look. He seemed to be reaching for the right words to say. I prodded him. "What could be these particular theological dogmas which some branches of the Church dogmatized?

"The Church in its 2,000 years of existence has declared only four dogmas in reference to the Blessed Virgin Mary. You know this, well-read as you are." I paused, waiting for an answer.

John kept his silence; that was typical of him, preferring to hold his peace when unsure of his grounds. In past conversations we have had, John often confided that he truly believed that God showered his Nanay with countless blessings and graces especially when she prayed for her son. Half-seriously he said that Nanay's implorations to the Lord clinched Sally's love for him over five persistent suitors.

When his beloved Sally passed away, John met and married Carol, a *probinsyana*, who hailed from a remote barrio and was thoroughly steeped in Maria Clara tradition. But Carol went against the grain and boldly proclaimed her feelings for John. She, a good woman, had no trouble stepping into the shoes of Sally and once more John attributed his extraordinary fortune in having two loving persons in his life to his unfaltering faith in the Lord.

At least in the matter of love and life partners, John could identify with what St. Paul wrote on the subject: "Love is patient, love is kind. It is not jealous, [love] is not pompous, it is not inflated, it is not rude, it does not seek its own interests, it is not quick-tempered, it does not brood over injury, and it does not rejoice over wrongdoing but rejoices with the truth. It bears all things, believes all things, hopes all things, endures all things" (1 Cor 13:4-7).

The four children that John had with Sally are all successful professionals. John is quick to acknowledge that they are what they are with God's grace. Still, comes now his only child with Carol, who with his God-given talent has already earned serious money for a design artwork commissioned by the United Nations. And he is only in his first year as a Fine Arts student at UP.

So I asked him one more time, "Doesn't that indicate how much God loves you? What more can God do for you?"

Still, John flitted on the periphery of doubt. Nanay succumbed to cancer just as he was starting to accumulate the wherewithal to afford the small pleasures of life. He had wanted to spoil her with frivolous gifts like a bottle of perfume which she wouldn't wear anyway, or a *quezo de bola* and roasted *castañas* for Christmas. He never got to do it and it cut him deeply. If God really cared, why did he deny his mother a few more years so she would share in the "harvest of what she painstakingly sowed in her son?"

John's inner self urged him to put his unconditional trust in God's design, but his earthbound mind strongly protested the passing of his mother. In his grief, he cried out, "My God, where were you when Nanay needed you most?"

I told John a story which he could easily accept. "More than 2,000 years ago, on the Hill of the Skull, a similar plaintive cry was uttered through parched lips, 'My God, my God, why have you forsaken me?' It rose up from the broken heart of someone who was suffering from the severest isolation of loneliness."

John was silent. I added, "Do you know that the man's biggest disappointment was not seeing his friends, except one, when he needed them most? His closest ally, the person he chose to lead his flock, denied him three times. Another sold him for thirty pieces of silver. He would have forgiven him who denounced him to the Pharisees had he sought forgiveness. For despite what his friend had done, his love for him never lessened."

I stood up to calm myself. My voice was on the verge of cracking. "He remained steadfast at his mock trial and endured the brutality of his captors. He did not lift a finger in retaliation. He suffered the pain of nails being driven into his hands and feet in silence. He was unmindful of the taunts of the jeering crowd to *come down* from the cross. He did not lift a finger in retaliation against his tormentors. Instead, he prayed, 'Forgive them, for they know not what they do.'

"What more could he have done for you, John? Are his shredded skin and torn flesh from the lash of his tormentors not enough? His dying on the cross saved us from hell's damnation. Does he have to come back, and suffer and die again before you fully accept him?

"Do you have to deny the Church that he created for you? Did he not hear you even when you said your prayers in anger?" I turned my back to hide my tears.

"My point, friend, is that you are not the first nor will be the last to question as you have. What is important is to never forget what he has done for you. Your mother gave you love even when that love sometimes kept you from doing what you wanted. But you never ran away from home, did you? You never gave up on your Nanay.

"Your issues are focused mainly on priests and lay leaders who do not come up to your standard. They are easy to resolve, John. You need to take courage to talk to them and tell them your concerns. If they give excuses and do not improve, talk to their bishops, they will help you."

"You are right, Rudy, priests who seem not to know the *ABCs* of their vocation are my nemesis. It makes me wonder whether there are a lot of politics and jockeying in the assignment of parish priests. I hope that the location and affluence of a parish don't come too much into the equation."

John looked at me for a reaction. I thought that it was best to let him talk now that he appeared to be opening up. He said, "Religion is of divine origin. However, the representation of organized religion is established by human beings with all their mortal failings. It is inevitable that flaws creep into these organizations. Why do Church leaders turn our religion into such boring and joyless affair? Surely, they can be less concerned with the minor niceties of liturgy, the subtle refinements of our doctrine. Then the churchgoers will eagerly look forward to Sunday mass and respond with enthusiasm and spontaneous joy."

I was about to say something when he raised his hand; he continued, "The Holy Mass is God's banquet where both the sinful and the sinless are always welcome. The invitation will never be appended with the earthly "RSVP," for everyone is expected to come. In spite of this, there are still many who ignore the invitation with their respective excuses. Then there are the invitees who showed up once, but disappointed with what went on during the party, stood up and left."

As John was carried on with his allegorical explanation, I searched my mind for other reasons why he had so many axes to grind against the Church. In his profession and up to the time of his retirement, John had traveled extensively around the country and abroad. This brought him into close contact with different cultures, traditions, and the many facets of humanity, including its frailties. His ever-expanding horizon included the latest development and discoveries in the scientific world. Once he noted the impiousness of an article published in *Time* Magazine based on a book, *"The God Gene: How Faith is Hardwired into Our Genes."*

The author, molecular biologist, Dean Hamer, postulates that in the process of human evolution, "spiritual trait became hardwired into the human gene." The implication of Hamer's research is that religious faith and experience are nothing more than a "misinterpretation of a biological phenomenon."

John, despite his many questions about religion, agrees with the counter-argument of American religious teacher, Jason Dulle, who wrote: "But for those of us who understand that religious faith is both rational and experiential, doubts cast on our experience are no match for the wealth of rational experiences in favor of God's existence. We do not believe in God merely of some experience, but because the rational evidence compels us to. Any scientific find claiming to explain away our religious experience can never explain away our faith."

This is the intuitive awareness of God's existence, John believes.

There is no denying that a fierce battle rages in John's mind. On one hand, he wholeheartedly believes in a Superior Being who holds reins to all of the known and yet to be discovered universes. On the opposite end, he cannot deny his own adverse experiences with the "dark" side of the religious ambassadors—the bishops and the priests.

John is turned off by the strident messages of the promoters of religious sects other than the Catholic Church. The leaders compete vigorously for the attention of prospective followers. It is not at all beneath them to engage in dirty tricks to put the other down. Invariably, their emphasis is on division and proving that "our group is more attuned to the teaching of Scripture than yours." This is what differentiates us from all the others: the central message of the New Testament is that God is our Father; therefore, we are all brothers and sisters!

While most definitely we are unable to see eye to eye on religion and theology as a whole, and on a host of other issues for that matter, why cannot we look beyond our differences and remember that we are all God's creation? He loves all of us with the same intensity!

John brought me back from my mental wandering. "But once in a while we get lucky. There was this young priest who was assigned to our parish. He filled our church with parishioners once more. Just like what Pope Francis is doing in churches in Europe.

"The priest, barely five feet tall, never failed to hold captive the audience's rapt attention with his thoughtful homilies which he delivered with much enthusiasm and the proper emphasis where it should be. He inserted a generous dose of humor relevant to the Gospel he'd just read. Then one Sunday, he somberly announced his impending transfer to a Tondo church which was easily five times larger than ours. He introduced a much older priest as his successor. Our petition for the former's retention was turned down by higher Church authorities.

"Our Church was back to a rambling monotone. The celebration of the Holy Mass led by the newcomer became even more humdrum rather than the glorious feast in which God is the real Host. The Mass should be a most anticipated event where to be invited is a singular privilege. Instead, our Sunday Mass celebrations turned out to be tiresome rituals where one couldn't wait to get out from; our current priest must have been a classmate in Homiletics of the previous ones," John sighed.

"John, excuse me for butting in but I couldn't help relating your explanation to the gospel of Mark."

On another occasion [Jesus] began to teach by the sea. A very large crowd gathered around him so that he got into a boat on the sea and sat down. And the whole crowd was beside the sea on land. And he taught them at length in parables, and in the course of his instruction he said to them, "Hear this! A sower went out to sow. And as he sowed, some seed fell on the path, and the birds came and ate it up. Other seed fell on rocky ground where it had little soil. It sprang up at once because the soil was not deep. And when the sun rose, it was scorched and it withered for lack of roots. Some seed fell among thorns, and the thorns grew up and choked it and it produced no grain. And some seed fell on rich soil and produce fruit. It came up and grew and yielded thirty, sixty, and a hundredfold." He added, "Whoever has ears to hear ought to hear."

And when he was alone, those present along with the Twelve questioned him about the parables. He answered them, "The mystery of the kingdom of God has been granted to you. But to those outside everything comes in parables, so that 'they may look and see but not perceive, and hear and listen but not understand, in order that they may not be converted and be forgiven.' "

Jesus said to them, "Do you not understand this parable? Then how will you understand any of the parables? The sower sows the word. These are the ones on the path where the word is sown. As soon as they hear, Satan comes at once and takes away the word sown in them. And these are the ones sown on rocky ground who, when they hear the word, receive it at once with joy. But they have no root; they last only for a time. Then when tribulation and persecution comes because of the word, they quickly fall away. Those sown among thorns are another sort. They are the people who hear the word, but worldly anxiety, the lure of riches, and the craving for other things intrude and choke the word and it bears no fruit. But those sown on rich soil are the ones who hear the word and accept it and bear fruit thirty and sixty and a hundredfold" (Mk 4:1-20).

I looked at John intently and asked, "Which one are you?"

St. Josemaria, the Saint of Ordinary Life

Would You Like to Meet My Spiritual Advisor?

John smiled.

I do not know Pope Francis, John's smile was full of meaning, a kind of smile that said, "Don't judge me just yet." Then he took a deep breath and said, "I am thirsty. Thirst is homologous to water. It can only be quenched by drinking water or any of its familiar variants—wine or juice. Thus when the guards at the foot of the cross heard Jesus say he was thirsty, their eyes instinctively turned to a nearby container that held the liquid. In their shortsighted vision, they concluded that he wanted a drink of water and saw yet another opportunity to ridicule him.

"I am thirsty for the Church of God, the way he intended it. Like Jesus, who was not 'physically' thirsty? I am suffering from 'spiritual' thirst which cannot be slaked by any liquid. One writer observed that *I thirst* was the same longing for the thirst for righteousness of the Beatitudes, 'Blessed are they who hunger and thirst for righteousness, for they will be satisfied' (Mt 5:6). I am thirsting for priests to show the teaching that Jesus gave to his apostles, one that is caring and nurtures faith.

"Jesus was thirsty for humanity's resolve to turn away from wickedness and sins, to move from disgrace to grace, to love his neighbors as well as those who are un-neighborly towards him, to be seriously repentant and be forgiven, to stand with head held up high, fully confident of his acquittal before God's bench of final judgment. That is what I am looking for from my priest.

"Now let me answer your question, *'Which one are you?'* to which of the seeds in the parable do I belong? I believe that I am in the seed that grew a hundredfold. Though, I will neither claim I am in that level all the time because I am not perfect, nor you, Rudy, nor anyone of us. I have many more questions in my mind bordering on doubt. But I deal with them. I think you are right, there are only two categories of people in our Church and I know at this moment that I am trying so hard to see your perspective, to be a practicing Catholic."

The waiter brought in our *lugao,* steaming hot and maddeningly aromatic with slices of fried garlic and chopped spring onions on top. The waiter had earlier suggested a companion dish of *tokwa't baboy,* a concoction of fried soybean cake and boiled pork swimming in soy sauce, vinegar, fresh ginger, and chillies—the perfect partner of *lugao.* John and I looked at each other and laughed. We turned down the suggestion. At our age, and with all the body aches that never seem to go away, we just weren't inclined to push our luck.

While enjoying our dish, I resumed our discussion by bringing up my association with Opus Dei. "John, there was a time when I was like you, with many questions about my faith. Then *Kuya Hesus* pointed me to a priest, a pious and saintly person in his manners. He patiently answered all my questions in our first dialogue. Before letting me on my way, he handed me a book for my home reading. In my succeeding visits, any anxieties or doubts that I had, I brought up to him and he provided the enlightenment I sought. He also advised me about the kinds of books I should read. I was somewhat intrigued that he should manage my reading.

"Fr. Joe said, 'Rudy, you are no stranger to modern technology. You know the meaning of GIGO—*Garbage in, garbage out.* The last thing I want to see is you reading books written purposely to create doubts in your faith.'

"I found our discussions more than just invigorating; he actually gave me a lifeline to God. The more questions I asked, the more books he would pull from his bag, books he wanted me to read. You are a voracious reader, John. You read as much as I do, perhaps even more. But I have an advantage; I have someone knowledgeable on whom to bounce off my questions and my doubts; and more importantly, someone to guide my thoughts on the true meaning of life, on the true meaning of Jesus' Gospels.

"Believe it or not, I have been with this saintly man almost half my life."

One of the lessons he taught me is how to be a good father:

Rudy, I am confident we see eye to eye that when a child, who is overly protected and habitually given whatever he wants, develops an "entitlement mentality" and always puts himself first. He is ignorant of his parent's efforts. When he matures and starts to work, he assumes that every person must listen to him; and when he becomes a manager, he is probably never aware of the efforts and hardship of the people under him. Moreover, he blames everybody but himself when things go wrong. He may achieve a measure of success but for people like this, success is never lasting nor does it give them a sense of achievement. And rarely are they ever satisfied; their grumblings never cease and they are clawing their way for more.

If we are these kind of protective parents, do we really love or are we destroying our children?

You cannot let your child simply live in a big house, eat three big meals a day, learn piano, watch big screen TV, and consider your duties as a parent done. When you are cleaning the house or mowing the lawn grass, let them try their hand at it. After a meal, let them wash their plates and spoon and fork together with their brothers and sisters.

It is not because you do not have money to hire a housekeeper, but because you want to love them in the right way. You want them to understand, no matter how rich their parents are, it is still *what you give is what you get*. And that lesson starts at home.

A most important thing for your child to learn is the ability to work with others. He must also learn to show appreciation for the efforts of his peers and subordinates to get the job done.

You can easily raise your children to the kind of person you want them to be, when you bring them up in an atmosphere of love, where there is respect for authority; because the same authority you have is founded on love and fear of God!

John looked at me fixedly. He already knew what I was going to say next. But I said it anyway. "Would you consider meeting my spiritual advisor?"

Pope Francis, in my continuing dialogue with John, I prayed to the Holy Spirit for guidance, believing always in your teaching, that in discussing the Word of God we must at all times have *humility before Scripture…* Whenever we attempt to discern the meaning of a text, Pope Francis says that we are practicing "reverence to the truth," which he defines as "humility of heart which recognizes that we are not its masters nor owners, but its guardians, heralds, and servants."

I seek your prayer for John that he may seriously consider my offer for him to meet Fr. Joe. With your prayers, he may still decide to take me up on my suggestion. Please pray for me, too, that I never tire of searching for ways to help John see the light.

Veronica

$\mathcal{P}$ope Francis, my understanding of our faith is miles away from what you know, your bishops and your priests, but I needed to write the little that I know in order to bring balance to the dialogue which I had with my close friend who finds fulfillment in the teaching of Christ in another Christian church. She wrote:

My name is Veronica.

I will never forget the time I enrolled at the Arellano High School. I was fortunate that AHS accepted me even though I was already a month late. As penalty, which I had expected, I was lumped in the lowest section, Section 57. I had imagined a miserable year in a class comprising mostly of the rejects and slow students but our teacher, Mr. Gallardo, knew how to inspire us to study hard and diligently, so after a while, it was fine. We formed a sort of drama group and I was assigned as leader. We presented skits during PTA meetings and special occasions in school; my first year AHS was a very good year.

I maintain regular contacts with some high school friends. It's a joy for the group to meet, kind of checking how each one is doing. We share happy moments reminiscing about the good old high school days, teasing one another about crushes and lost loves and other funny experiences., I believe that our Lord gathers us together for a reason: to love one another as brothers and sisters, to encourage and pray for one another, and to share at God's table of grace whatever our individual station in life may now be. We are generous with praise for those who have done well;

although we do not hesitate to gently rebuke any one of us who seems to stray and quicker still to reach out a hand to those who have fallen.

We are all in our 70s, and it is truly a gift that septuagenarians like us are still physically able and mentally and emotionally inclined to "flock" and "chew the fat." When I see all the happy faces, sagging and wrinkled as they may be, I think of it as a sort of mini-high school homecoming. Just for being around, you are thankful, no matter how our lives have been to us; for surely for some, it has not been all that smooth a ride. In these occasions, we feed off on each other, drawing strength and inspiration from the strongest of us. We make it a point to pray together and even share the Good News.

Although we were not rich in that sense, I was a spoiled brat growing up. My mother and siblings attended to all the house chores and took care of my needs besides; so in a way I was a pampered child. I never learned to clean house or cook because my older sisters were doing all that. After I graduated from high school, I started to work as a cashier in a gasoline station. This was the only time when I realized that I had to grow up and be a responsible person. The onset of maturity follows one's admission that you have to paddle your own canoe to get anywhere. But when I got married, I still didn't know how to cook. I blamed my mother and sisters for not teaching me how. The first time I tried my hand at cooking rice, I could only manage *lugaw*, porridge. My husband, Jonathan, came to the rescue; as it turned out, he was a natural-born wizard in the kitchen.

But Jonathan was not my first crush; it was Daniel, my childhood friend, who first awakened strange stirrings in my heart. Funny how things worked out, my eyes were on him but he had eyes only for my friend. Like in a *telenovela*, Daniel pleaded with me to connect him to the girl of his fancy and further more to get the dope on her—her likes and dislikes, her favorite color, etc. If he asked me for the moon, I would have given it to him—I had such feelings for him. So foolish of me that I did as requested, although God knows, my heart was breaking into a thousand pieces. But as usual with young love, Daniel and my *amiga* did not end up together. Daniel and I remained close friends up to the time his family migrated to America. He became a successful artist in New York, his oils fetching handsome prices. He has a good family life; I am so happy for him.

It's ironic but the man I married, Jonathan, has the same surname as Daniel: Arenas. Jonathan and I have been married for 53 years now. We wedded very young and reflecting on it,

Interreligious Dialogue

"I invite all religious people to view dialogue not only as a means of enhancing mutual understanding, but also as a way of serving society at large" (Pope Emeritus Benedict XVI).

Following the advice of Pope Benedict the XVI, our group which we call the Dream Team belong to different beliefs but we talk to each other as children of God.

it came to me how selfish and self-centered we both were in our early years. Life's frivolities were there for our picking. We did have our fill of the good times, especially when we first settled in the US. We felt like we were just starting life together—and in fact we were. We traveled all over, visiting relatives and friends in the US and Canada. It was like we were on our honeymoon: love is lovelier the second time around, although now and then we bared our fangs and claws at each other. As we grew older, we learned to accept one another for all that we were and that life is serious business after all. But over and above everything, our children brought true joy to the family as indeed children are God's blessings!

It is said that children bind marriages; it cannot be any truer than that. We have five children, five reasons to keep our marriage intact. I was wrong not to be strong for them when the big blow in my relationship with my husband came. Thank and praise God, I saw the light when I came to know him and started to seek him. It felt so good to be selfless and do what was best for my children.

I was only 21 years old when I had my first child. The sensation of holding your own child in your arms is so utterly indescribable. I remember putting her to sleep, cradled in my arms on a rocking chair. I would softly hum a lullaby and a smile would play at the corners of her lips and it was all I could do to hold back tears from the unmitigated joy that washed over me.

The children came one after the other and as they grew up, so did the treasure chest of pleasant family memories. My sons were close to one another and my *unica hija*, being the eldest, helped me look after her brothers; she was a second mother to them. Their ties remained strong despite the passage of the years and the physical distance between them. When we were struggling for economic survival back in those days, the children and the future we wished for them were the greatest factor to strive hard. I cannot be more thankful to our Lord that up to now, we are a strong family founded on God's love. The icing on the cake is having nine grandchildren and four great grandchildren. They are growing up so fast that our regret is that we won't have all that time left to spend with them while they are still young. I discovered that one of the most enduring joys that a person can lay claim to is to know God, learn about him through his Word, maintain a personal relationship with him, *and* impart all that to his or her children. In my case, it was not too late, to thank and praise God!

Life has its ups and downs, and as they say, you don't have to be a rocket engineer to figure that. It's tempting to dwell on the downs but it serves no purpose on earth except to bring back the pain. So I let it go and let our loving God do the rest. Better still, I lift it to our merciful Lord, on the strength of his promise that he will give me rest and inner peace. "Cast your burdens upon me and I will give you rest." If you believe this in your heart of hearts, then God's peace will be with you. It works for me every time.

When my son Joseph died at the age of thirty-nine, God favored me with his inner peace and strength. I entertained no doubt that his plan for Joseph was for the best. Joseph died a born-again Christian who served our Lord for many years through the music ministry. Joseph is indeed a testimony of a transformed life, thank and praise God! We were surprised to find out that Joseph had so many friends who showed up at his wake and funeral: friends from work, church, and the neighborhood who had only good things to say about him. Joseph was our "funny guy" in the family; he had a great sense of humor. Our Lord gave him a good singing voice and the talent to play musical instruments. He used his ability to serve God as a music leader in church. The thought occurs to me often that Joseph is now part of the heavenly choir.

I worked with one of the top multinational film exchanges in Manila for 17 years. It was a materially rewarding job—good money, enjoyable, and personally satisfying. After just four years, I was promoted as Publicity and Advertising Manager and I stayed there until I decided to migrate to America.

Why would I leave a very lucrative job with great incentives?

I must admit that the temptation to make more than my regular income afforded me was irresistible when we were raising five children, three of them going to college. My husband's business was failing and I succumbed to offers of cash "gifts" which went a long way to solve our financial problems. After a while, I was hooked and found it easy to engage in these anomalous practices. I reasoned that I was working really hard which always brought in great results for the company in terms of sales and revenues; as a matter of fact, the company became a trendsetter because of my efforts in putting together promotional tie-ins. I felt entitled to a little "extra" income. I became callous and my conscience no longer bothered me with the graft I had going on.

Life was good, in the material sense, at least. I enjoyed my work and derived great benefits from it. There was even a time that I was eyed by home office management to replace the branch manager who was set to retire. I declined the offer; I "loved" my position too much to give it away.

Then, just as I was sinking deeper and deeper in the quagmire of corruption, my brother, as if out of the blue, came to share the Word of God with us. And I didn't even know, to put it irreverently, that he has had "a bad case of religion." It was a wake-up call for me. I snapped out of my deadly existence as if from a dream, wondering where my life had gone. I realized that I had become so intoxicated with the largesse that my fraudulent practices were raking in that I had in fact sold my soul to the devil.

It was difficult for me to make things right but somehow God showed me the way. I started praying directly to him, imploring him to pull me up from the hole I had dug for myself so that I could start all over again. For this deliverance I prayed to God daily and to assuage the guilt that hanged like a sword over my head.

Months passed. Then unexpectedly, I received a call from my daughter who was living in California. Her petition for her parents to immigrate to the US had been approved. This was answered prayers! God was plucking me out of my old sinful life and giving me a chance to start all over again.

In Los Angeles, God surprised us with another answered prayer. I got a call from the Vice President for International Marketing of my old company; he was my former boss based in New York. He asked me to join him as his executive secretary at five times the salary I was getting in Manila. And I didn't even have to move to the Big Apple as the company was transferring headquarters to California.

I was ecstatic. Was this all a dream? Jonathan and I embraced in tears and started praying to God. With these gifts from the Lord, I realized that if we truly repent a sinful lifestyle and start trusting and obeying God, he will grant our hearts' desires more than we can ever imagine; that if we resist evil, the devil will flee from us: that is God's Word. Verily, one cannot serve God and Mammon at the same time. You love one and hate the other; that is the only choice. I chose to serve God, and break away from the enslavement of money. All praise, glory, and honor to an awesome God for what he has done for us!

Ours has not been a perfect marriage, just like any other marriages, I suppose. A broken family is the last thing that Jonathan and I would allow to happen to our union. Forgiveness is vital to any relationship, as at some point we commit mistakes. God's Word points out: we all fall short in the glory of God. But love for the family and reverence for God are the main factors that hold two people together. As couples age, physical love is the first to go. How often have we heard seniors say ruefully that their relationship with their spouse has become akin to that of brothers and sisters rather than lovers? But such is the nature of things and soon enough we begin to comprehend that God is using us as channels of blessings instead of allowing us to further manipulate each other for selfish reasons.

I will be less than forthright to say that I was always happy. Before I became a Christian, it was hard for me to accept depressing circumstances; I would immerse myself in work to free myself of negative thoughts, if for a while. An unfaithful spouse, a best friend's betrayal... I have been through trying times. I was the perfect picture of the martyred wife. I could not see how God blessed my life since I was swimming in self-pity for too long. And that derailed me, to put it bluntly. But somehow, God has a way of making his presence felt in the most unexpected places. I was surfing the TV one day and I chanced upon a Christian TV program. Something the host said caught my attention so I stayed tuned. The preacher talked about salvation and repentance and how God died for us. I don't know how it happened but right there and then, it was as if I received God's wisdom to understand it all—faith, trust, and obedience. I learned that our omnipotent God is bigger than any problem, that everything passes away but his Word remains, that everything is temporary in this world, and that he is our only hope. His wonderful invitation to accept him as my Lord and Savior and his gift of eternal life made me realize that all I needed was him. And that freed me to start living right with God.

Now in the twilight of my years, always in my mind is how to serve the Lord for the remainder of my life. By no stretch of the imagination am I anywhere near the caliber of the great evangelists like Billy Graham or the many doctors of our Church like St. Augustine, or St. Thomas Aquinas. All I have is time to give to my loved ones and friends. My advocacy is to help them to truly know and love God, and to live in accordance with God's ways and perfect will; this they can accomplish by constantly reading the Holy Bible and attending Bible studies, an effort that I vigorously encourage in them. Godliness is the only real legacy we can leave our children, something money cannot buy. I will help them know how good our God is by accepting Jesus Christ as our Lord and Savior, for he is "the way and the truth and the life," and no one comes to the Father except through him."

Pope Francis, I am awed at the steadfast acceptance of Veronica in her newfound faith which she never discovered in our Church. For my own education, I am tracing the path that non-Catholic Christians took beginning in the 15th century. I know that you are familiar with world history so I will straightaway proceed to the conditions that drove them to create their own versions of churches of Jesus Christ.

Foremost of these was the political chaos caused by the 100-year war between England and France, which diminished the influence of the Church on the kings and the feudal royalties. The inability to stop the bubonic plague which killed thousands, almost cutting to half the population of Europe, exacerbated the situation. People saw the ineptitude of the rulers of the known world at that time.

Into the swirl of this misunderstanding weighed in Martin Luther who unleashed his 95 "bulls" or theses against the Church. The worldliness of the hierarchy, clerical abuses, particularly in the granting of indulgences, had tarnished the authority of the Papacy. Indulgences were sold with forward effects. While the indulgence was in effect, one could commit any sin for the days; immunity was assured by the indulgence peddled by the clergy.

The abuses of the Church rankled Luther who sought to correct them by redirecting the people back to the Scripture as the sole basis of learning the faith, using principally as his platform, the letter of St. Paul to the Romans 1:17: "For in it is revealed the righteousness of God from faith to faith; as it is written, 'The one who is righteous by faith will live.' "

However, Luther's doctrine conveniently left out the Epistle of St. James 2:14-17 which teaches: "What good is it, my brothers, if someone says he has faith but does not have works? Can that faith save him? If a brother or sister has nothing to wear and has no food for the day, and one of you says to them, "Go in peace, keep warm, and eat well," but you do not give them the necessities of the body, what good is it? So also faith of itself, if it does not have works, is dead."

Luther's teaching was also based on the concept of *sola scriptura* which rejected tradition and the authority of the Magisterium of the

Catholic Church and the Pope. He put aside the Holy Spirit which continues to dwell and teach through the Church.

His teaching of faith alone dismisses the value of corporal and spiritual works of mercy. One is not saved through the sacraments but faith alone. "It is necessary to have faith to be saved, but following Christ cannot be theoretical; it must be shown in action, in deeds. Christ himself says the same thing in Mt 7:21: "Not everyone who says to me, 'Lord, Lord,' will enter the kingdom of heaven." Luther chose to accept only the sacraments of the Eucharist and Baptism. Luther's teaching of *grace alone* proposed that every good action is a direct result of God's saving grace, since it is beyond human capacity to do well; people cannot freely choose to do good but they can freely choose to do evil. He also taught the concept of *Christ only*, since Christ is the sole content of the scripture, perforce rejecting the Trinity.

Luther went against the core of the Catholic Church's teaching of *transubstantiation, where the substance of bread and wine completely changes into the body and blood of Jesus Christ, with only accidents or properties remaining.* Many miracles have supported this teaching, notably the miracle in the church of Lanciano, Italy, where the host and wine were transformed into the actual body and blood of Christ. His understanding of the Eucharist was based on a new word he coined, *consubstantiation where the body and blood of Christ are simply present only but are not fully transformed into his body and blood.* Christ is present in the Eucharist in the same way that heat is present in red-hot iron.

Finally, because his teaching disagrees with many passages in the Old Testament, Luther took out the books of Tobit, Judith, Wisdom, Sirach, 1 Maccabees, 2 Maccabees, parts of Daniel, and parts of Esther from his version of the Bible, including the Epistle of St. James because it opposed his teaching of faith alone.

Dr. Scott Hahn, a well-known Protestant minister who converted to the Catholic religion, explained in his book, *Understanding the Scripture* why Luther and other Protestant churches chose to ignore these books:

In the liturgy of the Word, the early Christians heard readings from the Scriptures, just as we do today. The Old Testament Scriptures were the same ones Jewish congregations heard in the synagogues; in fact, many early Christians continued to go to their synagogues until the synagogue authorities banned them. But they also heard letters from the Apostles and stories from the life of Christ. Which of these new books were suitable for reading in the liturgy? That was the question the early Church had to answer.

The "canon" is the answer to that question. Under the guidance of the Holy Spirit, the Church came up with the list or "canon," or approved books. The inclusion of a book in the canon meant it was divinely inspired. ("Canon" is a Greek word meaning "measuring rod" or "rule") Other books were rejected because they were not divinely inspired.

In the Old Testament, the Church accepts some books as canonical that Jewish tradition does not regard as scripture. These books are called "deuterocanonical," from the Greek word meaning "second canon."

These books are: Tobit, Judith, Wisdom, Sirach (Ecclesiasticus), Baruch, 1 Maccabees, 2 Maccabees, parts of Daniel, and parts of Esther.

Protestant churches usually follow later Jewish tradition, so most Protestant Bibles omit those books. But according to the Catholic Church, these deuterocanonical books have the same authority as the rest of the books of the Bible: they are part of the Scripture. These books offer quite explicitly, certain doctrines which are recognized as Catholic teaching and practice. For example, the book of 2 Maccabees shows conclusively the concept of creation that Jewish believers prayed for the souls of the dead (proving the existence of purgatory) many years before the coming of Jesus Christ. The book of Tobit demonstrates the existence and actions of guardian angels.

There was a division among the Jewish scholars between Septuagint or Alexandrian canon, a collection of forty-six books translated into Greek by 70 Jewish scholars and the Palestinian canon, which did not contain the deuterocanonical books. Protestant churches usually follow Palestinian traditions, thus Protestant Bibles omit those deuterocanonical books. The Catholic Church has determined the deuterocanonical books have the same authority as the rest of the books of the Bible. We know that the Palestinians, as the rest of the Arab world, are from the line of Ishmael and Jesus Christ is from the line of Isaac. We also know that Isaac and Ishmael are half brothers, sons of Abraham.

What did Luther say to the Epistle of James? Luther once referred to this letter "epistle of straw" and comparing the work to other parts of the New Testament, Luther considered "throwing Jimmy into the fire."

Luther also had problems with the book of Revelation, Hebrews, Jude, and 2 Peter. In addition to these New Testament books, Luther attacked the Old Testament deuterocanonical text although he did not take them out of his translation of the Bible.

The Catholic Church had only one response to all of Luther's demands: there are none within the Church who would refer to Martin Luther's actions as "religious reform." Martin Luther was a troubled soul, an apostate Augustinian friar, and the author of the great apostasy called the reformation. The Church's riposte to that apostasy was The Counter-Reformation which strengthened the faith through the pronouncement of the Council of Trent.

I will be seriously remiss and grossly unfair to your religious order, the Society of Jesus, which became the largest and most influential in the Catholic Reformation, if I do not include its historical vignette as it appears in Professor of Theology Alan Schreck's book, *The Compact History of the Catholic Church*:

The Catholic Reformation was ignited by the founding of new religious orders and groups, as well as the renewal of existing orders. One of the central concerns of the Catholic Reformation was the quest for a holy, zealous, and celibate clergy to lead the Church in its reform.

The religious order that led the way was the Society of Jesus, or the Jesuits, founded by St. Ignatius of Loyola in 1534, and recognized by the Pope in 1539. Ignatius was a Spanish soldier whose right leg was shattered in battle in 1521. While recovering, Ignatius read the life of Christ and a book of the saints, and it gave him such spiritual joy that he decided to spend his life serving God in the Catholic Church. After obtaining a good education, which later became a great apostolate of his order, Ignatius chose six men to join the brotherhood—including Francis Xavier, the great missionary.

Despite being constantly suspected by the Inquisition, Ignatius' order was finally approved by the Pope. Obedience to the Catholic Church and to the Pope in particular was a special mark of the Jesuits. The order began by educating the illiterate and poor, but within a few years it was educating princes and kings as well. The Jesuits also became great missionaries; Francis Xavier brought the gospel of Jesus Christ to India and Japan beginning in 1541. Later the battle to defend the Catholic faith became a primary work of the Jesuits.

Let me now bring you to my dialogue with my friend Veronica.

The Dream Team: Veronica is third from the left. Author is on the right of John

The Dialogue

$\mathcal{P}$ope Francis, the views of Bishop Raul comes back to my mind: Filipino Catholics have sacramentalized our faith; on the other hand, our non-Catholic Christian brothers and sisters are evangelized in the sense that they know and keep to heart our faith. Their words are carefully aligned to the teaching of the Lord.

Your encouragement to talk to our brothers and sisters of other faiths emboldened me to start a dialogue with Veronica. We actually had the dialogue over the phone. I saw the opportunity when she called to greet me on my natal day.

"Happy birthday, Rudy, enjoy another year of our awesome God's faithfulness."

"Thank you, Veronica. By the way, your religious affiliation is non-Catholic charismatic, is that right? Where do you usually have your prayer meetings?"

"Here at home, every Monday night."

"Do you conduct the prayers yourself?"

"Yes. We take turns in leading the prayers right after Bible study conducted by our pastor."

"How many members do you have in your community?"

"Eight to ten regulars."

"How about your total community?"

"I am with Greenhills Christian Fellowship Northwest. It's now on its 7th year, with over 300 members; we hold two worship services on Sunday."

"Great! Do you have a preferred Bible?"

"We use the New King James Bible in English, also Tagalog version during Home Bible Study which is good for some seniors, too."

"You were a Catholic before, right?"

"Yes, for 50 yrs."

"What was the compelling reason for your decision to move?"

"Compelling reason was mainly to grow spiritually and to continue life's journey pleasing to him. Only through his word can we know his wonderful plan and will for us."

"I just listened to a talk in our church about interfaith dialogue."

"That is good as long as God's Word is adhered to at all times. I am glad to have friends who truly know and love God, and are continuously in search for his truth, teachings, and promises, most of all, who delight in his word."

"Yes. How right you are! Do you see differences in our teaching and those in your church?

"Yes. God's truth gave me clear perspective on how I can be right with God. Most of the things I practiced before contradicted God's truths and teachings. Thank God, he opened my eyes to the realization that I needed to accept Jesus as my Lord and Savior, and totally trust him for his will is perfect."

"You will recall as a once-upon-a-time Catholic that our teaching comes from two sources: Tradition and Scriptures. Through oral Tradition the teaching of Jesus Christ came down from knowledgeable persons who were closest to him when he was still alive. We know that the first written gospel of the New Testament was written 70 years after the death of Christ, and without going back to Tradition, the gospels that formed the Scriptures would not have been written. Of course, the correct understanding of our teaching is interpreted by the Magisterium of the Church. Without questioning the basis of your belief, what do you think of these foundations of our own belief?

"Sad to say but during my 50 years in the Roman Catholic Church, the Church did not clearly establish how we can be saved so that we can have personal, intimate relationship with God which is the most important thing to personal growth. Traditional knowledge about God only results to temporary reformation, but genuine relationship in fellowship with God actually transforms us and we become born-again Christians. Sanctification follows after salvation as we keep on learning and studying God's words. What I saw then was too much legalism and traditional practices. Knowing God as a born-again Christian showed me that life is meaningful if you rely on his words. His teachings designed for us are so powerful to equip us for every good work."

"Again Veronica, who interprets your teaching when there is misunderstanding, how do you respond to gay marriages, contraception, abortion, and euthanasia?"

"In my humble opinion we need to adhere to God's word all the time in all aspects. He is omniscient, all-knowing God ready to give us wisdom to learn to do his will, as long as we trust and obey. It's all in his word; all we have to do is seek him with all our hearts. It's really a matter of relationship with him and whatever the issues at hand, we need to be standing firmly on his side."

"That is good Veronica. At the moment, the secular world is changing the rules of life as taught by Jesus Christ and no religious congregation has come out to challenge these changes except the Catholic Church. What role can we expect from your church regarding these secular changes?"

"Honestly, as long as the spirit of love is among us, there is always room for reconciliation as long as God's word rules. For unity in the spirit we must first seek his word to know for sure that we are right with him... as in what would Jesus do?"

"Yes, that is really the question, but the Lord is not here physically and the wanton disregard of the rules of God is happening before us. Who shall then interpret the question....What would Jesus do?"

"He is the Word."

"Yes, Veronica that is correct. But we are now faced with a new secular thinking that destroys his teaching. We cannot all be silent in our beliefs, contemplating his teaching while thousands of the unborn are dying every day. Someone has to pick up the cudgels in the open and openly fight the leaders of secularism and the evil before us. Will your church come and join our church and fight beside us?"

"Prayers are more powerful than anything else as long as they give glory to God. We are living close to end times where the prince of darkness is working double time; so it is a spiritual battle. For me, prayers are our weapons coupled with sharing the gospel as much as we can with guidance of the Holy Spirit. God will do the rest. I am not so sure how other Christians think about the changing times."

"There is now a growing partnership with other beliefs. In United Kingdom, the battle is joined. The Anglican Church, though they continue to receive their instructions from Queen Elizabeth, is fighting this onslaught of secularism. The Orthodox Church in the Eastern countries led by Russia, has banned gay marriages. In Africa, while there is respect for and understanding of the situation of homosexuals, the government enacted a law against activities of same-sex pleasures. In the US, the Catholic Church is defying Obamacare by not allowing abortion to be done in Catholic hospitals even if they are covered by health insurance—the heart of Obamacare. Every day there are more religious beliefs fighting alongside with us. Shouldn't your church fight with us, too? Like you, we believe in the power of prayer but we must accompany this with action, or else we become like Juan *Tamad* lying under the guava tree and praying for the fruit to fall so he could eat."

"Yes, Rudy, all we need is to read God's word and refer to the Scriptures in these changing times. But be of good cheer, these may be signs of the prophecies in the Book of Revelation."

"Again, Veronica, I agree with you. But will you allow secularism to progress and not do anything while the unborn are being killed? I don't know if the Book of King James has the epistle of St. James, if it is there, you will be able to read St. James' admonition, "Faith without action is a dead faith."

"Please don't get me wrong, I also strongly believe that faith without works is dead faith. But what I point out is I would prefer to act by prayers and most importantly, by sharing the good news of salvation to others whom I think are not aware of the biblical concept of salvation. I believe that sin is the cause of it all, when people persist in ignoring God and his Word. We can only know God's will for us if we look closely at what the Scriptures are saying. I'm sure you are in the know about this that our Lord Jesus Christ came to save us from sin so that we can be reconciled with God the Father. I also adhere to compassion with kindness or love with good deed. If you see someone in misery, it is good to pray for him and to extend help to alleviate his condition. Our church is quite active in evangelism but at the same time we lend a helping hand when called for, like visiting the sick, the poor, and those in prison. It goes hand in hand—feeding the body and the spirit.

"God is in total control even though situations are grim. To me, sincere prayers coupled with sharing the good news of salvation is most important so that many more souls and sinners turn to God. What is happening now is mainly due to the bondage of sin. The great commission is to be at our main task as believers in the midst of changing times. I also believe that he allows things to happen for reasons beyond our comprehension in the fulfillment of his plan and design for mankind.

"Let's pause for a while and continue tomorrow. Have a good one, *kapatid*, brother."

"Thanks, Veronica. Yes, let's pause for now. The differences in our beliefs are like two rivers running parallel with no signs that they will ever meet. I was hoping our interfaith dialogue could come to a point where our rivers can converge somewhere in the distance and flow as one. But thanks for helping me understand your church's teaching better."

"I do pray we'll come to that, God willing!"

"Yes, Veronica, let's accompany our prayers with action. As our teaching says, 'God helps those who help themselves.' "

"But always in his glory."

"Veronica, one last word, I know that you do not believe in saints but let me share the story of St. Francis, one of the two saints who carried the stigmata of Jesus Christ."

"Stigmatics are holy persons bearing the same wounds that Christ suffered during his passion and resurrection. Their wounds never heal. The nature of our body is such that wounds that do not heal decay and the body emits out a foul smell. In the case of St. Francis' stigmata, the wounds mimic the size and location in the body of Christ and emit a sweet smelling fragrance like the smell of an expensive perfume."

He dreamed of knighthood and longed for the adventurous life of chivalry. In pursuit of that dream, he joined in the war between Assisi and Perugia at the age of 20.

One night, a mysterious voice asked him, "Who do you think can best reward you, the Master or the servant?" Francis answered, "The Master." The voice continued, "Why do you leave the Master for the servant?" Francis realized the servant was Count Walter. He left Spoleto convinced God had spoken to him.

During the next two years, Francis sensed an inner force that was preparing him for another change. The sight of lepers caused revulsion in the sensitive soul of Francis. One day, while riding his horse, he came upon a leper. His first impulse was to throw him a coin and spur his horse on. Instead, Francis dismounted and embraced the leper. On his deathbed, he recalled the encounter as the crowning moment of his conversion: "What seemed bitter to me was changed into sweetness of soul and body."

Later, in a dramatic moment of prayer in the abandoned church of San Damiano, he heard a voice coming from the crucifix which challenged him to rebuild the church. At first he thought it meant that he should rebuild San Damiano. Gradually, Francis realized that God meant that he should "rebuild" the Church at large. From that moment, he learned that living a Christian life would place him in opposition to the values of his society and set him apart from family and friends and many of his own age.

The teaching of St. Francis, with the guidance of the Holy Spirit, converted many to live their lives daily according to the teaching of the Gospels. He touched many to see that God loves the poor because the poor are in need of God more. And so God gave St. Francis to the poor, and made them realize that living in luxury and the benefit of the material world is not the measure of God's love. Often, the rich become God's challenge. That is why he chose people like St. Francis, St. Augustine, and others who came from a life of ease and pleasure, to work with the poor, as if to drive home the lesson that being rich, with all its entitlements and comfort, is not necessarily the key to God's kingdom.

St. Francis gave the downtrodden, the poor, hope. After all, they realized that God is giving them priority in heaven (*Catholic New Advent*).

"In the history of the Catholic Church in times of crisis God always summons a person to help his church. St. Francis brought back the people to God. As a reward, Christ gave him his wounds until he died."

"Our present Pope, a Jesuit, gave himself the name Francis because he wants to bring back the people to God. Let's pray that Pope Francis will succeed."

"Rudy, I am now leaving for my *apo*'s birthday party. I will respond to your story of St. Francis tonight. Let us continue our interesting exchange of respective beliefs. Thanks for sharing."

Pope Francis, in my talk with Veronica, I cannot help but appreciate her steadfast belief that whatever circumstance confronts her, the strength of her faith and prayers will resolve everything for as long as she prayed with sincerity and a pure heart. I have personally seen how the non-Catholic charismatics allot regular time learning the Bible, something we Catholics are missing. I, myself, without the regular assignments of what book to read would not know our faith. Our Bible study, while sponsored by the Church, is purely voluntary. In Veronica's community, it is a must and the schedule of readings is assigned among the group so you are ready when your turn to lead comes.

In our conversation, we expressed our understanding of what we believed in and accepted them for what they are. We did not debate our differences because we both knew that they could lead to misunderstanding and possibly wreck an old friendship. What we accomplished, though, was learn more about our particular beliefs and respect them. We did not talk to convince each other which is the better teaching. Instead, our conversation was meant to strengthen what we believe in.

Pope Francis, the teaching that only the bearer of the Catholic cross is saved is a lesson of the past. Now our Church teaches a different dictum—all will be saved for as long as we believe in only one savior. When asked of your thoughts about non-believers, your response broke all grounds. Your "revolution of tenderness" confirmed it when you said, "Even atheists, who do not believe in God, can be saved, for as long as they do good."

Actually, you did not say anything new, you were just reiterating the teaching of our Church. In our book, *Catechism of the Catholic Church (CCC)*, this is clearly defined and it answers the question of my friend John, "If Jesus is the only Way to 'my Father's House' what happens to the spiritual efforts of Buddhists, Muslims, Taoists, and similar people?"

Those who have not yet received the Gospel are related to the People of God in various ways. When she delves into her own mystery, the Church, the People of God in the New Covenant, discovers her link with the Jewish People, "the first to hear the Word of God." The Jewish faith, unlike other non-Christian religions, is already a response to God's revelation in the Old Covenant. To the Jews "belong the sonship, the glory, the covenants, the giving of the law, the worship, and the promises; to them belong the patriarchs, and of their race, according to the flesh, is the Christ," for the gifts and the call of God are irrevocable" (*CCC* 839).

And when one considers the future, God's people of the Old Covenant and the new People of God tend towards similar goals: expectation of the coming (or of the return) of the Messiah. But one awaits the return of the Messiah who died and rose from the dead and is recognized as Lord and Son of God; the other awaits the coming of the Messiah, whose features remain hidden till the end of time; and the latter waiting is accompanied by the drama of not knowing or misunderstanding Christ Jesus (*CCC* 840).

The Church's relationship with the Muslims in "the plan of salvation also includes those who acknowledge the Creator, in the first place amongst whom are the Muslims; they profess to hold the faith of Abraham, and together with us they adore the one, merciful God, mankind's judge on the last day (*CCC* 841).

The Church's bond with non-Christian religions is in the first place the common origin of the human race: All nations form but one community. This is so because all stem from the one stock which God created to people the entire earth, and also because all share a common destiny, namely God. His providence, evident goodness, and saving designs extend to all against the day when the elect are together in the holy city… (*CCC* 842).

The Catholic Church recognizes in other religions that search, among shadows and images, for the God who is unknown yet near since he gives life and breath and all things, and wants all men to be saved. The Church considers all goodness and truth found in these religions as "a preparation for the Gospel, and given by him who enlightens all men that they at length have life" (*CCC* 842).

Fr. Charles Belmonte, in his book *Patience: The Path to Victory*, wrote, "If we look closely at Jesus we will see how patient he is with the defects of his disciples, and unwearied he repeats the same teaching over and over again, explaining it in detail, so that his slow minded and easily distracted friends can master his saving doctrine. He never loses patience with their obtuseness and failure to grasp his meaning. Truly, Jesus who is our Master and Lord at the same time is meek and humble of heart, acted patiently in attracting and inviting his disciples."

Pope Francis, my dialogue with Veronica is not meant to convert each other; the dialogue was meant to strengthen our own beliefs. Hopefully, our members who entertain thoughts of moving to another community will take the time to study our faith before concluding that "the grass is greener on the other side of the fence."

Whatever differences we have, they are meant to strengthen the source of our teaching… in your "revolution of tenderness." "There is emphasis on our divine call to live in community with others…

a message sorely needed in a time when so many are drawn on what could be described as the 'inactive solitude' of virtual communities. The fact that we have been created in the image of Trinity—the perfect divine communion—reminds us that we are meant to live with others that no one is saved alone. True faith in the incarnate Son of God is inseparable from self-giving, from membership in the community, from service, from reconciliation with others. The Son of God, by becoming flesh, summoned us to the revolution of tenderness."

Impossible Dream

Dear Pope Francis, we all have our own crosses to bear. For my dear friend, John, the cross that weighs heavy upon his shoulder are priests, or rather the lack thereof, that will satisfy his thirst in search for spiritual direction. He has come to the point where he has scratched them off as irrelevant to his existence. And John is not being facetious or merely symptomatic of a person who hides behind a lame excuse for his lethargy in attending to his religious obligations: he is truly being torn apart by his perception of priestly shortfalls. In the process, he has become a swirl of contradiction. He has the boldness to deny the Church of Jesus Christ as institution. But in the same breath, he affirms his faith in Jesus' teaching.

I do not judge whether John's action is born of conviction or simply a very human reaction of giving up on people whom he once respected as evangelizers of faith after he found them to possess feet of clay, just like you and I. Perhaps John could not help the comparison of the clergy of his experience and Judas with his bag of silver. Yet still it took a certain amount of courage for him to have done what he did—which is to come out overtly to announce to all and sundry, that as far as he was concerned, he was done with institutionalized worship.

I was reading William Bennett's *The Book of Virtues* and the following line struck me as fittingly descriptive of the situation of John: "The infectious nature of strikingly courageous behavior on the part of one person can inspire, and can also in part shame, a whole group... It was one key to the kind of courage displayed by those who silently suffered abuse when they joined ranks with Gandhi and

Martin Luther King Jr., in acts of non-violent protest directed at rousing the public conscience against injustice."

Paradigms of courage weave through our paths on a daily basis. When my children expressed their willingness—even eagerness—to push my wheelchair up the hill, it was to me, an example of courage, and the courage to display their unconditional love for me. They know that walking short distances on level ground leaves me gasping for air, not to mention walking uphill. But they were willing to push the wheelchair so I would not miss the sacrifice of love Kuya Hesus made for us.

Steve Jobs, the flamboyant marketing guru and co-founder of Apple who died at the young age of 56, recalled: "When I was 17, I read a quote that went something like this: 'If you live each day as if it was your last, someday you'll most certainly be right.' It made an impression on me and since then, for the past 33 years, I have looked in the mirror every morning and asked myself: 'If today is the last day of my life, would I want to do what I am about to do today?'"

Somewhere in the pages of this book I will share with you how the words of Steve Jobs, *If today is the last day of my life, would I want to do what I am about to do today?*, affected decisions I made that day.

On the eve of our departure for Lourdes, Bro. Millard briefed us on what to expect. It was a fair assumption that most of us silently wished that the Blessed Mother would grant our personal prayers; whether that would find favor with her... well, hope springs eternal...

Nevertheless, it was full anticipation for the best that energized us as we busied ourselves in the minutiae of the preparation for our trip. Who knows, this pilgrimage could very well spell the beginning of the rest of our days. Even in the schedule which Bro. Millard laid before us, I already convinced myself that the "Way of the Cross" was not for me. Viewing the hill to get to the Mother's shrine from a distance, I admitted to myself that this was an impossible feat; the hill of the "Way of the Cross" is much steeper to climb. It might as well be a trek up Mt. Mayon volcano in Albay for me. I looked forlornly at the hill, defeated.

It was not always this way.

I spoke to our Mother in Fatima

Life, come to think of it, is not different from a game of golf. Arnold Palmer said, "Success in the game depends less on strength of the body than strength of mind and character." Mastery of the game will refine your character and will make your goals easier to realize.

While the game aims at perfection, it never happens. "Golf is not won, it is played," said Jack Lemmon, great actor and golf aficionado. Therein the real value of the game lies. That is how I look at myself when my Kuya Hesus freed me from my asthma when I was young.

In the developing years of the sport, the golf ball was at one time made from a tree sap called *gutta percha*. The ball was molded from the heated sap and polished smooth. Because of this, the early golfers found it difficult to get a good, square hit on the ball—which meant less flight distance, requiring more strokes in their approach.

Observant players noticed, after some experience with the "gutty," as they called the tree sap ball, that they were hitting their old balls much farther and straighter; despite the fact that the balls were badly nicked and scuffed. Using hammers, they pounded a rough surface on the ball and got the same startling results: a ball with better flight characteristics. Further experimentation with material and design gave us the modern "dimpled" golf ball.

And so it is with life. When we are badly bruised, scuffed, and roughed up, and we somehow manage to pick ourselves up again, we come out stronger and fly higher than we used to do. What does not kill us makes us very sick, but it will also make us strong. Life's incessant buffeting never takes a break; that's just the way it is. Over the years, you have accumulated calluses and scars to show that you have survived. Like the golf ball, we need the dimples for distance and flying true.

When my old asthma came back, I accepted it. It happened after I was given bigger responsibilities in my old company. Stresses of the job triggered it. I didn't mind. Doctors have found new modalities of treatment and medication and I was able to push on quite vigorously aided along with constant puffs from my inhaler. I drew inspiration by one of the great figures in sports, Vince Lombardi. Lombardi was the first man ever to win three consecutive Super Bowls, while coaching the Green Bay Packers. Of success he had this to say: "Winning is not everything, it's the only thing."

He gave me the motivation to face the demands of work head-on and to win, despite my ailment. I was young and truly believed that I was some kind of invincible, like superman. Often I was in the golf course before the break of dawn, waiting in the tee box to make my first drive. By the same token, it was a rare occasion indeed to catch me home earlier than ten in the evening—that's the time I called it a day from work.

Golf's gift of focus, self-confidence, and equanimity probably benefited me more than the puffs I took from my inhaler. Asthma was my handicap but I trained my mind to beat it or at least keep it on a leash. I told myself that it should never get in the way as I rose to meet the challenge. If I surrendered this time and slackened my pace, my dreams would burst faster than a pricked bubble.

In golf, we turn in better scores with constant practice. Swings and putting greatly improve; and reading what the champions advice to play a productive game can bring down our handicap. Life is the same way; it is a constant struggle and if we want to win at the game of life, we have to work at practicing until we perfect the rules of the game. As in golf, we can strive to lower our handicap. And success depends on how motivated you are.

I did not want to just coast along. Each year that passed with relative freedom from asthmatic episodes and the horrifying experience of difficulty in breathing was a gift. Of course, I was aware that I might make a bogey. I could get laid up in bed for a few days. But that's alright. All I needed was to take it in stride. I let the gentle winds of faith and my trust in God put me on the green of greens… safely and in his appointed time.

I kept repeating my mantra: "When I get into a difficult shot, my constant practice will pay off." Difficult shot… practice… practice… payoff. I just had to correct my swing. I learned to adjust. As much as possible I had lunch at home, and afterwards a short nap to recharge my batteries before going back to work.

My routine became second nature to me. Deliver a good day's work… payoff… I'm OK that I have done the right thing for myself.

And so I thought.

Nobody will care to admit that physical aging changes the rules of the game—not while they are young, anyway. Age crept up on me and when it caught up with me, I was shocked. I was forced to slow down. From a dizzyingly fast pace, I sputtered to a slow walk. To hike uphill is difficult beyond what I can imagine. I do alright on level ground and with a bit of extra effort, can even tackle a gentle slope; but anything steeper than a 20-degree gradient or stairs that lead to the next level, is an absolute no-no. As my doctor says, "Don't even think about it." My heart may just give up!

I am one whose life has always been measured by impossible challenges, most of which I'd like to think that I conquered. *The Impossible Dream* was a song written just for me; so I identified with it. But today I admitted to myself, no matter what mantra, no matter mind-over-matter trance I willed myself into, this was going to be impossible.

Coming to terms with that realization made me sad and depressed; my shoulders sagged below the backrest of the wheelchair. Jun said, "Dad your chair seems heavy today. Let me stop and check the brakes."

It was not the brakes. The heaviness that Jun felt was the heaviness which I was carrying inside me. I finally gave up and admitted that I would not be able to walk the "Way of the Cross" to the top of the hill. I had long wanted to physically reprise the struggle of Kuya Hesus up the hill with the weight of the heavy cross on his shoulder.

I stared blankly at the hill, emptied of all motivation. You can understand what I was going through at that instance. It was a terrifying moment when the realization sank in that I couldn't make that walk, in fact couldn't do much of anything. I felt defeated and lost.

Jun sensed my mood and as usual, seemed to read my thoughts. He could, too, because when I requested him to write the introduction to the book I wrote about my own father, his words seemed able to probe deep into me as a person and a parent. Jun wrote:

A Son's Love for His Father

I am a selfish man, in a positive kind of way...

Ever since I was a child, I wanted to spend as much time as I could with my father. I wanted to get to know my father well—where he came from; what he did while growing up; why he did what he did; what his passions and hobbies were.

The only way to do this was to take up the activities my father did in his free time. One of these was sports. Basketball, in our country, is the national pastime so naturally, my father played the sport and so did I. He even put up a basketball court in our backyard so that we could all play at night after he got home from work.

However, after an injury he received from my brother during one of our scrimmages, he couldn't play with us anymore, not that he did not want to; he just couldn't because he was afraid that the accident he suffered would be repeated with either my brother or me at the receiving end. And basketball being what it is, a contact sport, and the possibility was indeed not far from happening.

During this time, he started introducing us to his other passion, tennis. He would take us with him to his tennis games and let us play with each other while he played with his friends. After playing with his friends, he made sure to spend some time with us and would play a few games with us to see how we progressed along. During these moments, among his friends, they would regale us with stories from their youth—stuff which they used to do, girls whom they serenaded, places where they went, and aspirations they had while they were growing up. It gave us a glimpse of my father's life before he had a family. I thought that it was a picture worth remembering.

When I was eight or nine, I spent an entire summer at the company swimming pool where my father worked. Back then, it was a special treat to be able to go swimming since only resorts, country clubs, and the rich had swimming pools. Every day, I would wake up very early so that I could accompany my father on his commute to work and when we got to his office, I would spend the entire morning at the pool as soon as it opened.

Lunch time was my favorite time of the day because I got to spend it with my Dad. After lunch, I would hang around the office while he worked or if he was in meetings, I would lounge in his office and explore the mementos he had displayed in there. His office mates would come by looking for him and would stay a while to chat with me. They would tell me stories of his days at work. Each person would have a story to tell about my father—his kindness and generosity, how he went out of his way to mentor and praise his people.

It also showed how much these people really appreciated my father because they took the time from their busy work schedules to spend a few moments with a youngster to tell him about the wonderful things that his father had done for them. As I looked back on that summer, I realize that the moments which I enjoyed most were when I was either spending time in my father's company or his coworkers telling me stories about my father's adventures.

I even took up golf when my father was bitten by the golfing bug. Golf is the only game that I play whenever my father is around. If I am not playing golf with my father, then I do not play golf at all. I love this sport because it has allowed my father and me to get to know each other more. What other sport gives you the luxury to converse with your playing partner for the next four to six hours without your game being affected?

When my parents would vacation in America, we would go on extended driving trips to visit vacation spots. I always drove during these trips not because I liked driving, but because my father always sat on the front passenger seat. During the times that he was not taking a nap, he would always be recounting stories from his youth or sharing funny anecdotes from work. The trips were always more memorable whenever my father shared his stories with us.

I even went back home after graduating from college so that I could spend more time with my father. But as you grow older and start your own family, you realize that you need to create your own memories, your own stories, to tell your children as they grow up. And as you tell your own stories to your children, they become entwined with the stories of your father's life and his stories become your own as well.

This book is not a book of collected stories but a legacy that my *Lolo* has given to my father and now he is giving to us. It is a treasure—these values that my Lolo left behind. His words and his wisdom will forever remain with us and our family and our extended families will always know where we came from.

In his own caring ways, my father made sure that my Lolo's legacy will be his own legacy to us that it will be carved in a stone of remembrance. His book will do that for us.

Thank you, Dad... (Excerpts from *The Courage To Be Pinoy: Lessons from My Father's Heart*)

"*Bakit*, Dad, *may problema ba*? [Do you have a problem?]"

"*Wala*. No problem. I was just thinking that I wouldn't be able to join you in the 'Way of the Cross.' "

"Why not? Wally, Paul, and *Kuya* Carlo are here, we will push you."

"It's okay. The hill is too steep. I will just wait down here."

The adjacent area for the "Way of the Cross" was like a golf course. While praying, I could breathe in the cool, clean air. I'd be hitting two birds with one stone. But thinking about it didn't make me feel any better.

Jun lived almost twelve years in America, six of those years as a student. He came home with a college and a master's degree. He achieved them with honors. He was a serious student but he knew when and where to have his fun. Being endowed with a better-than-average mental and emotional IQ, he practically breezed through college and his advanced course.

Hand in hand with what he learned in school, Jun also learned about independence and self-reliance; that is one of the side benefits of children who are fortunate to study abroad. Being alone and having to fend for themselves basically teach invaluable lessons about life and its interminable problem-solving opportunities.

Raising children is like making good wine. The entire process begins with planting and nurturing the vine. The viticulturist strictly controls the amount of water fed to the plant, for too much or too little will have a deleterious effect on the vine and the quality of the grape it will produce. He prunes the shoots of the vine mercilessly it seems, but the true purpose is to make the vine yield more and better fruits. The process is repeated over and over. Doing so, the best fruit to make the best wine is produced. And harvest becomes a time of celebration.

And so it is with bringing up children. It demands parental will and finding an acceptable balance between an iron hand and a velvet glove. And the pruning scissors. And most of all, knowing when to use them effectively.

If I knew one thing that the pilgrimage did for me, it was to capture once again the images that Jun evoked when he wrote the introduction to my book. Already the answer is forming in my mind when the Lord asks me for an accounting of my days on earth. I will simply reply, with all the humility I can muster, "You are our loving and just Lord. You gave me my children; judge me then on what they have become."

The exchange with Jun happened just before I felt Mama Mary's smile from where she was at the baths. Afterwards, I felt like she gave me renewed strength to beat anything, even my perennial breathing problem.

Did I imagine long lost youth resurgent through my entire being? Memories of how I used to do things the way God wanted them done flooded my senses; I wanted that hill if I had to die trying. Lines from my song came back to me: *"To dream the impossible dream... to reach the unreachable star."*

Ascent to Calvary Hill

Pope Francis, the object of the Stations of the Cross is to help the faithful to make in spirit, as it were, a pilgrimage to the chief scenes of Christ's sufferings and death, and this has become one of the most popular of Catholic devotions. It is carried out by passing from station to station, with certain prayers at each and devout meditation on the various incidents in turn. It is very common, when the devotion is performed publicly, to sing a stanza of the *Stabat Mater* while passing from one station to the next.

The hill before us was formidable. Fuelled by the shot of adrenaline I got from my encounter with Mama Mary, I requested my son Carlo to join me in the ascent of the hill. Believe it or not, my security blanket, the wheelchair, was missing. It didn't matter because as I walked, I held on to Carlo's shoulder. It was a long walk. I am used to stopping every 100 meters to do some breathing exercises and rest my lungs. But in this I really pushed my limit. The walk from our hotel was easily 400 meters. Add to that the initial climb, albeit slowly pacing myself, I was close to 500 meters on that walk and climb before I had to stop and rest heart and lungs. After two more stops, with longer paces, we were at the foot of the hill!

The members of the group began to arrive one by one. Paul, Leah, and Jun saw us and were surprised because they didn't expect to see me there. Jun and Paul raced back to the restaurant where they had parked the wheelchair; they wanted to make sure that I could make it all the way to the fourteenth station.

Then the main group started up on the trek again. Leah suggested that we stayed behind while waiting for the wheelchair to arrive; in the meantime she would lead in the prayers. But I wanted to join our group, "It's okay, Leah, I can walk until Paul and Jun get back, then they can rejoin us."

My daughter Ondine captured the drama of our ascent to Calvary Hill.

"No, Dad, let's not take the risk. God is not saying that you need to die while saying your prayers. Let's just wait."

Leah has always been decisive and determined, traits which she inherited from her mother. Our older children have already settled into their separate lives although they live near each other. The years which the children spent on the campus of the California State University taught them the independence which they could not have learned that fast if they were with us in Manila.

I remember how Leth, Nikki, and I would fly back and forth to make sure that the children in America were having their needs met. That was our routine until they finally earned their degrees. Jun and Leah came back from America after college while Carlo found his niche and decided to make his home there. After a few years, Jun went back to America, bringing his family along with him.

This pilgrimage was long on the planning board. As you must have guessed by now, it had been quite a spell since we were together as a family. In a sense, it was a nostalgic trip for us, a time to relive old memories and build new ones.

A parent relates to each of his children in different ways. I am close to daughter Leah in a way that is different from the way I am close to her sister, although they are both my jewels. Leah surprises me constantly. Once she wrote a letter to family, friends, and acquaintances to promote and encourage people to read my books.

A Letter from Leah

My father is a weaver of time. He brings people back and forth into his dreams. And in those journeys, I personally saw how his dreams never broke. They simply transform into something that was meant to be. And if we are fortunate enough to be like him, it might happen to us, too. You have all made it possible for him to be that way. His books and articles are your gifts to him. In sharing his stories and life journeys with you, you have all given him so much more than what you are taking away.

My father had many great teachers in his life. But I have been privileged to only have one. He has taught me about love and pain, laughter and sadness, and death. He taught me to learn what family means, why sincere friendship is beyond value, why a smile is important to just about anyone, and above all, what it means to honor your own country.

His dreams have become mine and now they are yours as well. And it is in tribute to my father that I celebrate my life today. One of the happiest moments of my Tatay was the day when he and my Nanay walked the aisle once again to celebrate their 40th wedding anniversary.

Their celebration and the memories of their love floods my mind until today, something my own children shares. As they stood before the altar renewing their vows, my Tatay's raspy voice came clearly throughout the church. He did not say, "I do." Instead, he happily recited the poem, "Roses Speak to Me of Love," a love poem he especially composed for my Mom. Everyone responded with applause. We all clapped and cheered. We all got carried away with the moment.

And now, we are the beau ideal of that love.

Leah (Excerpts from *The Road to Emmaus*)

I never had to worry about Leah. Never mind that she is someone faced with biases and discrimination because of her gender. My Leah is made of different stuff. In fact, she has always been as aggressive as her two brothers. And if I had something to worry about her, it would probably for her reckless abandon.

Leah can get into anything she puts her mind to. And she will do it with flying colors. But sometimes, she will also crash to the ground. As a young child she biked, swam, and ran right alongside with her brothers. At night, she slept with her doll collection. And oh... how she could read through me. She knew just how to get me to say yes to all that she wished for.

I remember when she was in high school and she had gone on her class' annual spiritual retreat. The activity was to conclude with a love letter written to the father. She wrote me a letter that so touched me that barely halfway through, I found myself teary-eyed. My little girl was begging me for more time with her. And she wanted me to know why I didn't hug her anymore and how she missed all the things we used to do together.

My sweet Leah, in her adolescent years, still wanted me to tuck her in bed at night and read her a story before she went to sleep. I was also the one she'd call in the middle of the night if she was having a bad dream. She and I were so much alike, especially when it came to our feelings.

Leah had her share of naughtiness and mischief, too. I remember the countless times she would ask me to get her a glass of water in the middle of the night when she was running a fever. Although I knew that it was good for her, I couldn't help but notice her playful smile when I had to get up again for that unending "last" glass of water in the wee hours of the morning.

I never forgot that letter she wrote from the retreat. Since then, I made sure to give her all the hugs she could handle, whether she asked for them or not. Her return hugs became the key to my heart as well. I don't think I ever said no to her for anything ever since that time! And I dreaded the day that she would grow up and live her own life. I knew that my Leah was mine, but I also knew that it won't be for long.

Leah is a woman with a gift of a prophet. She can read you like she owns your mind. She is as clever, as loving, and as strong-willed as her mother although she often tells people, "I may have gotten my strength from Mom, but mine is different."

That's because Leah's strength of character also has its gentlest side—a virtue that my wife, Leth, is now beginning to borrow from our daughter.

I saw Paul and Jun coming up the incline as Leah started to lead the prayers. There were a few pilgrims who waited for us. In my head, I had already worked out a plan. I would climb the hill to one station on foot and then ride the chair to the next. That way, I could rest and do my deep breathing in between stations.

But what we didn't anticipate were those ditch-like breaks in series of threes that sliced across the road! It presented a bit of a challenge because the cuts were deep enough so that when Paul and Jun tried to wiggle the wheels past the cut, the footrest of the chair got caught, bringing it to a jarring halt. I had to step out and cling to Paul's arm, which by this time was slippery with sweat from his exertion of pulling me up the path. Jun took to walking ahead like a point man to look for shallower crossings over which we could ease the wheelchair with relatively less effort.

I wanted to walk and just hold on to their arms but the boys insisted that I sat on the chair. They feared that the climb would put too much strain on my heart. So the routine was sit, get up, walk a little, and then sit again. This was "the way of my cross" until the 14th station.

Let me tell you: it was a struggle. So I led my mind to Jesus. He never complained when he walked on the same path. From the time they hauled him before the Pharisees, to the time they brought him to Pilate, to Herod Antipas, he didn't even say anything much less utter a sound. When they scourged him at the pillar with a shards-imbedded whip, pressed the crown of thorns on his head, he didn't whimper. And the ascent on the hill had not even begun.

When he finally walked the hill of Calvary, he carried the cross on his back willingly. He knew that he must do this. It was the only way he could give mankind another chance after the fall of Adam and Eve. It was the mandate he accepted from the Father. There was no other way or mankind would be doomed.

Even as he hanged on the cross, his thoughts were for us, "Father, forgive them, they know not what they do."

And dying on the cross, he told the thief on his right, "On this day you will be with me in paradise." It was the forgiveness that he meant for all of us if we mend our ways.

Before he finally expired, he looked at his disciple John, the only Apostle who had the courage to be with him at the hour of his need and with his dying breath said, "John, this is your mother." In his last moments he was still thinking of us; he was entrusting the apostles to his mother to calm their fears until his Spirit comes.

Who would take care of her? John, of course; there was nobody else.

And here I was with so little faith, worried that I won't be able to breathe, even as my children were there to take care of me. Would not Kuya Hesus take care of me, too?

I looked at Paul and Jun this time bathed in sweat yet with no signs that they were thinking at all of giving up. While I sat on the chair, Paul pushed and Jun pulled. I could hear Jun's labored breathing throughout the stiff climb. During "my way of the cross," I felt certain sharpness in my senses. Leah's voice was faltering as she read the prayers; the thinning air in the higher altitude had made even talking hard. Carlo had this time gone ahead to look for the easiest path for the unlikely caravan to traverse. But from the distance he kept glancing back, worried that I might fall off the wheelchair for the bumpy ride. In the meantime, Jun's wife, Ondine, worked her camera, recording the drama of my struggle and the sacrifice of my children—a sacrifice born of love.

In whatever way possible, every member of the family pitched in so I could complete my "way of the cross." I realized then that this was Kuya Hesus' way of letting me know how my children truly loved me!

Sitting in my chair and finally looking at the dying Jesus on the cross, I prayed silently and asked, "Do I deserve the love of my children?"

Having caught up with the first group, we paused to catch our breath and rest a while. I glanced at Paul who was seated on a rock, deep in his thoughts, his eyes never leaving his wife, Leah.

During the dialogue in the bus, I heard for the first time how the early death of his mother broke up Paul's family in some ways. He and a brother had to go and live with an aunt. He remembered the many times when he was left alone by himself. He looks at Leah as his savior and when his eyes cannot find her in a crowd or not see her from a distance, he would panic. "Leah, Leah, wait for me, don't leave me."

"No, Paul, in our family, you will never be left behind... not ever!"

And now back to Steve Jobs, *If today is the last day of my life, would I want to do what I am about to do today?*

Yes, I would definitely, with one exception: "I will never put my children again in that situation, the sacrifice they did for me."

"Mama Mary will not let me even if we were doing it for Kuya Hesus!"

The Dalai Lama in his book, *The Art of Happiness*, was asked, "What would you say is the most effective method... of connecting with others?"

> The Dalai Lama replied... "Now in looking at the various means of developing compassion, I think that empathy is an important factor. The ability to appreciate another's suffering. In fact, traditionally one of the Buddhist techniques for enhancing compassion involves imagining a situation where there is sentient suffering—
>
> "...for instance like a sheep to be slaughtered by the butcher. And then try to imagine the suffering the sheep is going through and so on... or ask a hunter to imagine the suffering of his prey, and you might be able to totally awaken feelings of compassion by beginning with him having to visualize his favorite hunting dog caught in a trap and squealing with pain..."

I guess that was how my children looked at me during that walk. They saw my suffering in themselves and it awakened their desire to help, to be compassionate to someone in need.

My breathing disorder gave me another food for thought—that indeed, there is innate goodness in everyone! Therefore, how can I be wrong when I answered the Lord, *"You are our loving and just Lord; you gave me my children; please judge me then on how they have served you and served me."*

Pope Francis, do you think it is too much to ask my friend John to forgive the sins of a few of your priests who, rather than embracing Jesus' love for the poor, preferred Judas' thirty pieces of silver?

And at the same time see the goodness of Peter's disciples helping to save the souls of many?

I pray your lesson of taking to heart… the wounds of Christ… that "sometimes we are tempted to be that kind of Christian who keeps the Lord's wounds at arm's length. Yet Jesus wants us to touch human misery, to touch the suffering flesh of others. He hopes we will stop looking for those personal or communal niches which shelter us from the maelstrom of human misfortune and instead enter into the reality of other people's lives and know the power of tenderness…"

And be the guiding light for us sinners.

The Law will be at our side with the help of the Author of the Law

The Accused

Dear Pope Francis, John rang me not too long ago and spoke of a dream he had. He was in The Great Judgment Hall in Heaven. A vast number of people were being ushered before the Supreme Magistrate for judgment. There were three lines of people. John found himself in middle line and with him were people upon whose faces a look of uncertainty and anxiety was markedly visible. They moved slowly as if dragging their feet, towards the massive bench behind which the Judge was seated. Flanking the line were two angel-scribes with parchment and quill to record the "proceedings."

The lines on the right and left comprised of people walking away from the bench. They had received the Judge's verdict, John concluded. Those on the right wore blissful smiles; while those on the opposite side had the most tormented and agonized expressions ever imaginable plastered on their faces.

As the line on his left came abreast, John recognized an old friend. On his friend's visage John saw distilled all the anguish and the terror as might be seen on the face of the damned; for indeed, the man had stood before the Judge and had been cast out.

In a voice trembling with indescribable fear and horror, the man cried out to John, "Why didn't you ever tell me?"

Tell what? John was even wondering what he was doing in the place, before a court that meted out final judgment. Everyone who came before the Supreme Judge was given the chance to speak and explain himself before he was pointed to the door on the right or to the left.

Then one of the angels beckoned John to approach the bench. As if from afar he heard the Judge ask, "Do you have someone to speak in your behalf?"

"No, sir," John replied.

"Would you like to call someone? Or if you wish, I can have someone represent you."

"May I speak for myself, Sir?" John asked, confident that he was the best person to plead in his own behalf.

With a gentle voice, the Judge replied, "I am sorry, I do not allow that. When you speak for yourself, you tend to lose your perspective when I begin to ask difficult questions. I cannot judge you after you've become emotional and lose sight of the facts."

"Well, Sir, I can only think of my friend Rudy."

The Judge asked an angel to fetch me. I was made to sit at the defense table beside John.

At this point, John woke up with a start. He was drenched in sweat, perplexed and disturbed by his dream which seemed so real. He decided to call me.

In a moment I realized that I was being presented with a glorious opportunity to share the Gospel with John. And that there was no better time to do this than this time! This was my mission, a God-given one, it was clear: *to shepherd my friend John back to the fold.* To reaffirm to him that Christ himself founded the Church, the organized religion, to which all must belong.

Frankly, I do not anticipate any serious difficulty in completing this self-assigned task. John is no stranger to the traditions and practices of the Catholic religion. Thanks to his mother, his pious aunt, and the religious instructions that he received in the *catecismo* of his youthful days when he joined an informal class in basic Catholic religion conducted by a senior student at the nearby Holy Ghost College. For a while, he was a member of a Catholic charismatic group where he developed a greater appreciation of the Bible. His insights on passages in the Holy Book which he generously shares with me are most enlightening.

I had mentioned quite a number of times that John is a personal friend. However, this same relationship presents its own problems. Absolute honesty is a requirement of such friendship—honesty about all aspects of the friend's personal life, about the good things as well as the bad. It is easy to share good news with our friends, but what about the really bad news?

Not once but countless times have I implored the heavens for the wisdom and guidance on the most effective way by which I can guide John.

"Well, John," I said, "if indeed you asked me to lawyer for you before the bar of the Last Judgment, first of all, let us discuss my acceptance fee and the subsequent amount you have to pay me per court appearance." We laughed.

"But seriously," I said, "let us for the sake of hypothesis, assume that it really happened as you dreamed, imagine this unfolding scenario:

John before the Bar

Then the Judge spoke, "Alright then, let's begin. You noticed that in your case there is no prosecution table. Normally, whenever we sit in judgment to decide whether or not it is time to elevate to Sainthood one who was earlier declared Blessed, a Devil's Advocate would sit behind that table. Otherwise called the "Promoter of the Faith," his main duty is to raise all possible objections and to bring out all significant arguments why the candidate should not be canonized as Saint. If the Devil's Advocate is convincing enough in his objections, then there will be no canonization. You will now understand that I did not provide that in this special court because my Father does not want to see anyone to challenge your "credentials." He has only one purpose and that is to see you enter the door on the left. I will ask all the questions and if I find your answers good enough then you will receive my favorable judgment. The alternative you will know also. Is that understood?"

"Yes, Sir," John and I answered in unison.

"Before we begin, I just want to ask a few questions to John. Please stand up, John. "What church are you with now and who sent you there?"

"My Nanay, Sir. I grew up in your church. Actually, in your church, the rules are very strict. We have to be baptized as soon as possible."

"Why do you think I imposed that?"

"Sir, I have always been told that Baptism erases the original sin inherited from Adam and Eve. However, please forgive me, Sir, for asking questions which I believe are very relevant to this, and which have puzzled me and I am sure many others as well."

I rose immediately before the Judge ruled us in contempt. But I saw Kuya raise his arm, "John, I will allow you to ask a question only once. Your question may force me to answer your question with another question. You may be placed in a situation where you are pushed in the corner, unable to explain yourself. When this happens, I may have to stop this proceeding because you already put yourself in a bind. Do you understand what I am saying?"

John, fearing his impertinence, lowered his gaze and stood with drooping shoulders as though to prepare for an admonition from Kuya. He kept still, not speaking a word, until Kuya said, "Alright, John, ask your question."

John slowly spoke, "Sir, with your death on the cross, didn't your supreme sacrifice serve as ransom for the original sin of Adam and Eve which we inherited? With my scant knowledge of your Book, I could recall only two times when baptism was administered, one of which merely inferred to the rite. Your baptism, Sir, as an adult, is clearly recorded. Circumcision of an eight-day-old infant was the "baptism" in the Old Testament, a prefiguring of Baptism in the New Testament. Even the latter has continued to confuse me. How can we be born with original sin before we are capable of 'sin'? How so, Sir, that you have to be baptized when you are sinless?"

I stood up immediately. I knew, John would fall in his own trap with his questions. "Kuya, I want to apologize for the impertinence of my friend. May I explain his issues to him?"

Kuya was about to speak but instead he settled back on his chair and waved his hand at me. I acknowledged his permission and faced John, "I am happy that you raised those issues which can only be asked by a true seeker like you. You are very familiar with the biblical account of Adam's transgression and his sin was imputed to all men, are you not?"

John nodded. I continued, "As you know, imputation is defined as a charge or credit of one's sin or righteousness to another. The concept of imputation is clearly stated in Romans 5:18-19, 'Just as through one transgression condemnation came upon all, so through one righteous act acquittal and life came to all. For just as through the disobedience of one person the many were made sinners, so through the obedience of one the many will be made righteous.'

"Allow me to cite you an analogy, admittedly a very remote one, but which illustrates how a mother's 'sin' can be transmitted to her yet unborn child. A leading Ob-Gyn specialist concludes that smoking cigarettes during a woman's pregnancy is probably the chief cause of adverse outcomes for babies. He has attended to complications too many times: premature birth, seriously underweight newborn, worse, still births.

"Common complaints of pregnant women include diabetes and hypertension. These conditions can be controlled through proper medications. But when a pregnant woman insists upon her bad habit of smoking, nothing can protect her baby from danger.

"Then there are the so-called inherited diseases or genetic diseases. These diseases are inherited because genetic material is passed on to the offspring from the parent, and can include heart ailment, high blood pressure, Alzheimer's disease, arthritis, diabetes, cancer, and obesity. They are known as inheritable traits like fingerprint patterns, height, eyes, and skin color."

John listened intently, slightly nodding his head. I felt reassured and went on. "John, as to your other questions, I quote your favorite author, Bishop Fulton J. Sheen, in his book, *Life of Christ:*"

Human infirmity touched him [Jesus] so deeply, because deafness, dumbness, leprosy, insanity were the effects of sin, not in a person afflicted but in humanity. Because his death would remove sin which was the cause, *though the final release from sickness and error would not come until the resurrection of the just,* he said that it was just as easy for him to one as the other.

By submitting to this rite, baptism, which he need not have done because he was sinless, the Son of God made man satisfied with the demands of his nation, just as he was to keep all the other Hebrew regulations. He kept the Passover; he observed the Sabbath; he went up to the feasts; he obeyed the Old Law until the time came for him to fulfill it by realizing and spiritualizing its shadowy pre-figurations of God's dispensation.

Kuya spoke, "John, are you satisfied with the explanation of your friend?"

"Yes, Sir. And please forgive me for my impertinence."

"Alright, Rudy, do you have an opening statement?"

"Yes *po*, Kuya."

He looked at me with an amused expression on his face; perhaps I was one of the few who addressed him in thus manner. This will be a fine day, I told myself.

"When John confessed to me, quite hesitatingly, he no longer believed in organized religion, I was flabbergasted and tongue-tied. Not John, my friend of 50-plus years, which span our teen days up to the present when we find ourselves in the "pre-departure area"—as we joke about being septuagenarians. Our high school years we alternately refer to as the "*kotong*" period, in memory of the pock-like scars left by the usual adolescence pimples, the scourge of our pubescent years. Those were the years when we were clueless on whether we are coming or going. We were not yet full adults but no longer children. At the Arellano Public High School, somewhere across the classroom aisle where the girls sat were our respective crushes. How sweet the first faint stirrings of our hearts!

"John was not spared this harmless attraction to the opposite sex but alongside that, his Nanay made sure that his first *catecismo* lessons was not forgotten and relegated to a corner. Besides, the woman was herself the perfect example of a person living and breathing Christian values and practices in full view of a son maturing into manhood. This religious template handed to John was further reinforced by an aunt who could only be adequately described as another *catolico cerrado*, a diehard Catholic, to whom John was equally exposed during the years he stayed with her family."

I paused for a moment. The Judge spoke, "Continue."

"Kuya, if you please, imagine that I am a doctor and John is my patient. He consults with me a lot; I shall describe to you now the type of disease that afflicts him. As you know, Kuya, we can only give the right medication when our diagnosis of his condition comes as close as possible to what is actually happening to him. Even then, we can still give him the wrong prescription. I know, Kuya, you are the greatest physician of all times and should you wish to interrupt and ask some questions, please do so."

"OK. You have all the time; after all, your friend's soul is in your hands."

I shivered at what struck as a thinly veiled warning. "I will give him only my best, Kuya."

Proceeding, I said, "John's main complaint is his disillusionment with formal religion precipitated by his bad experiences with some clergymen whom he came in contact with. There was the partaking of meat in a parish dining room on a Good Friday; an officiating parish priest who accommodated an out-of-the-ordinary request for a baptismal event after he was offered a generous amount; the not-to-be-forgotten embarrassment suffered by him and his bride on their wedding day. Plus a few more incidents which left a severely wounded and badly scarred John—in the spiritual sense.

"Still and all, John exerted enough efforts to hear Mass in the parish church of his neighborhood. Perhaps as a sign of respect to his departed mother who admonished him to attend church consistently? Or perhaps he felt some vague yearnings in his soul that drew him to your table. Alas, subsequent events only made matter worse.

"John chafed at the long-winded ramblings of the officiating priests who seemed not to be mindful of their listeners; carrying on in a coma-inducing flat voice spoken yet into an antiquated address system that made everything sound unintelligible."

Kuya signaled that he wanted to speak.

"Excuse me, Rudy; I want to ask John a question again. John, why do you judge my church against a few of my misguided priests? Did not your Nanay's example and sacrifices to keep you alive not good enough for you? You know that she died with my name on her lips. Why throw all that away because you are unhappy with my priests?"

John did not expect the question. I thought that he might stumble. I butted in, "Kuya, if you don't mind, may I answer for him? (*Sabi n'yo po kaya kailangan may magtanggol sa kanya ay baka may tanong kayo na mataranta siya.*) You said Sir, my friend might get confused when you ask difficult questions. I think this is one of those questions, Kuya. "

Kuya looked at me, "Go ahead."

For the Defense

Pope Francis, I began my defense of my friend John with a relaxed tone. "Kuya, life is a grand journey everyone makes. We traverse different routes. But whatever kinds of road we travel on, be they strewn with rocks, deadfalls, and bends, is not by itself important: what finally matters is the finish line. Just as there are straight and smooth highways, there are also unforeseen detours that delay the journey. But we push on, day after day, year after year, until we reach the journey's end.

John was in tense anticipation of the hearing, more so, the verdict

What confronts us during life's passage and how we circumvent them is truly indicative of our response to you, Kuya.

"A beautiful butterfly, resplendent in its color and graceful in flight, was once an ugly, hairy caterpillar. A high-leaping frog lived its early development underwater with an ungainly tail as a tadpole. An eye-catching macaw with its multi-colored feathers started out as a stark naked, disproportionately large-headed nestling.

"I can only say that John might well be the hairy caterpillar which no one would want to touch. Or the frog. Or the macaw.

"The birth of John in the circumstances that you planned, the attitude of some of his blood relations, even some of his friends—well, they were traumatic experiences that burned into his young mind; he could not forget them. But the final straw was the actions of your priests; John knew that this was not the teaching which you entrusted to them—and that pushed him to the edge. If your priests could do this in your Church which is the only Church, John would rather not be with your Church or with any other for that matter."

The Supreme Judge did not speak for a while, then, "OK, Rudy, I will take that into consideration. You may continue."

"Kuya, a number of eminent psychologists and sociologists have put forth theories about the several stages of certain aspects of life. There is Abraham Maslow whose theory describes the stages of growth in humans. He used the terms: psychological, safety, belongingness and love, esteem and self-actualization. He postulates that these are the needs to describe the pattern that human motivation generally moves through. And when they are not able to mature in these stages, they get lost or remain stagnant in the stage they are in.

"Just to relate it to the issue on the table, Kuya, my friend John is in the stage of *belongingness and love*—from the point of view of his church community. But John does not feel this sense of belongingness and love; he has cast himself as an outsider. Would we rather wish that he remained stuck in that emotional stage, and let it swallow him like a bottomless quicksand?" I waited for an answer. Kuya was in deep thought. He looked at John, and then shifted his eyes.

"Rudy, I know what you are saying. I will never wish that on John or any of my people. But I gave him all the chances to look for a better way without leaving my church; I know that you are helping him. Does he have to leave without exhausting all means available and seek true enlightenment?

"There was a time that you, too, like your friend here, were searching for answers: why was my teaching seemingly so difficult to understand? But even as you sought for answers, you remained in my Church. Your biggest obstacle had been your own Tatay. Your heart stirred because your family's church, the Aglipayan Church, was not my Church. Your family belonged to a church whose teachings are not those I fully intended. You did not accept my sacrament of Confession and your priests did not practice celibacy. But that was not what was nagging you.

"You asked your mother why you didn't go to church on Sundays and your Nanay answered, 'Our church is too far away.' How old were you then?"

"Nine years old *po*, Kuya," I replied.

"Yes, that's right. Then you asked your Nanay if you could go to *my* Church and she said, 'Go ahead if your *Lola* Maria will have you.' Do you remember that?"

"Yes, *po.*"

"Your Lola Maria was one of my disciples on earth; she is now with me. Ah! But your mother bore the brunt of your Tatay's wrath. He gave strict orders to your mother and your siblings never to speak to you about my Church, least of all, about my teachings.

"But the tables were soon turned, for this time they were the ones asking you about my Church and what it was that you found there that kept you coming back. Just what did you tell them, Rudy, to convince them to seek my teaching?"

"Kuya, I just shared what I felt. The first time I went to your church I had this unexplainable sense of calm coming over me. Like I was at peace with the world and the world was at peace with me. I still feel that whenever I sit down to talk with you—wherever I am."

"Yes, Rudy, all my children feel the same way. But do you know what is your greatest gift to me?"

"No, *po*, Kuya, I cannot recall having given you anything. I know that I have received a lot from you, even now. I don't know *po*, Kuya."

"Do you remember even as your Tatay refused to talk to you about my Church, you would pray my Mother's Rosary every night, night after night, kneeling down, your arms outstretched, until numbness caused them to drop? But when that happened, you would gather all your strength, fight the numbness, and finish your Rosary despite the grave physical discomfort to you."

I gave Kuya a big smile. And in a higher pitch, as though I was speaking in my voice when I was young, I said, "Yes *po*, Kuya. The ache in my arms made me feel your suffering as the nails drove through your hands and feet."

"I know, I know. What happened after that?"

"On Sundays, Kuya, we used to have those big family breakfasts. During one of these family gatherings, Nanay whispered to me that Tatay had something to tell me. It was the first time I ever heard Tatay speak of your Church. 'Rudy, please arrange with your Fr. Cruz our simultaneous baptism and marriage.'"

"That is your gift to me, Rudy. No less do I expect from your friend John; he needs to exert more effort to change the attitude of my 'fallen' priests. The last thirty years that you have been in constant dialogue with one of my priests, you've asked him to talk to John; has that happened yet?

"John is seriously considering that, Kuya."

Kuya nodded.

"Is there anything more that you want to add?" Kuya concluded with a question. There was an edge to his voice.

"We rest our case, Kuya."

"Alright, since I did not allow a prosecutor to present the position of my Church I will now discuss from my perspective. I have many disciples expressing my faith in the way that they know best. John Pastor Bevere has come to mind and directly addresses John's reasoning for leaving my Church:

'Who sent you to the church that you presently attend?'

He answered, 'God did.'

If God sent you, do not leave until God releases you. If the Lord is silent, he is often saying, *don't change a thing. Do not leave. Stay where I have placed you!*

When God does instruct you to leave, you will go out with peace, no matter what the condition of the ministry: *Yes, in joy you shall go forth, in peace you shall be brought home* (Is 55:12). Therefore, your departure will not be based on the actions or behavior of others but rather on the Spirit's leading. So *leaving your church* is not based on how bad things are. To leave with an offended or critical spirit is not the plan of God. It is reacting rather than acting on his guidance. Rom 8:14 says, *For those who are led by the Spirit of God are children of God.*

Notice that it does not say, *For those who react to difficult situations, these are children of God.* Almost every time the word *children* is used in the New Testament, it comes from the two Greek words *teknon* and *huios.* A good definition for the word *teknon* is one who is a child by mere fact of birth.

When my first child, Addison, was born, he was John Bevere's child by mere fact that he came from my wife and me. When he was in the nursery in the midst of all the other newborns, you could not recognize him as my child by personality. When friends and family came to visit, they could not pick him out except by the nametag above his crib. He did not possess anything that set him apart. Addison would be considered a *teknon* of John and Lisa Bevere.

We find *teknon* used in Romans 8:15-16. It says that because we have received the spirit of adoption, *the Spirit itself bears witness with our spirit that we are children [teknon] of God.* When a person receives Jesus Christ as Lord, he is a child of God by fact of the new birth experience (See Jn 1:12).

The other Greek word translated *sons* in the New Testament is *huios.* Many times it is used in the New Testament to describe *one who can be identified as a son because he displays the character or characteristics of his parents.* As my son Addison grew, he started looking and acting like his father. When Addison was six, Lisa and I took a trip and left him with my parents. My mother told my wife that Addison was almost a carbon copy of his daddy. His personality was like mine when I was his age. As he has grown, he has become more like his dad. He now can be recognized as John Bevere's son, not only by the fact of his birth but also by the characteristics and a personality that resemble his father's.

So, to put it simply, the Greek word *teknon* means *babies or immature sons*, and the Greek word *huios* is most often used to describe *mature sons*.

Looking at Romans 8:14 again, it reads: *For those who are led by the Spirit of God are the children [huios]of God.* We can see clearly here that it is the mature children who are led by the Spirit of God.

Immature Christians are less likely to follow the leading of the Spirit of God. Most often, they react or respond emotionally or intellectually to circumstances which they face. They have not yet learned to act only on the Spirit of God's leading.

As Addison grows, he will progress in character development. The more mature he becomes, the more responsibility I will entrust to him. It is wrong for him to stay immature. It is not God's will that we remain babies.

One way the character of Addison has grown is by facing difficult situations. When he started school, he met up with some "bullies." I heard some of the things these rough kids were doing and saying to my son, and I wanted to go and deal with it. But I knew that would be wrong. For me to intervene would hinder Addison's growth.

So my wife and I continued to counsel him at home, preparing him to face the persecutions at school. He grew in character through obeying our counsel in the midst of his suffering.

This is similar to what God does with us. The Bible says, *Son [Huios] though he [Jesus] was, he learned obedience from what he suffered"* (Heb 5:8).

Physical growth is a function of time. No two-year-old child has ever been six feet tall. Intellectual growth is a function of learning. Spiritual growth is a function of neither time nor learning, but rather of obedience. Now look at what Peter says: 'Therefore, since Christ suffered in the flesh, arm yourselves also with the same attitude (for whoever suffer in the flesh has broken with sin' (1 Pt 4:1).

A person who has broken with sin is a perfectly obedient child of God. He is mature. He chooses God's ways, not his own. Just as Jesus learned obedience by the things he suffered, we learn obedience by the difficult circumstances we face. When we obey the Word of God that is spoken by the Holy Spirit, we will grow and mature in times of conflict and suffering. Our knowledge of Scripture is not the key. Obedience is.

Now we understand one reason why we have people in the Church who have been Christians for 20 years, who can quote verses and chapters of the Bible, who have heard a thousand sermons, and have read many books but still wear spiritual diapers. Every time they meet with difficult situations, rather than responding by the Spirit of God, they seek to protect themselves in their own way. They are *always trying to learn but* never able to *reach knowledge of the truth* (2 Tm 3:7). They never come to the knowledge of the truth because they do not apply it.

Truth must be allowed to have its way in our lives if we are going to grow and mature. It is not enough to give mental assent to truth without obeying it. Even though we continue to learn, we never mature because of disobedience.

Kuya banged his gavel once after concluding his rather lengthy lecture. He signaled one of the angelic scribes to gather his notes and said, "Let's take a fifteen-minute recess. I want to study your arguments carefully before I make my final judgment."

Kuya stood up and retreated to his chamber.

Souls I want to
meet in Heaven

(Photo taken from purplecookiejar)

Mama Mary and Sally are constantly praying for John

Friends in Heaven

*P*ope Francis, in the interim I requested John to come with me to the chapel beside the court. John hesitated because we would be entering one of Kuya's churches. I told him, "What have you got to lose, John? In a few minutes, it will be over. Maybe the short time you spend in Kuya's church could well spell the difference between heaven and hell for you."

John relented.

When we were in the chapel, I prayed as I have never prayed before. The chagrin of my friend John came to a head after his questing mind and impressionable soul finally balked at the clerical anomalies that had accumulated over sixty years since his age of discernment. If truth be told, he considered himself fulfilled in the human aspects of being; but the spirituality that he sought remained elusive try as he might, to grasp the perfection of Christ's teaching. He measured St. Peter's workers and found them wanting. His life reached a point when the clergy became the catalyst of his dissatisfaction with the Church. In them he saw a scowling Judas reaching out to the poor only if they were clutching thirty pieces of silver in their bony hands.

So, I thought that I should seek seven souls that are close to me, and who in turn consider me as someone close to them; and among them, three souls who will pray for John with unrelenting intensity. They will lay siege to heaven with their plea for John's enlightenment—that he may take a deeper look into his decision to leave the Church. Surely, Jesus Christ is waiting for him to come back to his Church, for he is not blind to the basic righteousness of John as a person.

Yet still a lingering fear haunts me that it may be too late. Shall we instead pray that John receives pardon for his indiscretion and still merits the reward of heaven?

I am thrown into a kind of panic as I scour my mind for applicable expositions on the seemingly intractable problem of John. William Bennet spoke about compassion and compared it to courage when people take a stand in a challenging situation. He says, "There is some benevolence, however small, infused into our bosom, some spark of friendship for human kind, some particle of the dove kneaded into our frame along with the elements of the wolf and the serpent."

As he continues to explain the meaning of compassion, he quoted David Hume: *Compassion is a natural feeling which by moderating the violence of love of self in each individual, contributes to the preservation of the whole species. It is this compassion that hurries us without reflection to the relief of those who are in distress.*

Pope Francis, author and lecturer Leo Buscaglia, talks of exactly the same thing as do Bennet and Hume. But he reduces it to terms and images which we can easily connect with through this lovely little tale:

> Once he talked about a contest which he was asked to judge. The purpose of the contest was to find the most caring child.
>
> The winner was a four-year-old child, whose next-door neighbor was an elderly gentleman, who had recently lost his wife.
>
> Upon seeing the man cry, the little boy went into the old gentleman's yard, climbed onto his lap, and just sat there.
>
> When his mother asked him what he had said to the neighbor, the little boy just said, "Nothing, I just helped him cry."

I want to give more meaning to the example of this little boy with the stories of the souls whom I asked to pray for John:

As I sat in the chapel praying, a scene played in my mind. I saw a distraught woman in a splendid garden kneeling before the altar of the Holy Trinity. She was clutching the Holy Rosary to her breast. From where I was, I couldn't make out her face. Then another woman, with a radiant aura about her, approached the kneeling woman and helped her to her feet. She led her to a stone chair by the altar. I still couldn't see the first woman's face but I knew that she was crying, for I could hear her silent sobs and her shoulders were shaking. I inched closer to the pair and heard the weeping woman ask, "Mother, where have I failed?"

The radiant lady reached out and cupped the face of the other woman in her hands. Gazing at her tenderly, she said, "You have not failed. It is my Son's will. He knows that your son is losing his way. Maybe if he excludes him from his Church, he will wake up. You and I should pray for John to recover his senses enough to realize the importance of my Son's gift, all the more after one loses it."

"I always pray for him, Mother. I have never stopped. I hope that John is aware how much I love him and how his decision tears my heart apart. But I cannot help thinking that it is my fault that John rejected your Son's Church. I made the mistake of falling in love with a man who did not love John and me enough to give us dignity. Maybe John is blaming me for that; I pray not. And I pray hard that he does not use my mistake to reject the Church of Jesus."

"I will pray with you, Nanay. John will return. My Son will help him; he never says no to me."

"Mother, please also pray that John always remembers my promise to him. *"Mahal na mahal kita. Walang makakakuha sa iyo mula sa akin. Igagapang kita sa gitna ng ating kahirapan at bibigyan kita ng magandang kinabukasan.* In everything you do, I will always pray for you."

With Mama Mary and John's Nanay praying for him, I know that everything is well.

Pope Francis, a touch of compassion is all that is needed to calm a grieving heart. Empathy, kindness, and generosity spring in our hearts almost as if by instinct: a consoling voice makes all the difference, presence is enough to show compassion just like the little boy who helped the old man cry.

Let me share a secret with you but remember, discretion requires the story of Manny, a classmate from high school, be kept from prying eyes.

My freshman year was spent with students whom the teachers in school absolutely abhorred. I belonged to the group of kids who were in school only because the law required it. Had secondary education been a choice, our class would not have been formed, not a chance. To put it bluntly, we were the school outcasts and the social pariahs of Arellano High.

All they said about us was true. We were a bunch of rowdies and louts. The teachers were jail wardens rather than patient mentors tutoring us on the three 'Rs. Our classrooms were like cells, hot and stuffy with little air getting through the windows. The teachers wanted the lectures over as fast as possible. Joe Enriquez belonged in our section. He was the founder and leader of our gang, the Blue Boys. He towered over most kids in school and don't anybody forget that. Sometimes he came to school reeking of alcohol. The teachers feared him, except perhaps Miss Difontorum who loved teaching and made every day worth staying in class.

We were all in awe of Joe, especially we of the Mayhaligue Branch, an offsite of Arellano High. He was our hero: someone we all wanted to be but knew that there could only be one like him. My, he was a tough 'un. But to his credit, he knew his limits. His story ends here however, because after that, there was really nothing much to write about him anymore.

I remember being seatmates with a boy named Manny who came from one of the roughest districts in Quiapo. He was a frail kid with Chinese features who looked as though a good breeze could sweep him away in one huff. He never admitted to anyone that the feared OXO gang used him as a gofer to buy their cigarettes, gin, or run just about any errand that they pleased. Not one squeak of protest was heard from Manny; slaving for the gang gave him protection and even a sort of power. Even school bully Joe steered clear of Manny. Between Joe and Manny, I was like *nakasandal sa pader*, I was literally backstopped by a solid wall to buttress me; no one dared mess with me because of the company I kept.

We had a classmate named Stella who, everyone said, had a crush on me. But my skinny friend Manny had his eyes on her. My personal memories of Stella are as clear as the days of our high school life. I even remember the lyrics of the song with her name, Stella by Starlight: "*The song a robin sings, through years of endless springs. The murmur of a brook at even tide, that ripples through a nook where two lovers hide…*"

The way it was with Stella and me was no spring; it was more like the gloomy dampness of the rainy season. And the applicable lyrics in our situation goes this way: "*Jim's in love with Jane, Jane's in love with someone who's not in love with her…*"

Manny was madly in love with her but never had the courage to tell her so. Stella, on the other hand, had eyes only for me. When the three of us hanged out, it was only I that she looked at, though, to return her gaze would have been a mistake, a fatal one. Often I caught Manny casting the same lovelorn look at her. But sadly, their eyes never met.

Manny's mother almost died giving birth to him. The attending *hilot,* inexperienced and using primitive ways, nearly cost the woman her life. Manny grew up just like any other kids, although he looked somewhat emaciated compared to the other neighborhood children. It didn't bother him; what did was the sight of mothers picking up their boys and girls from school. There were no welcoming *besos* or *abrazos* for him at the school gate; the very poor do not usually practice such affectation.

Poverty was relentless and brutal in Manny's family. He had an artistic bent to him but he shied away from joining school presentations because it required money to obtain costumes and show paraphernalia. He never knew how it felt to kneel at the pew to receive First Communion; that would have called for a white shirt and a white pair of pants. He wondered why families woke up early on Sunday to hear Mass together. *Simbang Gabi* and Christmas Eve Midnight Mass held no meaning for him; all the important milestones of a boy's growing up went past him and left for good.

Manny's father was the classic absentee parent who was never around for the family. So the boy grew up without really knowing a father. The things that father and son normally do together were a mere abstraction in Manny's experience and therefore contributed nothing to his personal development.

That notwithstanding, Manny tried to make the best of the situation and somehow he managed. He was emotionally more mature than other boys his age. He became cunning, suspicious, somewhat devious, and inquiring about life in the sense that he wanted no surprises. His was a life without frills; it was survival in that particular jungle of Manila.

Manny and I were always seen together in school whenever our class schedules permitted. We shot baskets during countless one-on-ones, playing for peanuts or a bottle of *sarsaparilla*. Most of the time Manny, his reedy frame slipping past my defenses with ease, won and I had to ante up. I thought nothing of sharing my *baon* with him, for he almost always never came to school provisioned to quell the grumblings in his stomach.

In retrospect, I am quite thankful to have known and befriended Manny. As it turned out, he was a strong believer in God, albeit in a crude way. He convinced me to join the procession of the Black Nazarene, my first time to do so. I found myself among the hundreds of thousands jostling for a place at the ropes that pulled the carriage of the Nazareno. It was a totally different experience to be one among the multitude expressing total devotion to the miraculous black image of Christ. And I have only Manny to be grateful to for the privilege.

Getting a college education was tough but somehow Manny made it. Right after graduation, he joined the police. The old neighborhood OXO gang that gave him such a bad time in the past thought that they could pursue their deeds with impunity this time that they had a friend in the force. But Manny was uncompromising and the gang took great pains to steer clear of him. He proved a good officer and quickly earned his sergeant's stripes. He married and had children; life was looking up for my high school chum.

One evening, when Manny was on duty at the desk, a robbery-in-progress call came in. All the policemen on the shift were out responding to earlier calls and Manny had no choice but to act on the report himself and hurry to the scene.

Manny rushed to the spot alone without any backup. Shots rang out and in a moment Manny was on the pavement bleeding profusely.

It took a while for an ambulance to arrive because of the usual traffic. When finally the paramedics got to Manny, it was too late.

Manny left four children and a grieving wife. His son read a very touching and emotional eulogy. He spoke of how his father made them feel; of how, for no reason, he would hug them. Why, Dad? they asked. *Nothing, just to say I love you.*

Yes, he was like that so his children felt an overflow of his love. It was something he wanted for his children. He never wished for them to miss it. A hug costs nothing but offers so much. His son could not understand why God had to take their father just when they were getting to enjoy each other's company. Manny's eldest son left the podium crying. There was not a dry eye in the crowd.

I stood up, hoping to alleviate his pain. "I speak from experience when I say that I know the hurt you feel at your father's passing. I also understand why you're holding back acceptance of God's desire to have your father in his side. You are right; death brings a kind of pain that is difficult to accept. Keep your father alive in your dreams and in those moments of consolation, you will feel his arms around you and hear him whisper, *"Sleep not with your sorrow, may your fears for tomorrow never come."*

Manny knew how it felt to miss the love of a father. He and John are kindred souls and he will lead in breaking down the wall of John's doubts.

I knew that we have a good case with Mama Mary praying for us. Manny's pleadings could be the icing on the cake. But my previous experiences tell Manny that it will not hurt if we siege heaven with more souls.

Who else to call on?

Not Guilty! Declared my Kuya Hesus

The Verdict

And then there is Sally, John's late wife. She was the first love of John. I had not seen John in a while but I bumped into him and Sally in one of the doctors' clinics I visited in the course of my job. They were seeing a cancer specialist. Sally was undergoing chemotherapy. In a high percentage of cases, cancer patients fight a losing battle. Sally showed all signs that she had given up the fight; she was listless, morose, and defeated.

John himself looked miserable. You could read it in his face. I hardly recognized him. He had aged a lot and although he is years younger than me, that day I saw an old man.

John and I lost touch again after that chance encounter in the doctor's clinic. Actually, it was him who avoided making contact; I knew him well enough to know that he wanted to spare me his grief.

Pope Francis, John had happy memories of Sally and they soon supplanted his grief at his loss.

When loneliness visited him, he simply redirected his thoughts to the fun things Sally and he did together. This one was very fresh in his recollection: he'd moved to a new assignment at Columbian Rope. He was given charge of marketing the passenger amenities in their ocean-going vessels.

One Saturday, John was asked to join the boarding party of one of the ships anchored off the breakwater of Manila Bay. Saturday was also the day when Sally and he usually went out on a date. There was a long delay before the boarding launch returned to shore where Sally waited. It was almost ten in the morning when John landed ashore.

When he got back to the office, he was surprised to see Sally talking with one of her former suitors. Before she could utter a word, John said gruffly, "*Akala ko ba binasted mo na yan* (I thought you told him off already)," and left without waiting for her to speak.

After thirty minutes his telephone rang. It was somebody from the office. "Hey, John, Sally said to tell that she's left already."

"*Salamat,*" was all he could say. Now it was his turn to worry. What if she accepted an invitation from her suitor to lunch and then to a movie afterwards?

He gathered his things and left the office in a huff. Maybe Sally decided to watch the movie alone which they had planned to see that afternoon. On a strong hunch he called the movie house. He asked the receptionist if she noticed a pretty lady in a polka-dot dress enter the theater. "*Sandali lang po.* I will take a look."

A familiar voice came to the phone. "Sorry I left without you because you're mad at me. I am sorry, please hurry. I will wait for you."

He was the one at fault and rude, too, and here she was apologizing. How could John not love her so? Such a person was Sally whose ever-present radiant smile turned a bad situation around and made everything alright again.

And that Baguio experience he would always remember. It was John's first time in the city of Pines. As the bus was negotiating a right turn towards the city transport terminal, he immediately espied Sally and her welcome crowd. His eyes were focused on her only, in her pedal-pusher getup which was the '50's version of the denim pants.

Sally's smile was sweeter than mangoes in season—her *pasalubong!* If it were today, John would have gotten a hug and a kiss, even just on the cheek. Instead, she gave his arm a firm squeeze and asked, "*Nag-lunch ka na ba?*" (Read: "I missed you.")

John had always been an early riser. Early morning chores at home ingrained the habit in him from the time he and Nanay were living with his uncle. Sally's aunt met him in the hallway of the house where they were staying in Baguio and said, "Sally is still in bed, wrapped like a cocoon. Do you want to peep in her room?"

True enough, there she was all wrapped in her blanket, her pretty mouth slightly open, deep in slumber.

Leaving Sally to continue with her beauty sleep, John made ready to take his customary morning shower. There was only one problem: there was no hot water and it was freezing cold. He had to bathe but was too *macho* to ask for hot water.

At the breakfast table he was the topic of conversation. "Wow! John, we didn't know you could handle ice-cold water in a bath. Why didn't you ask to have heated water brought in?"

Sally was listening to the banter but apparently had another thing in her mind, for she suddenly butted in and said, "Auntie, why did you let John come to my room? You knew I was still asleep. Did I have my blanket to cover me?"

"So what's your problem?" the aunt retorted with a big laugh. "It's good for John to see how you look when you're sleeping."

"Yes, I did peep in and saw you with your pretty mouth slightly open," John admitted. "I thought you looked cute, like a baby Eskimo and it made me love you more!"

Everybody at the table sighed... "ooo... oooyyy!" The aunt said something in Ilocano to her husband, who responded, "Absolutely!"

Whatever it was, it was definitely a good sign for John.

On the return to Manila, Sally sat beside John in the bus. But John was for the most part silent. He was in deep thought. He had always been a firm believer in God. Everything happened for a reason. He believed that certain events and encounters in his life were in fact gifts from the Lord. Meeting Sally was one of these. God gave us free will to make our final choices in life. God's foreknowledge of what we would do, does not limit our decision on what we wanted to do. In fact, when we recite the Lord's Prayer, we are putting ourselves in God's mercy. We are his players bowing to his cues and curtain calls. What remains is for us to trust totally in the Lord!

Ah! What pleasant memories.

Sally will storm the doors of heaven to save her one true love, John.

Pope Francis, let me tell you of the other soul whom I asked for prayers for my friend John.

Jim Dale Black is the 7th soul.

There is a beautiful story of friendship in the New Testament that led to a miracle. This is the friendship of Jesus Christ with Martha, her sister Mary, and her brother Lazarus whom he brought back to life. I love this story because it reflects my own friendship with Jim Black which also produced incredible results; by no means miraculous but certainly remarkable.

I first met Jim in the 1970s when Unilab, my company then, forged a joint-venture alliance with G.D. Searle, an American pharmaceutical company that had been operating in the Philippines for quite a while but appeared to be getting nowhere. Unilab was the dominant player in the industry, accounting for almost 25% of the market, when the alliance was made in 1974; it made good business sense for Searle to partner with us.

In the '70s, the most popular sport was pelota, a hybrid of squash and racquetball. In pelota you played against two walls and whoever controlled the left corner of the walls was the odds-on favorite to win the game. Jim was an avid sportsman and we played both tennis and pelota.

After our rounds in Cagayan de Oro, a city in Mindanao, we were invited by a local enthusiast to an evening game. Jim and I played fluidly as a team and won all the games. We followed the same pattern in the neighboring city of Iligan. We met with the doctors and pharmacists in the day and played with them in the evening. By the time we got to Ozamis City across Iligan bay, words had reached our prospective customers that there was this team that made mincemeat of the top *pelotistas* of the cities we visited.

Let me digress a bit. We were not aware that the regional champions for the whole of Mindanao were from Ozamis. On the day we arrived, they were to inaugurate a new pelota court. We were in a doctor's clinic when we were advised that we were being invited to an exhibition game against the champions in their new court.

Jim and I were surprised when we arrived for the game. It seemed that the whole town was present! Folks wanted to see their champions teach us a lesson which we would never forget. But we shocked the champions instead. Of the three sets, we trounced them in two. We were ready to rest when the organizers approached Jim with a request:

"Can we extend the game to three out of five?"

Did I hear right? The sets we'd just finished lasted more than two hours. Jim, being an athlete, would have no problem going through three more games. But I was beat. Several nights of playing the fast, tough game had finally taken its toll on me. And the sets we had just gone through fairly sizzled with blazing speed and seesawing scores.

Still, we were guests and it wouldn't have been nice of us not to give our host a chance to recover. Besides, I was the Filipino side of our team and it would not sit well with the locals if I didn't give in to their request. So on with the games.

Jim played well. But pelota is a doubles' game and I was not in it. So we lost the third and fourth sets. Our score was this time 2-2!

The crowd was ecstatic. They saw our team's Achilles heel… and it was I!

Jim sued for a break and beckoned me to the locker room. Once there, we washed up, changed shirts, and combed our hair. It had an amazing effect on me. The cool water gave me a fresh surge of energy. My mind shouted, "We've just begun to fight!"

The fifth set was ours. It should have been a runaway win. But Jim gave our opponents some shots that were easy to retrieve, shots that were easy kills.

After the game Jim and I had a long talk. I learned three lessons from him that night. First lesson: be always ready to meet the unexpected. Life is full of constantly changing challenges and one must learn to adjust and meet them. The refreshing wash in the locker room was his way of telling me that there's always a way to adjust.

When I asked him why he gave our opponents easy shots, he smiled and said, "Rudy, I am a guest in your country. As a guest, I am an ambassador of goodwill for myself and my country. You are a proud people. You can accept defeat, but not humiliation. Didn't you notice that after the game we were the toast of the crowd? That's because we saved the face of their champions."

The second lesson was clear to me. In Asian culture, "saving face" is like a code of honor. And Jim was sensitive to that cultural nuance. That sensitivity gave me an epiphany into Jim's character. That night it was my honor to request him to stand as godfather to my youngest daughter, Nikki.

The friendship we built and the new relationship we forged with our customers made us meet the goal for Searle earlier than targeted. We did it in two and a half years. He was consequently made President of Searle Philippines and I was moved to the Corporate Offices of Unilab as Executive Vice President and General Manager. That was the third lesson. When you love your job, it is not a job.

My friendship with Jim lasted through the decades, even after we parted ways. We managed to always keep in touch. I was grief-stricken when I received the news that Jim had gone on to meet his Maker.

Good-bye, Jim. *Vaya con Dios*!

John and I heard the bells chime announcing the resumption of the trial. We quickly went back to Heaven's Court. We sat at our assigned table and waited. Kuya noticed that I made the sign of his cross. He nodded at me and smiled.

"John and Rudy, rise and I will render my judgment.

"Rudy, I find your defense compelling. You did well in presenting the case of your friend John; I am sending him back with you on earth. Help him to search for more meaning of my teaching. I will wait for his return. But I will not wait for him forever. This is the chance I am giving him. You may go!"

"Well, John," I said. "That ends our imaginary court of Final Judgment scenario. We won! Cheer up, friend, lest you become a man of constant sorrows!"

"Ah, well," John said with a sheepish smile on his face.

"But here," I said. "Let me give you the bill for my lawyering services."

Pope Francis, in my life I saw the companions of compassion... prayer and patience. No problem remains unsolved when people demonstrate more patience towards each other. Wars will not be a consequence of disagreement when leaders practice the virtue of patience and not allow pride to dictate their actions. Even my friend John would not be thinking his thoughts of leaving our Church if only he had more patience. I say that without condemning him for his decision. If he prayed more for his priests, he would not have come to the tipping point of disgust and declare, "I no longer believe in organized religion."

Patience is like the parable in the gospel when the vineyard owner, finding no fruit in the fig tree, wanted it cut down. The vineyard keeper stayed the hand of the owner and said, "Let it alone sir, this year also, till I dig about it and put on manure. And if it bears fruit next year, well and good; but if not, you can cut it down."

It is Jesus who intercedes for us before the Father, since we are the fig tree planted in the vineyard of the Lord. St. Augustine commented: "The vinedresser intervenes, he steps in when the axe is about to fall upon the sterile root. He intercedes like Moses before God… he who acts like a mediator is full of mercy… "Let it alone sir, this year also…" How many times has this scene been repeated: Lord, give us another chance! To realize that you love me so much, my God, and yet I haven't lost my mind."

That is the same second chance that Kuya Hesus offers us, especially to John.

In keeping with our faith and our Church, you always teach us… *Faith is always a cross…* and remind us that this powerfully echoes Galatians 2:19-20, where St. Paul tells us that he has been crucified with Christ so that now it is Christ who lives with him, and Colossians 3:3 where he applies this to us: "For you have died, and your life is hidden with Christ in God."

Pope Francis, I know that God loves my friend John and will not let him leave his Church. Did he not just save him?

When we are at the edge, it's time to bend our knees

I Quit

Pope Francis, the statement sprang on me by my friend John, "I no longer believe in any form of organized religion," so consternated me that almost daily, I pored over books and resorted to search engines, including Google, for any possible explanation why he should lose faith in organized religion—if indeed his quarrel was not with God but the hierarchy that managed the Church of Christ.

I am emboldened to share the thoughts of Rabbi David Wolf on *The Limitation of Being "Spiritual but Not Religious."* Do you like feeling good without having to act on your feeling? boosting your self-esteem no matter what your competence or behavior? Then I've got the religious program for you:

Spiritual but Not Religious

All of us can understand institutional detachment. Institutions can be slow, plodding, and dictatorial; they can enable and shield wrongdoers. They frustrate our desires by asking us to submit to the will of others.

But institutions are also the only mechanism human beings know to perpetuate ideologies and actions. If books were enough, why do we have universities? If guns are enough, why do we have the military? If self-governance is enough, let's get rid of Washington. The point is that if you want to do something lasting in this world, you will recall the wise words of French

Catholic writer Charles Peguy: "Everything begins in mysticism and ends in politics."

...Spirituality is an emotion. Religion is an obligation. Spirituality soothes. Religion mobilizes. Spirituality is satisfied with itself. Religion is dissatisfied with the world. Religions create aid organizations... enable churches to help those in need.

To be spiritual but not religious confines your devotional life to feeling good. If we have learned one thing about human nature, however, it is that people's internal sense of goodness does not always match their behavior. To know whether your actions are good, a window is a more effective tool than a mirror. Ask others. Be part of a community. In short, join. Being religious does not mean that you have to agree with all the positions and practices of your own group; I don't even hold with everything done in my own synagogue, and I am the Rabbi. But it does not mean testing yourself in the arena of others.

Another article I read concerns a man talking to God about his frustrations and decision to quit. I paraphrased the story a bit to give it presence and bring it closer to home; the fellow about to throw in the towel is John. Towards the end, I join the drama because I want to personally beseech God to help my friend.

One day I decided to quit

I quit my job, my relationship, my spirituality; I wanted to quit my life. I went to the woods to have one last talk with God.

"God," John asked, "can you give me one good reason not to quit?"

God's answer surprised John, "Look around," he said. "Do you see the fern and the bamboo?"

"Yes," John replied.

"When I planted the seeds of the fern and the bamboo, I took very good care of them. I gave them light. I gave them water. The fern quickly grew from the earth. Its brilliant green covered the floor. Nothing came from the bamboo seed. But I did not quit on the bamboo."

"In the second year," God continued, "the fern grew more vibrant and plentiful. And again, there was nothing from the bamboo seed. But I did not quit on the bamboo."

"In the third year, there was still nothing from the bamboo seed. But I would not quit. In the fourth year, still nothing from the bamboo seed. I would not quit on it," God said.

"Then in the fifth year, a tiny sprout emerged from the earth. Compared to the fern, it seemed small and insignificant. But in just six months, the bamboo rose to over 100 feet tall. It had spent the five years growing roots. The roots made it strong and gave it what it needed to survive. I would not give any of my creation a challenge it could not handle."

He asked John. "Do you know, my child, that all the time you have been struggling, you were actually growing roots? I did not quit on the bamboo. I will never quit on you. Do not compare yourself to others."

God continued, "The bamboo has a purpose different from that of the fern. Yet they both make the forest beautiful. Your time will come. You will rise high."

"How high shall I rise?" John asked.

"How high does the bamboo rise?" God asked in return.

"As high as the bamboo can?" John asked.

"Yes," God said. "Give me glory by rising as high as you can."

"You should never, never give up," God said. "You are my Christians. I gave you my Church, did I not? When you are in doubt, pray. For I am always listening. The chance to pray is not an option, but an opportunity. Don't tell me how big the problem is; tell me how great I am!"

When the heavens opened its doors this morning, God asked me, "My child, what can I do for you?"

And I said, "Protect and bless my family, all our friends whom we love and who love us, and especially, protect my friend John."

God smiled and answered, "REQUEST GRANTED."

I also read the work of C.S. Lewis, a well-known Catholic writer whose books are respected by churches of different persuasions. In his work the *Illustrations of the Tao,* he says, "...a human being without faith, without reverence for anything, is human being morally adrift. The world's major religions provide time-tested anchors for drifters; they furnish ties to a larger reality for people on the loose."

The work of Fr. John Flynn, LC, touches on the contribution of the Catholic Church to human development not just on spirituality but on every aspect of life. He depended heavily on the writings of Dinesh D'Souza, a research scholar at the Hoover Institution at Stanford University, author of *What's so Great about Christianity.*

"One of the biggest problems," he argues, "is that many are ignorant about the role played for centuries by Christianity. A common belief is that after the high point of civilization during Greek and Roman times, the world was plunged into darkness during the Middle Ages, rescued only by the return to classical sources during the Renaissance. The destruction of the Roman Empire was not the work of Christianity. It was a combination of Roman decadence and the invasion of barbarians. It was Christianity, largely through the contribution of Catholic monks, who preserved learning and science, and also converted the barbarians. Western art, literature, and music also owe an enormous debt to Christianity. For many centuries, even artists who rejected Christianity produced work that was shaped by Christian themes."

Human dignity is another prized contribution of Christianity examined by D'Souza. Not only does Christian teaching maintain the dignity of the sinner and those who fail, but it also calls for respect for those who are poor and lowly. "Christ produced the transformation of values in which the last became first, and values once scorned came to represent the loftiest human ideals," explained D'Souza.

The Universal Declaration of Human Rights adopted by the United Nations in 1948, D'Souza pointed out, "is based on the premise that all human lives have worth and that all lives count equally—not a teaching to be found in all cultures and religions, but one derived from Christianity." D'Souza warned, "If the West abandons Christianity, it may well put in danger the egalitarian values that Christian teaching brought into the world."

Turning back to the political realm, D'Souza added, "The Christian notion of leaders who must consider themselves as servants of others provided the basis for political and social accountability. As a consequence, the political leader, the merchant, and the priest are called upon to serve the people by attending to their needs.

"Another vital contribution of Christianity is the high importance given to marriage and the family. The premises on which family life are based were introduced by Christianity into society. No longer was family life subordinated to that of the state, but it was elevated through the sacrament of marriage. Christianity also introduced the concept of consent by both spouses as being a prerequisite of marriage, a vital instrument in preventing people being pressured into marriage against their will. The Christian precepts of mutual love and charity were also behind the development of institutions such as hospitals and orphanages, taken for granted today by many who forget their origins."

The Catholic Church is seen by another authority as a force for good. Religion's contribution to society is not limited to the past. Iam Buruma, writing on September 29, 2013 in the opinion columns of the *Los Angeles Times*, observed that recent best-sellers would have us believe that religious faith is a sign of backwardness and the mark of primitives. "Religion, we are told, is responsible for violence, oppression, poverty, and many other ills," noted Buruma.

Religion is not perfect, he admitted, but in many cases it is a force for good. He cited the recent example of Burmese monks, who defied the security forces of an oppressive regime. Christians have stood up for democracy in countries such as the Philippines, South Korea, and China. "In a world of political oppression and moral corruption, religious values offer an alternative moral universe," argued Buruma.

When religion is greatly weakened, as in the Canadian province of Quebec, many social problems result, the tensions between religions and cultures in Quebec are largely due to a loss of the traditional culture, combined with a crisis in the family and in education.

Citizens, have been left "disoriented, unmotivated, subject to instability and leaning on transient, superficial values."

A similar alarm was sounded by Ireland's Bishop of Limerick, Donal Murray. "We live in a time of conflict between faith and the ideology of secularism," the bishop observed.

"Secularism," Bishop Murray added, "would have us believe that there is no answer to the fundamental questions about the meaning and destiny of human life. Faith, however, recognizes that we do not live on bread alone and places us on solid ground, free to pursue what we are really seeking as individuals and as a society."

My research brought me to the website of Grace Bible College, a Christian Institution. They declared that religion is man's attempt to have communion with God. The Christian faith is a relationship with God because of what he has done for us through the sacrifice of Jesus Christ. There is no plan to reach God, "he has reached out to us" (cf. Rom 5:8).

"The people have to be evangelized to know the teaching of God. To reach them, Jesus organized his Church through Peter and his Apostles. Being organized is not the problem, focusing on the rules and rituals of religion is the problem."

Pope Francis, I quite believe that herein lays the problem of John; he has lost his focus and allowed mere rituals to sidetrack him. That things should come to a head as we enter the Advent season is providential for me, and in the spirit of Lent, I am certain that I shall find the courage, patience, and the readiness for self-sacrifice for the sake of my friend.

When John texted me that he no longer believed in organized religion, he followed it immediately with another bombshell: "Yes, I may now be called as a Christian agnostic. I borrowed the term from the late Rev. Leslie D. Weatherhead. The word is an oxymoron or a combination of contradictory or incongruous elements. Rev. Leslie explained:

'I feel that it is no sin to be an agnostic. By agnostic, I do not, of course, mean, the atheist, who declares that there is no God. The simplest reader of my book will realize that no one can prove a negative like that. To me, it seems a strange mentality by which a man can look up into the starlit sky or even down into a humble flower or listen to a haunting tune or watch a sunset, meditate on some deed or utter self-sacrifice or on the mystery of human love, and say, 'I know that in this whole universe there cannot possibly be God!' Since I have talked with many self-styled 'atheists,' I have come to believe that the true species does not exist, and that atheism, so called, is either an emotional deviation in the same category as neurotic illness and with a similar causation, or else the denial of the existence of a mythical figure that certainly does not exist. The latter type of 'atheist' is welcome, for he helps us to find the true God and to exclude false ideas about him.

"By Christian Agnostic I mean a person who is immensely attracted by Christ and who seeks to show his spirit, to meet the challenges, hardships, and sorrows of life in the light of that spirit, but who, though he is sure of many Christian truths, feels that he cannot honestly and conscientiously 'sign on the dotted' line that he believes certain theological ideas about which some branches of the church dogmatize; churches from which he feels excluded because he cannot 'believe.' "

In reply, I assured him that I would never give up winning him back to the fold. He said, "You have a humongous job ahead of you."

I resolved then and there never to turn my back on John because I knew that he has a place in Jesus' heart and therefore is never beyond redemption. I remember that John always spoke proudly of his first wife, Sally, who never allowed herself to be affected by the actuations of a few members of the clergy. By the same token, it puzzles me that John should give up his religion merely on the basis of errant behavior of some priests and, moreover, should take such an intractable stance as could be inferred from his statement, "You have a humongous job ahead."

Pope Francis, the Lord always listens. He never gives up on his children, especially those who, like John, after going through a series of dreadful ordeals in life, feel that God has abandoned them.

The cliché that "a rotten apple in the barrel does not make all apples in the barrel rotten," hits the mark when one considers that even if the leadership of the Church and its clergy make mistakes, it does not define the Church because other leaders and clergy come forward to rectify the mistakes and make the teaching of God even more vibrant.

Pope Francis, you, of course, recall the conversation you had with Eugenio Scalfari, founder of "La Repubblica," where you clarified your position on the issue of "negligence and mistakes" of the clergy.

Scalfari: *Jesus in his preaching said that agape, love for others, is the only way to love God. Correct me if I'm wrong.*

"You're not wrong. The Son of God became incarnate in order to instill the feeling of brotherhood in the souls of men. All are brothers and all are children of God, Abba, as he called the Father. I will show you the way, he said. Follow me and you will find the Father and you will all be his children and he will take delight in you. Agape, the love of each one of us for the other, from the closest to the farthest, is in fact the only way that Jesus has given us to find the way of salvation and of the Beatitudes."

Scalfari: *However, as we said, Jesus told us that love for one's neighbor is equal to what we have for ourselves. So what many call narcissism is recognized as valid, positive, to the same extent as the other. We've talked a lot about this aspect.*

"I don't like the word narcissism, it indicates an excessive love for oneself and this is not good, it can produce serious damage not only to the soul of those affected, but also in relationship with others, with the society in which one lives. The real trouble is that those most affected by this—which is actually a kind of mental disorder—are people who have a lot of power. Often bosses are narcissists."

Scalfari: *Many church leaders have been.*

"You know what I think about this? Heads of the Church have often been narcissists, flattered, and thrilled by their courtiers. The court is the leprosy of the papacy."

Scalfari: *The leprosy of the papacy, those are your exact words. But what is the court? Perhaps you are alluding to the curia?*

"No, there are sometimes courtiers in the curia, but the curia as a whole is another thing. It is what in an army is called the quartermaster's office; it manages the services that serve the Holy See. But it has one defect: it is Vatican-centric. It sees and looks after the interests of the Vatican, which are still, for the most part, temporal interests. This Vatican-centric view neglects the world around us. I do not share this view and I'll do everything I can to change it.

"The Church is or should go back to being a community of God's people, and priests, pastors, and bishops who have the care of souls, are at the service of the people of God. The Church is this, a word not surprisingly different from the Holy See, which has its own function, important but at the service of the Church.

I would not have been able to have complete faith in God and in his Son if I had not been trained in the Church, and if I had not had the good fortune of being in Argentina, in a community without which I would not have become aware of myself and my faith."

The Ibañez family with Bishop Raul and Bro. Millard during our Marian
Pilgrimage

The Better Side

On Christmas day, I asked myself if John would reconsider his position against the Catholic Church if I shared with him my experiences with priests that made me glad I am a Catholic.

Of the sincerity of John I have no doubt when he talks of priests who have allowed themselves to be "disciples of Judas in their quest for thirty pieces of silver." Pope Francis has intimated that he accepts that the anomaly does exist. While there may be truth in the observation, my own experiences more than adequately serve as a counterpoint...

Fr. Guido

Sometime in the '70s my family transferred residence to Greenhills in Mandaluyong. Our parish was the Santuario de San Jose in honor of the foster father of Jesus; the parish priest was Fr. Guido, a missionary from Italy who had spent most of his time as a priest serving the poor. We first met him after morning Mass. I remember we were seated in the front row and he approached us, looking bright and cheerful. "Aren't you the couple in the movie now showing in the Greenhills Theater?" He asked with a smile.

Leth and I looked at each other. We returned his smile and I asked him, "Why do you say that, Father?"

"Your wife's face is familiar. Isn't she Miss Amalia Fuentes?"

I almost fell off the pew laughing. Leth was giggling girlishly, thrilled at the compliment. "Thank you, Father. What a nice thing to say." Amalia was then the reigning local movie queen and one of the prettiest faces on screen, although to be honest, I really thought my wife was more beautiful and charming than Miss Fuentes. Of course, I could be biased.

Our friendship with Fr. Guido literally got off to a laughing start. His kind words and disarming smile immediately opened our hearts to him. He was instrumental in making me more committed in serving Christ. He blessed me to be one of the Extraordinary Ministers of Holy Communion. Holding the consecrated host in my hand gave me the feeling of blessedness. The first time I served God as his minister so moved me to the point of tears. I had the feeling that it was a tremendous privilege to touch the Lord repeatedly in the solemn ritual of serving the communicants his sacred body.

Fr. Guido was known in our parish as "The Church Builder." In *sitios* or *barangays* whose faithful had to travel long distances to access a church in a distant town or city, Fr. Guido built magnificent houses of the Lord, to the joy and gratitude of citizens.

The good priest had an almost playful way of soliciting funds. Usually my wife and I would tarry in church after Mass to spend some quiet moment in reflection and prayer. In a while, we would see Fr. Guido walking towards us, flashing his warm Italian smile as he neared us. As we conversed, he played with his ballpoint pen and then, in a conspiratorial tone he would ask Leth, "Would you like to hold my pen?"

Then, sounding more and more like a royal court intriguer, he would ask Leth to ask me if I had my checkbook with me. The three of us would break the stillness of the church with our laughter; Fr. Guido needed some help for his new church project and he certainly knew how to go about getting it. I'd hand my checkbook to Leth and she would write out an amount. It was a pleasure giving him the check.

Fr. Guido came to visit us at home quite a few times. He would be dressed in his priestly habit that was somewhat yellowed with age and frayed at the edges. But he wore it with consummate dignity as befit a true man of God to whom external appearance was no longer of any moment. The truth was, every peso of donation he received, and even his meager allowance, went to the church he was constructing at the time.

When he died, it seemed as if our entire village came out and joined the funeral cortege to his final resting place, in his religious order's church in San Jose, Batangas. His name shall live forever in the many churches that he lovingly built. When you visit any of the churches of the Oblates of St. Joseph, even neophyte priests would speak of him with pride. "Fr. Guido? He provided houses of refuge for our parishioners!"

I am a Rotarian. At one time, I served as president of my club and among other socio-civic activities we conducted outreach programs in marginalized communities. It was in one of these sorties that I was introduced to the Provincial Superior of the Servants of Charity.

Fr. Luigi

His mission sent him to the Philippines years ago to help those with special needs. In time he learned to speak passable Tagalog and Cebuano albeit heavily laced with the intonation of his original European language. He sounded more like a twittering bird, the locals fondly joked about him. Fr. Luigi's religious order is dedicated mainly to serving children with physical and mental disabilities and those who are malnourished. The order's center has truly become the hub of Christian love in the community.

One day before Christmas, I took time out from my busy schedule to join fellow Rotarians in distributing gift packages to informal settlers (a euphemism for squatters) who lived along the banks of a creek that divided two luxurious villages in the city. Eager hands reached out to claim the bag of "goodies" and the gratefulness of the recipients overflowed. *"Maraming salamat po,* sir. You've made our Christmas happy." I took the extra effort to make small talk with each beneficiary and, of course, to greet them with the customary courtesies of the season.

Some pressed my hand as they claimed their bags, *"Ang bigat,* sir, *mukhang may* corned beef *at sardinas."*

A lady with a child in her arms awarded me with a toothless smile, *"Naku,* sir, *makakagat ko kayo, kaya lang wala akong ngipin* (If I had my teeth, I'll bite you, too)."

The crowd roared in laughter. *"Hoy! Umalis ka na d'yan at baka mahilo si* sir *sa amoy mo.* (Leave now before sir faints from your smell)," somebody in the back shouted.

So the friendly banter went on until I noticed some of the older men doubling back on the line. One even elbowed a child out of the way to get ahead. Not wanting to embarrass anybody, I pretended not to notice. I knew they were taking advantage of our generosity, but I let it pass.

But the incident sort of put a damper on my enthusiasm and after a while, I decided to move away and sit quiet in a corner. I tried to rationalize the action of the few who joined the queue twice. Maybe they had many mouths to feed. As the local saying went, *"Ang taong nagigipit, kahit sa patalim kumakapit* (Even to a sharp-edged knife, a desperate man clings)."

Sensing my sudden change of mood, Fr. Luigi asked what was wrong.

"I feel a little bad, Father," I replied. "I was really enjoying myself, you know, mixing with the people and exchanging pleasantries with them. It's been awhile since I've mingled with these people, and I really felt a genuine sincerity in their gratitude for our gesture. Then I noticed some of them getting back in line. One even had the audacity to say that he had not gotten his share, *tinulak pa 'yung bata na nauna sa linya* (he even pushed the child in front of him)."

I could no longer keep my annoyance out of sight even before a priest.

Fr. Luigi listened and nodded sympathetically. "Rudy, you have to be more patient with them. Their lives have always been one of survival. Pangs of hunger wake them in the morning and their day is spent wondering where their next meal is coming from. Can you imagine how the parents console their children when they cry for food? I am sure you can't because even they can't. Only the threat of whipping stops the children from crying but the hunger doesn't go away. At night they go to sleep on empty stomachs."

Fr. Luigi continued, "Rudy, I know how you feel. I felt the same way the first time it happened to me. But when you really get to know their kind of existence, your heart will bleed. This is not to say that what they did was right; nothing can ever justify that. But sometimes you just need to be more compassionate and not quickly judge people at face value.

He smiled and asked me a question,. "When people call your name, do they associate your name to your face?"

I was a little puzzled and not sure if I understood the question. But I answered anyway, "I guess so, Father. Why?"

Fr. Luigi's eyes twinkled, "You're one of the many who are able to say that. But have you ever wondered how it feels not knowing who you are?"

I met the question with silence. "Let me tell you the story of a little boy."

The Face with No Name

His was a face with no name. He made a sort of guttural sound when he attempted to speak, for he couldn't form words. No one was able to say where he came from, much less, who he was. He was simply a face with no name. But there was something different about this nameless boy. He was nowhere like the sunburned, dehydrated infants you see sucking at their mothers' breasts while the latter begged in the streets.

"What made him different? Nothing much really, except that those children with their beggar-mothers are also the faces you see in Caritas posters, 'Do you care enough to help?' But this boy had no one to take care of him. No one knew him. No one looked after him, not even Caritas.

"A policeman saw him scavenging for food, took pity on him and gave him some bread and a Coke. He was brought to the DSWD. Efforts were made to locate his family but nothing happened, so the government agency gave him to us.

"I was told that the boy couldn't talk. They said he must have been living by himself with no one to talk to. I patted his head gently and he looked up at me. I thought I'd try and ask his name. He said nothing and just stared at me. Slowly, I noticed a smile break on his face. He said, 'Jesus?' "

Fr. Luigi wiped his tears. "His word sounded more like recognition than a question. I didn't know what to say."

His voice breaking, the priest continued, "Rudy, that was one moment I will never forget. I do not know how long I held him in my arms. I was tingling all over because this boy who seemed to know nothing just uttered the only word he knew. You know what, Rudy? As we held each other tight, the first thought that came to my mind was the Child of long ago, born in a manger, named Emmanuel. Ah yes, I said to myself, we shall call this boy Emmanuel."

Fr. Luigi waited for my reaction. I stood up and, without a word, went back to the waiting line. The priest smiled. (Excerpts from *Courage To Be Pinoy: Lessons from My Father's Heart*)

My association with Fr. Luigi was put on hold during the incumbency of President Cory Aquino. Several coup attempts were mounted during her term, and always the target of the mutineers' attack was Camp Aguinaldo, the headquarters of the Philippine army. Troops set up checkpoints around the Greenhills area. My family lived in terror during those times. Our village was almost directly in front of the military camp, and it was not only once that stray bullets rattled our wall and roof of our house. We sold our property and moved to Ayala Alabang. But the travel was killing me. The company where I worked is located in Mandaluyong and traffic then was so bad that it took almost two hours one way from home to office. When the political situation normalized, we decided to move back to a place nearer work and bought a house in Acropolis Greens in Greenmeadows Avenue. This is where I met...

Monsignor Dan

Leth and I are enthusiastic participants in Parish Renewal Experience seminars. During a break in one of the programs, I found myself seated beside Msgr. Dan. I took the occasion to thank him for the lessons he'd just shared. Somewhat hesitantly, I said, "You know, Monsignor, ST PAULS Publishing has just completed the printing of my new book. The title is exactly the talk you just gave, *The Road to Emmaus*."

"Why, Rudy, do you write?" he asked, surprised.

"*Opo*. Yes, Monsignor. I even have an award-winning book."

"Congratulations. I hope your new book also wins. Why don't we launch your book in the parish?" the Monsignor offered.

I agreed, thinking Msgr. Dan would gather a few people in one of the smaller function rooms for the launching.

A week passed. Then I received a call from Msgr. Dan. He excitedly told me of his plans. The book would be blessed in an anticipated Mass to be officiated by Bishop Honesto Ongtioco of the Diocese of Cubao. The launching and cocktails would follow at the Social Hall. Msgr. Dan would give a message, and invite lay leaders of the church to receive copies of the book. I was dumbstruck and my hesitation showed. "Don't worry, Rudy, Bishop Raul, our resident bishop, and I are celebrating 75 years of apostolic service and would like to present your book to the parishioners as part of our celebration.

"By the way, Rudy, you need not worry about preparations for the event. Everything will be taken care of; all you have to do is just show up," Monsignor Dan said cheerfully.

"Monsignor, if you don't mind, may I take care of printing the invitation? And it will be an honor for our family to donate the proceeds of the book sales to your favorite Stewardship Program."

The Monsignor flashed a big smile, no bigger than the smile in my heart… (Excerpts from *The Road to Emmaus)*

As the practice in all dioceses, parish priests are rotated every six years; we were saddened in losing Msgr. Dan but happy welcoming…

Fr. Bong, our parish priest, with the knights of Columbus

Music to My Ears

The man that made the difference in our Parish is Fr. Bong.

Our church is assisted by different mandated organizations. One of these is the Knights of Columbus (KOC) of which I am presently the Grand Knight. Most Knights are active leaders in the Church. In our desire to help the parish, we do fund-raising even without the explicit permission of the church.

Our priest does not mind. He knows that we use the fund to help the needy. During the time of Msgr. Dan, we relocated marginal residents in our parish to a *Gawad Kalinga* housing site to give way to a new skyway being constructed in the area.

Since the parish priest also serves as chaplain of the KOC, he suggested for us to become even more involved in church activities by being one of the social arms of the parish. He would provide the entire budget we need. We are currently managing the educational assistance program of the church which he funded with close to a million pesos.

Recently, he requested the KOC to help out-of-school youths join the Dualtech Training Center. The program requires a six-month classroom training at a tuition fee of twenty-one thousand pesos plus eighteen thousand pesos for board and lodging per student. This is followed by an eighteen-month internship program with allowance provided by the sponsoring organization. In the first six months, our parish spent five hundred thousand pesos to cover the cost of the scholarships.

Fr. Bong makes it a point that the educational grantees receive not only training for their economic need but spiritual education as well. To this end, all the students are enrolled in regular catechism lessons.

The experience of being in direct contact with the poor and needy was another spiritual awakening for me. While we tried as much as possible to accommodate those who wanted to benefit from the efforts of the church, we could only do so much. One of the guidelines we followed was to reach as many families as we could. To accomplish this, we limited the educational assistance to one child for every family. Related to this, I cannot help but share the following story with you:

Marjorie, the Child of Libis

Marjorie is a grade seven student at Camp General Emilio Aguinaldo High School. She was in Section II of her batch-class in elementary school and graduated with a grade average of 81%.

The Sunday Fr. Bong and the Knights met with the children who qualified in the program, we discovered that there was a child in the list whose sister was already a beneficiary of the program. Unfortunately, we learned about the situation only belatedly.

We sat down with Marjorie to explain the error. Marjorie spoke to the lady volunteer, "Auntie, the money you will give will be for my school projects. This was the reason why I could not get higher grades because I lacked the projects required by the school. If you will not include me, what will I do?"

Then she began to cry. Our hearts went out to her but there was nothing we could do. Rules were rules and we didn't want to set a precedent, besides there were just not enough resources to go by. Still, she stayed behind, hoping and praying for a miracle. Later in the afternoon, she accompanied a classmate who was picking up her allowance. We had a Knight stationed in the office to keep procedures running smoothly and in an orderly manner. Marjorie fell in line and when the Knight requested for her ID, she handed it over. For some reasons, we had overlooked to inform the Knight and the lady releasing the money that Marjorie was no longer entitled to the allowance even if her name was still on the list.

We had not expected that Marjorie would attempt something like that. The money was not much. But to her it meant the world. She reached out and took the allowance. It was a few days later that I learned of what happened. I requested to meet with Marjorie and her mother. The night of the meeting, I had with me Kuya Buddy, Ate Chat, and Ate Carmen, our acknowledged church leaders in Libis.

We requested Marjorie to tell us what happened. "I accompanied my classmate to get her allowance. I was thinking if I, too, had the allowance, I could buy the things I needed in school. While we were in the line, Mr. Joe (our knight member) asked for our IDs. I thought it was not wrong to give my ID. I didn't know that they were using it to release the allowance. I accepted the money."

"I was told that you have been informed this morning that you are no longer qualified because your sister is already a recipient of the church's assistance. Is that true?" I gently asked her.

"That is true, sir," She replied.

"Why did you still get the money? Didn't you know that was wrong?" She was silent. Then I asked, "Can you return the money?"

"I already spent it to buy my books." Her head was bowed and I felt she was about to cry. Somehow I had a feeling that some of the money was used to buy some food for the house since public schools provide for the books.

I took pains to carefully explain the consequences of her action. "I am sure that you realize what you did was wrong. It cannot go unpunished. Do you remember in your application form there is a statement that says, 'I attest that all information in this application form is true and correct to the best of my knowledge and if proven not true, assistance will cease automatically.' Do you remember that?"

"Yes, sir."

"It is likely that if the money is not returned, you will no longer be allowed to join the program. Your sister will graduate in four years; you have ten years before finishing your studies, even if we take away the four years that is allocated to your sister, you still have six years all the way to college. As it is now, even your sister is in danger of losing her privilege, I am sorry to say."

The mother finally said something in quite a disconsolate tone, "Sir, I will answer for the money. We will return it. I just request that you give us up to the end of the month to pay for it, I will scrimp and save to raise the amount."

I knew that the father was not regularly employed and to put food on the table, the mother was doing a bit of buy-and-sell of whatever small item she could get her hands on. I knew, too, that that they were obsessed with the desire to give their children a proper education as the only means out of poverty. I pulled out my wallet. I said, "I want to help but I can do only so much. I will entrust Ate Carmen with seven hundred pesos, so you only need to come up with five hundred pesos more."

The room was silent. I looked at Marjorie and I could see the tears welling in her eyes. I quickly changed the subject.

"Marjorie, you have not asked this. But let me share the struggle of my own Tatay. He started schooling at the age of 13. His father had died early. To support the family, his mother did odd jobs just to earn some money.

"They were four in the family. My father was the eldest. He sent his brother and sister to school with his meager earnings. He would go to the public market very early in the morning and offered his *kargador* services to women with heavy loads. He took whatever they could afford to give. In the afternoon, he would go in the nearby forest to look for fallen trees. He would chop the tree to a certain length and burn the pieces to produce charcoal. One morning, after seeing his brother and sister off to school, he looked at his mother and asked, 'Nanay, can I also go to school?'

"My Lola did not say a word; she put on her bandana, took something from a glass jar and left. When she returned, she told my father, 'The principal said that you can start tomorrow. He also said that you should take a bath. You will smell up the whole classroom.'

"My Tatay graduated valedictorian. He actually finished elementary school in only four years because he was accelerated twice. He wanted to continue his studies but there was not enough money. His brother and sister were almost through with high school. Tatay was lucky to work as an apprentice mechanic. He was a voracious reader and read anything which he could lay his hands on.

"When the big war broke out, the corps of professionals in the country was decimated. The government came up with a Commonwealth Act that allowed those with work experience to take government examination despite the lack of a diploma. My father passed. He was given a license as a mechanical plant engineer. We, his children, fulfilled his dream to earn a diploma and find honest employment. His legacy to us was, 'No matter how poor we were, not once did I feed you with food bought with stolen money.'

"In fulfilling our father's dream, we also promised that we will share whatever we have with the needy, the reason that I am taking pains talking to you. No matter how poor we are, we must do what is right in the eyes of the Lord."

We parted on those words; and my deepest hope then was that they found a home in the consciousness of Marjorie.

That Sunday—it was the 14th of July, 2013—Fr. Bong read, "The Parable of the Good Samaritan." In his homily, the good father said, "The way to life is not primarily through knowing; it is through doing. The scholar of the law knows what he must do to inherit eternal life. He has knowledge of the law but is unaware of the spirit of the law. The Lord told him, 'Do this and you will live.' And when he realized what the Good Samaritan did, Jesus said to him, 'Go and do likewise.'"

And the final lesson shared by Fr. Bong that fateful Sunday was, "We have a heart for God, if we have a heart for the needy."

As of this writing, eight months have passed. Marjorie's mother is making a tremendous effort to return the money; she still has two hundred pesos to go to complete the amount to be paid back. We don't mind. We know that the family has learned the meaning of honesty and integrity.

I learned the greater lesson: the lesson of compassion.

For almost thirty years, I have been having weekly chats with my Spiritual Advisor of the Opus Dei. Inevitably, my sons Carlo and Jun were both intimately exposed to the Opus Dei before they left for the US to study. They had all the intention to come back home but better opportunities made them choose to stay there. But whenever they are home in Manila, they always make it a point to touch base with **Fr. Joe, My Spiritual Advisor.**

My struggle with asthma became a major battle when I was diagnosed with COPD, a condition which is characterized by three continuing conditions: the presence of phlegm, coughing, and shortness of breath. I don't have the phlegm and coughing, thank God!

At the height of my struggle, I came in for a talk with Fr. Joe who immediately sensed my despondency. He rose quickly from his chair and walked towards me with outstretched arms. Not wanting to cause him any unease, I backed away. Fr. Joe's face clouded with pain. He dropped his arms and stood very still. Finally, he sat down and pointed me to the other chair. I wanted, above all things, to shield the good father from my pain now, I was the source of his anguish. But if Fr. Joe was disappointed, he hid it very well.

In a soothing voice, he said, "Rudy, do you remember our last talk?"

I was not ready. I had come in to listen to some words of encouragement. Talking was difficult for me. It was extremely hard just forming the words and making the sounds come out. I gave Fr. Joe a nod.

"You recall what I taught you about sickness and pain?"

I forced myself to answer though it required great effort. "Yes, Fr. Joe, I am sorry if I am unable to carry a decent conversation. I lose air just talking."

I felt frustrated, angry even. I couldn't vocalize the disappointment I harbored in my heart and the disappointment I had at the Lord for allowing me to suffer so.

"It's alright, just sit and listen," he said.

"It is easy to worship God when things are going great in our lives," Fr. Joe began, "when he has provided family, friends, food, happy situations, especially good health. But circumstances are not always pleasant. The deepest level of worship is praising God despite the pain, thanking him during trials, trusting him when tempted, even afflicted, surrendering while suffering and loving him when he seems distant."

Fr. Joe paused and looked at me with measuring eyes. He was waiting for a sign that I understood. I sat motionless. He continued, "How often have we studied the meaning of the cross in our lives. The language of the cross is not easy to understand. Nevertheless, we are disposed, albeit with general intention, to go along with what Jesus wanted. We should not place any limits on how far we are willing to follow our Lord. And so when we make a petition for something, when we pray, we ought to be disposed towards accepting, above all, the will of God; even if it does not run in accord or parallel with our wishes. His majesty knows best what is suitable for us, for he can rightly reply that we know not what we ask (St. Teresa, *The Interior Castle*, 2, 8). He wants us to ask him what we need and what we want, but above all, he wants us to conform our will to his. He will give us what is best.'"

I knelt before Fr. Joe and asked him to hear my confession. He said, "Jesus loves all of us like a child. The innocence of child is what he wants because a child is pure of heart" (Excerpts from *A Love That Never Says Goodbye*).

Fr. Joe's teaching kept me going.

Pope Francis,

Fr. Guido, Fr. Luigi, Msgr. Dan, Fr. Bong, and Fr. Joe are truly Peter's disciples. There are thousands, if not millions, of them throughout the world. The wayward priests that caused my friend John to look at the Church with disdain are few, as few as Judas' disciples.

I rested after writing this part of my letter because John once more loomed large in my mind. Despite my hesitancy to greet him that Christmas day, I decided to do it anyway:

Hi John,

I don't know if it's still appropriate to greet you "Merry Christmas" because the word connotes belief in God who freed us from the sin of Adam and Eve. I wrestled with this thought all day. Finally, I decided that it will do no harm to greet the one person who helped me so much in writing the stories that reflect on the word of God. Merry Christmas, my friend, for whatever good it brings you and let me apologize if somehow the greeting offends your sensibilities. Thanks.

Hi Rudy,

I'd very much be hurt if the one person who is leading me to the Fold (not that I left it. Not in a million light years!) did not greet me on Christmas Day. I know that I commented that even the Evangelists did not agree on Jesus' true birthdate. I hasten to say that that is not crucial to me. What is, is that he came in human form, with all his frailties, warts, and boils. He can then empathize with mortals like me, and forgive me for my human failings.

I quarrel with organized religion and its purported system. Of course, system is a must in our affairs lest anarchy takes over. But a system is there to serve and not be the master. It must create doorways and entrances to Jesus' advocacies. This system must not be held back, and be overcome by traditional expectations.

The author, A.C. Lewis wrote: "We may ignore, but we can nowhere evade the presence of God."

"We will not 'spend' Christmas… nor 'observe' Christmas. We will 'keep' Christmas—keep it as it is… in all the loveliness of its ancient traditions.

May we keep it in our hearts that we may be kept in its hope. I wish you a Blessed Christmas.

John

Actually, a few weeks earlier, John related to me his meeting with an elderly Jesuit father. John said that that was part of his efforts to reconnect with his paternal relatives. It was years ago when he met some of them during the interment of his father. John is particularly close to an older first cousin, Ursulita, who together with her father, Dr. Pedro Reyes, were the only ones who gave him "official recognition." In fact, John's Nanay was his Ate Lita's Ninang at her baptism.

The priest used to be an official of the Hagonoy Parish Priests Association, who may be able to furnish John with solid leads as to the whereabouts of his Ate Lita and other relatives. Dr. Reyes has been a prominent Hagonoy resident having owned the biggest hospital in that locale.

Even at the start of their meeting, the kindly Jesuit corrected John when he apologized to the priest for disturbing his retirement. "John, you must know that we priests do not really retire, in fact I am tempted to say—we cannot retire. When we took our vows in the Holy Orders, we committed ourselves in the service of our Lord for a lifetime. As you know, Jesus Christ called himself as the Bridegroom. On earth, the relationship between the bridegroom and the bride is on a "till death do us part basis." I am afraid that that does not apply to us priests. We are on call even in our next life in heaven."

During the course of their conversation, John asked the Jesuit whether or not subscribing to organized religion is a sin. To which the priest replied, "Sin can be described as a conscious, responsible, and deliberate act of the will, by which, recognizing the existence of a moral choice, one chooses wrong, knowing it to be wrong, because, for the moment, at any rate, it is desired more than its alternative.

"You were traumatized by your previous encounters with certain religious groups and individuals. I do not fault you for your present attitude towards what you call organized religion."

The priest continued, "I believe that at present you have this very strong stirring in your soul, and because of what you have experienced, you are very much confused where this is pulling you. Allow me to share with you what Her Majesty Queen Elizabeth II said in a special assembly of her church group: 'If we have faith and courage to seek it, we shall be shown new truths in the Gospel of real and immediate relevance to our own time, and we shall be given new insight to understand the unexampled problems which arise, almost every day at home and abroad."

Pope Francis, Rappler, a local news agency reported your "10 Best Quotes in 2013" which is now seen by readers all over the world as the New Year's resolution everyone should have. Here is one of those quotes:

Befriend those who disagree. You surprised Mario Palmaro, who wrote the article, *"The Reason Why We Don't Like This Pope,"* when you visited him because he was gravely ill. When asked what you told him, Palmaro said, "He just wanted to tell me that he is praying for me."

Pope Francis, this is one of the important purposes of my letter, to request for your prayer, please pray for me and my friend John because we know that *"faith is always a cross...* this powerfully echoes Galatians 2:19, where St. Paul tells us that he has been crucified with Christ so that now it is Christ who lives with him, and Colossians 3:3 where he applies this to us: 'For you have died, and your life is hidden with Christ in God.' "

I pray and believe that my friend John will awaken and come back to the Church that Jesus Christ asked Peter to nourish. That day will be here sooner than later!!

Pope Francis, as I am putting the final touches on this letter, I called my friend, "Hi John, Fr. Joe asked about you. May I tell him you are ready to meet?

"Yes."

His reply was music to my ears.

Praise the Lord!

My Daughter Nikki

Dear Pope Francis, the issue of the Reproductive Health Law raging in our country has divided us. One camp insists on allowing all forms of contraception, but their cry points to a flawed reasoning that contraception merely prevents the meeting of the woman's ova with the male sperm and ergo that no killing of life happens. Abortion is not allowed in the law. The purpose of the law is to protect the health of women whose lives are at risk, especially in far-flung areas where medical attention is limited, if not totally absent.

Your position on abortion is clear but deliberately misinterpreted by those who look at your statement as some form of license that opens a window for Catholics to use contraceptives, short of practicing abortion. To set the records straight, let me quote you verbatim:

> "We cannot insist only on issues related to abortion, gay marriage, and the use of contraceptive methods. This is not possible. I have not spoken much about these things, and I was reprimanded for that. But when we speak about these issues, we have to talk about them in a context. The teaching of the Church, for that matter, is clear and I am a son of the Church, but it is not necessary to talk about these issues all the time.

> "We must warm the hearts of the people, who walk through the dark night with them, by first professing Jesus' undying love for each and every single one of them, and reminding them that the promise of salvation is offered to every human person, in spite of their sins and moral failings. I see the Church as field

hospital after battle, it is useless to ask a seriously injured person if he has high cholesterol and about the level of his blood sugars! You have to heal his wound."

Pope Francis, with that said, what is the worldwide data on abortion today?

Of the estimated 210 million pregnancies that occur throughout the world each year, about 38% are unplanned, and 22% end in abortion, according to a new report by The Alan Guttmacher Institute (AGI).

- In developed countries (where average desired family size is small), of the 28 million pregnancies occurring every year, an estimated 49% are unplanned, and 36% end in abortion.
- In developing countries (where average desired family size is still relatively large), of the 182 million pregnancies occurring every year, an estimated 36% are unplanned, and 20% end in abortion.

"It is clear that women the world over go to great lengths to terminate an unplanned pregnancy. It is not only our responsibility but our duty to respect that decision. We must do our best to ensure that abortion takes place only under safe conditions and to see that women have the means to prevent pregnancy in the first place," comments Jeannie I. Rosoff, AGI's president.

But why is this happening? Clearly you saw the reason for this and your statement is manifest:

"Don't be afraid to say 'forever.' " Today, there are those who say that marriage is out of fashion; in a culture of relativism and the ephemeral, many preach the importance of 'enjoying' the moment. They say that it is not worth making a lifelong commitment, making a definitive decision, 'forever,' because we do not know what tomorrow will bring.

"I ask you, instead, to be revolutionaries, to swim against the tide; yes, I am asking you to rebel against this culture that sees everything as temporary and that ultimately believes that you are incapable of responsibility, that you are incapable of true love. I have confidence in you and I pray for you. Have the courage 'to swim against the tide.' Have the courage to be happy."

As you say, "*Today, there are those who say that marriage is out of fashion; in a culture of relativism and the ephemeral, many preach the importance of 'enjoying' the moment.*" And that is where it all begins. Couples enjoy the pleasure that marriage brings but do these pleasures

Nikki's Wedding Day
From left: Kuya Carlo, Ate Leah, Dad, Nikki, Mom, and Kuya Jun

outside of marriage thereby the sacrament of Marriage, the first institution that God created is sacrificed.

My wife and I made that mistake even as we thought that we had the permission of the Church. Let me tell you the story of Nikki, the apple of our eyes.

We arrived late in Fatima. It was cold; everyone was tired, showing symptoms of irritability, and very hungry. I myself was in a morose mood, for some reason worried that our room would not be spruce clean which would then trigger my allergies; I almost dreaded the prospect of entering an unfamiliar place.

I patiently waited for Brother Millard to announce our room assignments. From the corner of my eyes, I could see my daughter Nikki coming towards me with my son-in-law, Wally in tow. They had just finished helping the lone porter with our entire luggage, most of which were bulging with souvenirs and religious items.

She smiled at me. She must have noticed the worry on my face. Her question surprised me. "Dad, why did you name me Maria Fatima?"

The sweet girl was obviously trying to distract me from whatever it was that was bothering me.

But I guess that she was truly curious to know; after all, we were right here where Our Lady of Fatima made an apparition. Why, we were even billeted in a place called "Hotel Fatima." But Nikki's question did sidetrack me from my concerns and in fact, made me feel a bit guilty.

I suddenly remembered that one of the reasons why we were here today was to finally have the chance to thank Mama Mary in person for giving us our daughter right here where it all started. How self-indulgent of me to be only thinking of my allergy. How I returned Nikki's smile, my thoughts drawn back to the interesting history behind her name.

I pulled Nikki away from the chattering crowd so I could tell her the full story of how her name Maria Fatima came to be.

Children are gifts from God; that is how we always look at them. Nikki, in particular, came when we needed her most. My wife and I have always been ardent believers in God. We would never in our wildest dreams go against his teachings.

So in the life that we built together, the Lord's presence has always been in our midst. But somehow, somewhere along the way, the bond that kept us glued to the Lord loosened. That was the time we needed to focus on our older children, build a career, and create the future that we all wanted to have. The kids came one after the other. In fact, Leah and Jun's age difference is just a year. Actually, they almost met in the same year Leah was born.

Although it was true that I was earning more than enough for our daily needs, it still seemed natural that I wanted more for our family. But wanting more meant more time away from our children. Thus, adding another one did not seem right.

My wife and I went to see a priest, a family friend. I guess we misread his message when he said, "Rudy, the Church allows for family spacing."

We took that to mean as license to practice family planning, and not necessarily the natural way. We did not entertain any guilt feelings; after all, we were following the priest's advice.

My career blossomed.

Our older children grew up in a comfortable environment, though not in excessive luxury, for this was not what we intended for them. We continued to pray to the Lord and pray the family Rosary, specifically to our Lady of Fatima who had become our constant companion. She protected us in spite of us not being completely in accord with her Son's teaching. We were violating his rule: *the purpose of marriage is procreation.*

Mama Mary had to do something. She somehow put me in touch with Opus Dei. In this personal prelature, I had the opportunity to meet my Spiritual Advisor.

Nikki is just one day shy in completing the monthly calendar in the number of years she's been in existence on earth—that's how long I have known Fr. Joe. Whenever time permits, I see him weekly. In one of our profound conversations, he opened my eyes to the mistake my wife and I were committing. We stopped immediately and let God do what he wanted. That same month, Nikki was conceived.

Carlo, Leah, and Jun welcomed the arrival of their youngest sister with great joy. The coming of Nikki fourteen years after Jun was born changed our lives. We began to look at things in a more positive light. With her coming, the grass seemed greener, the roses redder, the sun brighter, and the light of the moon more silvery. God had indeed given us everything we prayed for. Nikki's siblings simply spoiled her.

God reminds us that he, too, wants to share in our joy. In our case, he delivered his message in a runabout way. When Nikki was three months old, her pediatrician noticed her fontanel was closing much too fast than normal, beyond what was average for her age. The doctor wanted to operate; the other alternative was just to let things be but that came with the certitude that Nikki would grow as a child with special needs.

We hesitated letting the older children know that something was wrong, fearful that they might not be ready to accept the reality that such medical anomalies happen. For my part, I felt an overwhelming sense of sadness at Nikki's condition; but my true sorrow came from seeing how deeply Leth was suffering as she watched over our youngest child. I would leave for work in the morning and return home in the evening to find her exactly as I left her, sitting forlornly by Nikki's crib, her face drawn and tear-stained.

We would then kneel by Nikki's crib side and pray the Rosary intently to our Lady of Fatima. We prayed for understanding, to accept the gift of Nikki for whatever she was.

Soon, Carlo noticed the gloom in our house. Being the eldest, he was more perceptive but chose to keep his suspicions to himself. But not for long. Leah and Jun were this time themselves conscious of the heavy pall that hanged like a dark cloud over the entire household. Their mother's usual light disposition had been replaced by a noticeable introversion, and while she tended dutifully to everyone's needs, she spoke and answered in a monosyllabic monotone as if something dreadful had completely drained her and caused her to lose interest in anything that went on around her.

Still, Leth and I tried to keep it from the children, explaining away the perceptible change in their mother's bubbly outlook as the result of some vague malady that was bothering her. All the while, we continued with our intensified prayers to Mama Mary. And like I said, God acts in mysterious ways.

One day, my mother-in-law came to visit. She quickly noticed her daughter's tears-swollen eyes. "What's wrong, *anak*?" the older woman asked. Like a dam bursting, Leth poured out in wracking sobs all the emotions she had been keeping inside her for such a long time. Nanay Fely embraced her tightly. "Hush, hush, it's okay. Tell your mother all about it."

Nanay Fely listened patiently. Afterwards, she wiped Leth's tears with the hem of her dress and with a soothing voice, said, "Be happy, nothing is wrong with Nikki. All my children, including you, had the same peculiarity. When you were barely six months old, your fontanel was almost completely closed. And look at you, why, you are one of my brightest children."

I imagine, it was God's way of telling us that in spite of the wrong we did, he had forgiven us with the precious gift of Nikki. Of course, when she was baptized, she formally became Maria Fatima in honor of our Blessed Mother.

As Nikki was growing up, the thought, she might still harbor some ill effects from the early closing of her fontanel stayed with me. So I made up a game we played between us. We would hug each other tight and I would whisper in her ears:

"Who is daddy's most beautiful baby?" And she would answer, "Me!"

"Who is daddy's most intelligent baby?" And she would answer, "Me!"

Then in a really low whisper, "Who is the baby that daddy loves the most?"

And she would answer, "Me!"

Finally, I would end our game with the question, "And who are you?"

At this point she could hardly contain herself and would burst out with, "Meee, Nikkiii!!!"

Somehow because Nikki came much later than our older children, my bonding with her is more intense. Even today I feel that she is still my little girl. My mind refuses to completely accept that she has grown to a fine lady, married to an equally fine gentleman. No, I never resented her marrying Wally. For that matter, I look at him as the perfect match for Nikki.

The older children went on to adulthood while I was focused on my career. And I have to admit, I missed a lot of important occasions with Carlo, Leah, and Jun. It was Leth who acted as a surrogate father most of the time then. With Nikki it was different; I never passed up any of her important milestones. Weekends, though, except under extreme circumstances, were fully devoted to the children. My excuse was that I was assuring their future by giving them quality time. I think that I was using the praise "quality time" long before child psychologists and guidance counselors highjacked it as their very own.

When Nikki was five years old, the political situation in the country took a turn for the worse. Much against our wish, we were forced to send our older children to the US to continue their studies. The political unrest that followed the assassination of Ninoy Aquino brought things to a head. Classes were suspended almost on daily basis. Removing the children to the US entailed great sacrifice on our part as parents but we knew that the children would be better off there. My parents and siblings were living in the US and would be within easy reach just in case the children faced any emergency there.

At home, the absence of the older children was compensated with Nikki's presence. Yes, Nikki indeed came when we needed her most. We did not want to let her go when she was old enough to study abroad. The sadness of the separation from our other children was almost too much for us and the thought of Nikki going away was something that would simply be unbearable for Leth and me. Nikki understood. There was never a time when she made us feel that she missed out on anything by studying at the Ateneo.

After I finished telling Nikki her story, she was teary-eyed. She leaned on Wally to hide her tears, for this time she finally learned the details of how she came to be named Maria Fatima. And she knew that being here, face to face as it were with her namesake, was a lifetime experience that not too many could enjoy.

Recalling Nikki's troubled beginnings, I was inspired to write her story which revolves around her smile.

The Smile of Nikki

The scientific pronouncement is that it takes only seventeen muscles to smile and forty-two to frown. So why overwork oneself? Besides, a smile is infectious, lighting up a room as a candle spreads its glow. Imagine, then, that little smile catching like wildfire and turning the world into a world of peace, a world of love, and a world of beauty. Quotes the Bard of Avon, "If eyes are made for seeing, then beauty has its own reason for being." And from a more contemporary time, a song that optimistically proclaims, "Everything is beautiful in its own way."

It is often enough said that "life begins at forty," but I argue that life begins at any age because age is a mind game and you are as young as you will yourself to think. I feel that I am just in my twenties and my passion for life flows on unhindered. Not a day passes that I am not challenged by the need to be innovative, to create. Ideas and words vie for space in my mind, juggling to be committed to paper with the bright hope that someone somewhere might encounter them and depending on his state of being at that particular moment, be moved or even inspired.

As my years cast ever-lengthening shadows, I see only beauty and peace around me. I will it so, because there is only so much time left for it to be wasted on frivolities.

Today, when I hold a blade of grass in my hand, I see an ocean of green awashed in morning's dew. A butterfly flits on gossamer wings from flower to flower and on each bestows a kiss as an errant lover might on his many loves.

Nature offers a treasure chest of heart-stopping beauty: a cloud-cladded mountain, gentle waves lapping at a pebbly shore, a warm rain that falls without warning on a summer's day... In my mind's eye,

I see lovers caught in the sudden downpour rushing to seek cover under the trees. The rain lingers and ushers in a certain chill in the air. Then a rainbow arcs across the sky with its eternal promise that a thunderstorm cannot last forever. It is the Supreme Being at work again. He gives us reasons to rejoice, then allows our hearts to be wounded at little, then heals and makes us whole again.

"Beauty," St. Thomas said, "is the splendor that comes when the pieces fit together. When we are what we are supposed to be, when we do what we are supposed to do." The beauty of a sunrise lies as much on the dawning of another God-given day as on the diamond sparkle it gives to the morning dew. The beauty of a sunset is the curtain it rings down on a day dedicated to the workings of the Lord, no less than the exploding colors it deigns to clothe the sky and the low-lying clouds.

On a good day, as I go near our farm, I see from the distance, children running about in abandon, vainly chasing after some winged insects. I hear them shouting and laughing in carefree glee; and lost among them is my Nikki. Guileless innocence is etched on the children's sunburnt faces. What freedom! What utterly unbelievable, uninhibited joyful laughter coming from them!

Frankly, I cannot distinguish the smile and laughter of a child from a home of some means from the smile and laughter of a child from a home of more humble circumstance. Our Nikki is fortunate to be growing up surrounded by material comfort but when she chases a dragonfly, her shrieks are as pure as that of the children of the farmer folks. When she is offered a toy or a piece of candy, her face breaks in a smile and brightens up the same as any other child. For to retain forever the honesty and the sincerity of youth surely must be a gift from God.

Do we realize that the only time in our life that we are incapable of putting labels on people is when we are young? To the young, there is no rich or poor, no black or white, no pretty or ugly; for their mind is a camera that captures a picture as it is and not what we want it to be.

The English writer Fynn wrote about the extraordinary story of Anna, an orphan girl he rescued from the slums of London. And from her, he borrowed some of the deepest insights that can only spring from the unclouded vision of the young: "If you live in a house, and you let the window get splashed and dirty and you look out the window, it looks like the world is dirty, but it is not. If you look inside the house, it looks like the house is dirty, but it is not because only the window is dirty. All people have two windows. All people have an eye window and then a heart window. The eye window is to look out and see things from. The heart window is to see inside to see you when you cry; your tears wash the windows, so that you can see well."

We should allow the smile to inhabit the very essence of our lives. A smile is the handmaiden of a good heart. Our daughter Nikki transcends her humanness and becomes for us the smile in our existence and everything is but a note in the love song that is her smile. And for Nikki, I penned this poem:

It Rains Tulips in the Spring

I look at the daffodils and see
candlelight glowing for me;
fillet mignon, mushroom toppings,
beans almandine, and apple *ala* mode to go.

I hear raindrops, like tulips
dropping still on my rain-soaked lawn,
a gentle veil, light as feather,
a little girl dancing on tiptoes.

For spring has sprung unannounced
and tulips pour on me.
A little girl chases her shadow;
and everything, on its own way, is beautiful.

And yet the battle for the unborn has just begun!

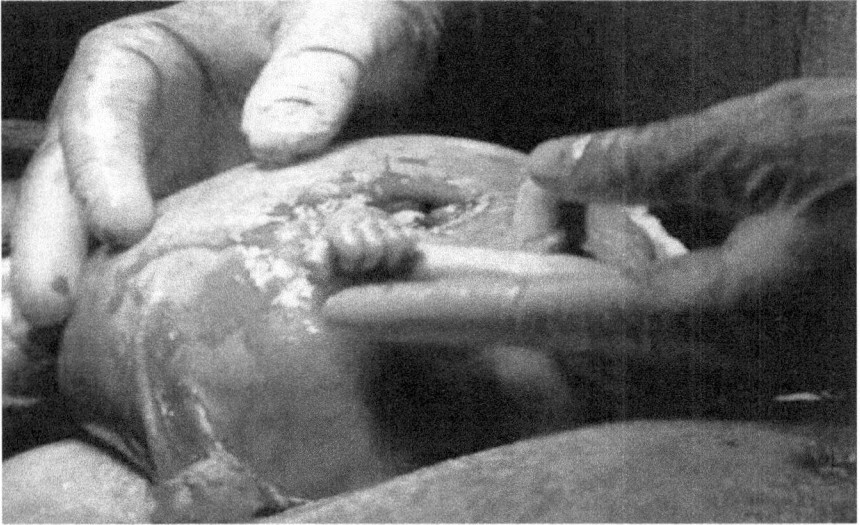

Samuel Armas
21 weeks in the womb

Samuel Armas
3 years out of the womb

The Battle for the Unborn

Pope Francis, on our first night in Fatima, I was gifted by Mama Mary with praying a decade of her Rosary in front of a huge international crowd gathered in her honor. Those invited to recite the Rosary were requested to do it in their own language.

I was literally on "pins and needles," for this is the night, I was given the chance to talk to our Mother and thank her for our wonderful life, our children, and most especially Nikki whom she granted with a normal, healthy life.

When my turn to recite my decade of the Rosary came, I said it with as much power of voice as I could muster:

> *"Aba ginoong Maria, napupuno ka ng grasya.*
> *Ang Panginoong Diyos ay sumasaiyo.*
> *Bukod kang pinagpala sa babaeng lahat,*
> *at pinagpala naman ang iyong anak na si Hesus."*

I prayed in Filipino and the people answered in their own languages. Deep in my heart, I wanted to reach out to Mama Mary. As the sound of my voice reverberated across her hallowed grounds, I prayed for her to hear me. Her place is sacred and she is always present here. Yet, I imagined her seated beside her Son in heaven and I had to shout to reach her. I wanted everyone to hear how much we loved her!

As Mary's image was slowly moved to begin the procession, Leth murmured, *"Inay, Inay, salamat po!"*

I knew that Mama Mary heard our prayers, for as the image passed before Leth, Mama Mary's presence embraced her so strongly that my wife cried with joyous tears. I told her how Mama Mary must love her so. In Lourdes with the crowd trying to get as close to our Mother, she was invited to stay in front of her image; in Fatima she felt the grace of her presence. How Mama Mary truly loved the mother of my children!

I want to end Nikki's story with two spiritual events which Bishop Raul gave us on a silver platter. To appreciate these events, let me first bring you the meaning of Mama Mary's "secret" messages to Lucia, Francisco, and Jacinta. The importance of the Bishop's actions dawned on me as I was reading the book, *Fatima in Lucia's Own Words*.

Below, I quote word for word Mama Mary's explanation as Lucia shouted in fear from what she saw during the 13th of July 1917 Apparition of Our Mother:

> "You have seen hell where the souls of poor sinners go. To save them, God wishes to establish in the world devotion to my Immaculate Heart. If what I say to you is done, many souls will be saved and there will be peace. Then war is going to end; but if people do not cease offending God, a worse one will break out during the pontificate of Pius XI.
>
> "When you see a night illumined by an unknown light, know that this is the great sign given you by God that he is about to punish the world of its crimes, by means of war, famine, and persecutions of the Church and the Holy Father." (As the Blessed Mother promised, World War I ended in 1918.)
>
> "To prevent this, I shall come to ask for the consecration of Russia to my Immaculate Heart and the Communion of reparation on First Saturdays. If my requests are heeded, Russia will be converted and there will be peace; if not, she will spread her errors throughout the world, causing wars and persecutions of the Church. The good will be martyred; the Holy Father will have much to suffer; various nations will be annihilated." (Here the Blessed Mother foretells that Russia would soon embrace communism. History tells us that after World War I ended, the Russian revolution erupted and Russia embraced Communism.)

"In the end my Immaculate Heart will triumph. The Holy Father will consecrate Russia to me, and she shall be converted, and a period of peace will be granted to the world."

What actually happened with Our Mother's request?

After the apparitions at Fatima, Lucia lived in a monastery in Pontéverda, Spain, where the Blessed Mother visited her often.

"On December 10, 1925, the most Holy Virgin appeared to me, and by her side, elevated on a luminous cloud, was a Child. … Then the most Holy Virgin said, 'Look my daughter, at my Heart, surrounded with thorns with which ungrateful men pierce me every moment by their blasphemies and ingratitude. You at least try to console me and say that I promised to assist at the hour of death, with the graces necessary for salvation, all those who, on the first Saturday of five consecutive months, shall confess, receive Holy Communion, recite five decades of the Rosary, and keep me company for fifteen minutes while meditating on the fifteen mysteries of the Rosary, with the intention of making reparation to me.'

"On June 13, 1929… Our Lady then said to me, 'The moment has come in which the Holy Father, in union with the Bishops of the world, to make the consecration of Russia to my Immaculate Heart, promising to save it by this means. There are so many souls whom the justice of God condemns for sins committed against me, that I have come to ask reparation: sacrifice yourself for this intention and pray.'

"I gave an account of this to the confessor," said Lucia, "who ordered me to write down what our Lady wanted done.

"Later in an intimate communication, our Lord complained to me saying, 'They did not wish to heed my request! Like the king of France, they will repent and do it, but it will be late. Russia would already spread her errors throughout the world, provoking wars, and persecutions of the Church: the Holy Father will have much to suffer.' "

Still, our Mother told Lucia, *"In the end my Immaculate Heart will triumph."*

In Rome, before the statue of Our Lady of Fatima, Pope John Paul II, with all the bishops of the Church, renewed the consecration of the world and Russia on March 19, 1984.

It took 67 years for the Church to fulfill the request of Mama Mary.

Let me now bring you back to the spiritual gifts from Bishop Raul: it rarely happens that when receiving the Body of Christ, we are allowed to come up the altar, take the Holy Eucharist, and dip it in the Blood of Christ. Bishop Raul did this for us with the request that as we went back in our seats to reflect on the message of the gospel, to think how blessed we were to be here in Fatima, a rare gift from our Mother.

After the Mass, he gathered us outside the chapel so that he could consecrate us to the Immaculate Heart of Mary. He was connecting us to the request of Our Mother to consecrate Russia to her Immaculate Heart.

But the consecration of Russia was a long time ago. What then did our consecration mean?

When we personally took the Body of Christ and dipped it on his Blood, the bishop was consecrating us to the Sacred Heart of Jesus through his Body and Blood. Reciting the prayer to the Immaculate Heart of Mary, he was consecrating us to Mama Mary's Heart; consecrated to her, our Mother, would keep us in her care and protection until we meet her in heaven… a gift few ever received.

In our hearts, my wife and I realized that in praying the Holy Rosary, we, too, consecrated our little Nikki to Mama Mary's Immaculate Heart in the hour of her need.

I know now that Leth, Carlo, Leah, Jun, Nikki, all my children-in-law, our *apos* and I, look at Mama Mary as the true apple of our eyes.

I dare to say, Mama Mary is in the heart of God and our good Bishop Raul Martirez is also in God's heart. Hail Pilgrims!!!

Pope Francis, Mama Mary's heart is truly in the heart of God. Here is a heartwarming true story of love for the unborn. The parents of Samuel did not believe in abortion to end the difficult pregnancy of his mother. Instead, Samuel's parents fought to keep him, a tribute to God's teaching that all life is sacred.

Tribute: Fetal Hand Development

Samuel Alexander Armas (born December 2, 1999) became known as the child—shown in a famous photograph by Michael Clancy—that grasped his surgeon's hand from a hole in his mother's uterus during open fetal surgery for spina bifida.

The true story behind the photo!

The famous photograph was taken during a pioneering surgical procedure performed on August 19, 1999. At a mere 21 weeks of gestational age—long before it was time to leave his mother's womb—Samuel underwent a bold and experimental surgical procedure to close a hole at the bottom of his spinal cord, the telltale characteristic of myelomeningocele, or spina bifida.

Samuel's parents, Julie and Alex, could have terminated Julie's pregnancy at 15 weeks when they learned about their son's condition, which could result in lifelong physical and mental disabilities. But the Armases do not believe in abortion. Instead, in August 1999, they drove 250 miles from their home in Villa Rica, Georgia, to Nashville, Tennessee, where Dr. Joseph Bruner, of Vanderbilt University, performed a surgery bordering on the fantastical. Bruner cut into Julie's abdomen, lifted her balloon like uterus out of her body, made an incision in the taut muscle, removed the fetus, sewed up the spinal defect and tucked him back inside.

Fifteen weeks later, Samuel Armas "came out screaming," says Julie, mother of Sam.

Pope Francis, the battle for the unborn is a never-ending fight of good against evil. Patrick Henry was an American patriot who rallied the colonists in their fight for independence against the British. Let me quote the words of Patrick Henry in a speech he made at the Virginia Convention: "There is no longer any room for hope. If we wish to be free, if we mean to preserve inviolate those inestimable privileges for which we have so long contending, if we mean not basely to abandon the noble struggle in which we have been so long engaged, and which we have pledged ourselves never to abandon until the glorious object of our contest shall be obtained, we must fight, I repeat it, sir, we must fight! An appeal to arms, and to God of Host, is all that is left us!"

Pope Francis, we must fight for *the most vulnerable—the unborn...* "Among the vulnerable for whom the Church wishes to care with particular love and concern are unborn children, the most defenseless and innocent among us... human beings are end in themselves and never a means of resolving other problems. Precisely because it involves the internal consistency of our message about the value of the human person, the Church cannot be expected to change her position on this question... This is not subject to alleged reforms or modernizations. It is not progressive to try to resolve problems by eliminating a human life."

In Search of God

$\mathcal{D}$ear Pope Francis, thousands of years before Jesus came into the world, God promised Abraham that he would have children as numerous as the stars, beginning with his son Isaac, and onward down the generations to Jacob the father of Joseph, husband of Mary. The Lord's coming foretold of peace among men of goodwill.

Unknown to Abraham, God made the same promise to Hagar the slave girl who gave birth to his other son, Ishmael.

Isaac became the father of the Jewish nation and Ishmael of the Arab nation. The Jews were promised a Messiah who would free them from the clutches of the sin of Adam and Eve. Isaiah prophesied the coming of Jesus Christ who would later build his Church on the rock that was his first vicar, Peter. "Arise! Shine for your light has come, the glory of the Lord has dawned upon you" (Is 60:1).

From the line of Ishmael came the Prophet Mohammed; and Islam grew along with Christianity. Regrettably, if inevitably, friction between the two nations arose and bitter rivalries and quarrels ensued. God gave the founders of the two nations the free will to do as they saw fit, whether good or bad. Even as God knew that discord would shortly take place, he could not stop it; foreknowledge of what would happen could not prevent Ishmael or Isaac from pursuing their chosen paths. The paths they chose, following parallel lines, were doomed from ever converging, and a balanced coexistence has since continued to elude the inheritors of the legacies of the sons of Abraham.

The same tension has spawned the different "isms" of today, beginning with terrorism. Terrorism applies to both nations, each one perceiving acts of war or fear created by intention to make war, as acts of terrorism. Terrorism and materialism and relativism, its ever loyal companions, combine to become the triple-headed evil that consumes with insidious rapacity at any hope of universal harmony. While the world tries its best to live God's commandments, the people breathe fear and death constantly. God must be shaking his head, "Why did I give you free will?"

Faith in the people's respective beliefs suffers because the peace that was foretold with the birth of the Lord continues to be elusive. Remember, God only promised "peace to men of goodwill."

A basic tenet of Communism is the denial of the existence of God. Russia became a nation of atheists. Finally God said, "Enough is enough." Mama Mary promised that when Russia was consecrated

The Marian Pilgrims of Bishop Raul Martirez

to her Immaculate Heart, she would bring peace. St. John Paul II led the world in prayer and peace came, uneasy though it was.

Communism has lost its foothold and its spread came to a grinding stop. But a new thinking, to live only in the present, has given birth to a new "ism," secularism, where people turn their backs on their piety; and they choose to live only in the present since secularism erases the concept of heaven and hell. Secularism does not respect any belief: Christians, Muslims, Buddhists, Taoists, and oriental mystics are all victims of secularism. Will secularism provide the impetus for all religions to unite?

Who will lead?

In Europe, a Euro-Barometer Poll was released in 2010 that focused basically on three aspects of people's frame of mind in relation to God. I did a simple averaging of the data among six countries where Christianity progressed after the resurrection of Jesus Christ. The countries with large populations like Italy, Spain, Germany, France, Portugal, Denmark, Belgium, and the United Kingdom give credence to the gathered data.

The statistics are staggering. Belief in God in these countries is 51% or just about half of the total population. Those who believe in some sort of spirit-god or life force are at 23.3% of the total population and those who no longer believe in God are at 21% of the total population; the balance is presumed to be followers of Islam.

However, the shift to secularism does not happen overnight; the change gradually sets in as the faithful is confronted with experiences and events, spread over the years that erode his faith until it comes to that point where interest in any kind of organized religion completely disappears.

The situation of my friend John points unerringly to the new enemy. He titters at the very threshold of secularism. The next progression is to question the existence of God while retaining belief in some form of life force or life spirit. According to Pope Francis, they are the agnostics not yet fully convinced that God does not exist. They are in stage of denial although they continue to do good.

From there it's a toboggan slide downhill. The agnostic graduates to atheist, fully convinced that God does not exist, but still doing good.

The final stage is when he discards all forms of holiness; and doing good is not differentiated from doing evil. At best, he takes an ambivalent view towards abortion, contraception, gay marriages, euthanasia, etc.; they have become non-issues to him. At this stage, heaven and hell are rejected; his life is wrapped around the present only. After all, life ends on earth when one dies. Nothing else follows.

Why is the world facing this new enemy?

After the crucifixion of Jesus Christ, many of his disciples lost sight of the meaning of their struggles. They had joined him on the mistaken notion that the Messiah was one who would lead armies to free them from the eagle claws of Imperial Rome. Once again, the glory of Israel would be upon them. One of the followers who gave his entire life to this belief saw no further purpose to stay in Jerusalem. But deep in his heart, he was convinced that there was a promised Messiah; but it was not the man who was crucified.

He was still out there.

Disappointed and dejected, the man left the city and embarked on a quest that would satisfy his restless spirit, searching for the man who would bring peace to the descendants of Abraham, and return once more the splendor of the time of his ancestors. The man was not unlike the two disciples of Jesus on their way to Emmaus. "That very day [the first day of the week] two of [Jesus disciples] were going to a village seven miles from Jerusalem called Emmaus... but their eyes were prevented from recognizing him" (Lk 24:13, 16).

The man, a disciple of Jesus, like him, was a Jew. He was a learned man. He had met Jesus in one of those occasions when he spoke in the synagogue. He was so mesmerized by his teaching that he joined Jesus and became one of his loyal followers. But this time he was certain that the man they called Jesus was not the promised Messiah.

The loss of his Messiah hardened the man's thinking that there was even a God; that the God of Abraham and Moses and King David was just a myth. If there were no God, maybe there was a place where people banded themselves together to live the life he was looking for...

In his quest, he met a man who similarly did not believe in God. In the case of my friend John, he still believes in God, but has left his Church. But both of them are searching for the truth. The man was looking for the Messiah and John is searching for his true Church. "But how can anyone know about truth when it is humanly impossible to exhaustively try all the alternatives?" asks my friend John.

Available numbers point to Europe as the seat of secularism where non-belief in God is searing the very hearts of people. To a man who has lost belief in God, understanding that there is God is a dim prospect. Attempts to change his thinking shall come to naught; family, friends, and those recognized as experts in the propagation of the faith shall fail and fail miserably.

But all is not lost. I just read two stories on faith: one man searching for his God, the other searching for his Church.

The man searching for his God fell in love. A beautiful girl raised and bred in the teaching of the Lord brought him up short. He marveled at her innocent acceptance that there was a God. In her naivety she would talk of the beauty of creation, of the teeming life that abounded wherever one looked; and how everything that happened in the world happened for a reason, and how only the Mighty Being knew all the reasons. Quite ingenuously, she insisted that without God the world would not even be here.

The atheist spent hours discussing the same subject with the girl, over and over. He finally admitted to himself that the girl's faith was unshakable. She told him that she knew he was looking for a reason—even one—to believe that there was a God. And she loved him for that, she confessed. She knew, too, that he was a good person. She could read his desire to want to believe that there was a God, and to do all the things she was doing for God.

For an atheist to accept God is an impossible struggle. He is convinced that God does not exist. Believing so, he has never experienced the beauty of God and the fulfilling realities, the emotion of joy, the pain of suffering, emptiness of love lost, and the triumph when God answers prayers.

But what finally convinced the man to look for God in earnest were his beloved's words spoken with finality, "You know I can't make this decision for you; you alone can face the reality that there is a God. However, you must realize that God is not going to wait for you forever. Be that as it may, I cannot also imagine the dark side waiting for you."

Those words finally jarred him to his senses. He closeted himself within himself and examined the negative reasons that convinced him there was no God. But this time, instead of searching only for the reasons why there was no God, he examined evidence that purported the existence of a God. He was a student of history, aware that mankind owed the great writers of the Gospels even if there were points of disagreement in their writings. His question, "How can anyone know about truth when it is humanly impossible to exhaustively try all the alternatives?" could be answered.

Even to the seeming disagreement among Gospel authors Matthew and Luke regarding the genealogy of Jesus, there was an answer, the man found out.

> St. Luke (2:4) says that St. Joseph went from Nazareth to Bethlehem to be enrolled, "because he was of the house and family of David." As if to exclude all doubt concerning the Davidic descent of Mary, the evangelist Luke (1:32, 69) states that the child born of Mary without the intervention of man shall be given "the throne of David his father," and that the Lord God has "raised up a horn for our salvation within the house of David his servant"...
>
> In St. Luke's genealogy, the name of Mary's father, Heli, agrees with the name given to Our Lady's father in a tradition founded upon the report of the Proto-evangelium of James, an apocryphal Gospel which dates from the end of the second century. According to this document the parents of Mary are Joachim and Anna. Now, the name *Joachim* is only a variation of *Heli* or *Eliachim*, substituting one Divine name (Yahweh) for the other (Eli, Elohim).

...As Joachim belonged to the royal family of David, so Anna is supposed to have been a descendant of the priestly family of Aaron; thus Christ the Eternal King and Priest sprang from both a royal and priestly family (*New Advent Catholic Encyclopedia*).

In addition, the *Christian Community Bible* says:

Luke then presents a list of Jesus' ancestors which is quite different from that of Matthew. Luke not only goes back to Abraham, he also supplies the legendary list of Abraham's ancestors all the way back to the first man, (Adam) as if to emphasize that Jesus comes to save all humanity. Moreover, from Joseph to Abraham, the list of ancestors varied depending on whether one counted natural parents or adopted parents, since adoption was a frequent practice among the Jews.

Both Matthew and Luke teach the same dogma: Jesus Christ as Man not only descended from Abraham, but all the way from Adam and Eve; and in his divinity, is Son of God the Father.

But where is he?

God spoke to us and we kept his words in our hearts

Love, the Language of God

Pope Francis, the man searching for his God concluded that the evidence for the existence of God as taught by the Catholic Church was there. The reality that there were good people in the Church who would help him firm up his acceptance of the presence of God was so strong that it made sense that God existed, as opposed to the idea that there was no God. Finally, he realized that he must study the teaching of his Church from a new perspective, "For we, too, are his offspring" (Acts 17:28).

He knew why: we are the offspring of Jesus Christ, born of his Church bequeathed to Peter. "And so I say to you, you are Peter, and upon this rock I will build my church, and the gates of the netherworld shall not prevail against it. I will give you the keys to the kingdom of heaven. Whatever you bind on earth shall be bound in heaven; and whatever you loose on earth shall be loosed in heaven" (Mt 16:18-19).

He realized that as God's offspring, the people were the Church— the living, moving, breathing Body of Christ. The Church was not the building, the Church was not the steeple; the Church was the people.

Then he recalled the two disciples who walked with the risen Christ on their way to Emmaus: "Oh, how foolish you are! How slow of heart to believe all that the prophets spoke! Was it not necessary that the Messiah should suffer these things and enter into his glory?" (Lk 24:25-26).

The man was the wandering Jew who finally found Jesus Christ the Messiah.

The story of my friend John, the man searching for his true Church, is different. It will be easier for him to accept that the Church is the people and being human make us prone to mistakes. Often we err unwittingly and intentional harmful acts are rare, because the people of God ideally live in the teaching of doing well to others, as they do well to you.

My friend John will come back to the fold for only one reason: the deciding factor will be the Holy Eucharist. He misses the love of his Christian community, the personal relationships which he shares with his fellow members; the knowledge that with the Eucharist one is never alone.

The Lord walked with the two disciples, as he walks with John. There is never a time when he is alone; Jesus is right beside him all the time.

It is true that there are moments when we take a misstep and seem ready to fall. But God's teaching is always there. "Put on the armor of God, that you may be able to resist on the evil day and, having done everything to hold your ground" (Eph 6:13). Author Bill Crowder of *Our Daily Bread,* gives a thoughtful meditation on this passage:

> For the last few years my wife Marlene, has suffered from inner problems that caused her to lose her equilibrium. Without warning, something inside her ear is upset and she becomes dizzy, if she tries to sit or stand, a condition called vertigo makes that impossible, and she has to lie down. No amount of effort can compensate for the power of the inner ear to disrupt and disturb. An active person Marlene finds these unwelcome episodes frustrating.
>
> Sometimes life is like that. Something unexpected upsets our routine, and we are knocked off balance. Perhaps it's bad news about our job being eliminated or disturbing test results from our doctor. It may even be attack from our spiritual enemy. In its case, our emotional equilibrium is hammered, and we feel we can't stand.

Those moments should cause us to turn to God, when we feel we are losing our balance, he can help. He provides spiritual resources to help us stand. Paul says, "Take up the whole armor of God, that you may be able to withstand in the evil day, and having done all, to stand" (Eph 6:13).

When life knocks us off our feet, we don't have to be frustrated. With God's strength lifting us up and God's armor protecting us, we can still stand strong. "We can endure anything if we depend on God for everything."

I know that John will let go of his inner controversies, and let Christ Jesus do the rest.

In the midst of the challenge of secularism, we prayed for a miracle to give us a man of goodwill to lead in this new battle. God gave us two.

Pope Emeritus Benedict XVI, who resigned his papacy, because he is no longer capable to answer the needs of the world, physically, psychologically, and emotionally, is the first miracle.

Pope Benedict XVI is a reluctant miracle. He debated with himself the impact of leaving the papacy when he was most needed. But in his humility, he realized that someone younger, charismatic, was called for, one who could best put in effect the changes he introduced to strengthen the doctrines of the Church, which at the time was being questioned as to their relevance in "modern times."

As he neared the momentous decision to leave the papacy, Pope Benedict introduced changes in the Mass that would enhance the beauty and substance of the celebration of the Eucharist. The additions, which in English amounted to five words inserted after the Eucharistic Prayer, were issued by the Vatican's Congregation for Divine Worship and the Discipline of the Sacraments. The new words, "with blessed Joseph, her spouse," follow a mention of Mary and are included in three different versions of the prayer.

However, before the changes received final approval, Pope Benedict resigned. The change reflects the Church's growing interest in "fatherly care," says the Rev. Dan Merz, associate director of the Secretariat of

Divine Worship for the United States Conference of Catholic Bishops. "It's emphasizing that St. Joseph was someone who protected the Blessed Virgin and who cared for Jesus. We call him the foster father of Jesus, but we have to think of that word in the sense that he fostered the humanity of Jesus," says Merz. "He nurtured and helped Christ grow into an adult."

To his credit, Pope Francis hasn't shied away from his own interest in St. Joseph. He chose March 19, the feast of St. Joseph, as the date for his inaugural Mass, and has a flower on his coat-of-arms symbolizing the saint. "St. Joseph appears as a strong and courageous man, a workingman, yet in his heart we see great tenderness, which is not the virtue of the weak, but rather a sign of strength of spirit and a capacity for concern, for compassion, for genuine openness to others, for love," Pope Francis said at his inaugural Mass.

Pope Francis approved the change in the Catholic Mass to include prayers referring to St. Joseph.

The election of Pope Francis, the Pope who came from the ends of the earth, is God's gift of a second miracle.

His first statement is to bring back the Church to the poor in spirit and substance. The world is living in an imbalance. The rich get richer and the poor get poorer. This imbalance causes hunger and uneasiness of the spirit, hunger and uneasiness that lead to all form of negative "isms."

Jesus Christ wanted to be born among the shepherds, the poor, and the downtrodden. He wanted to bring balance to the world. His message is clear but the world responded with deaf ears.

Pope Francis, you rekindled that message. We have to bring the Church to the poor. Lip service is not enough. You say, *"Sure, we donate to charity. But this is not enough. Commitment to the poor must be "person to person, in the flesh. It is not enough to mediate this commitment through institutions, which obviously help because they have a multiplying effect, but that is not enough. They do not excuse us from our establishing personal contact with the needy. The sick must be cared for, even when we find them repulsive and repugnant. Those in prison must be visited."*

Pope Francis, you called for long-term commitment. *"Hospitality in itself isn't enough. It's not enough to give a sandwich if it isn't accompanied by the possibility of learning to stand on one's own feet. Charity that does not change the situation of the poor isn't enough."*

God loves the poor. He also loves the rich, the rich who are men of goodwill.

You defined your papacy with your first exhortation, *Evangelii Gaudium* or "Joy of the Gospel." Your *Evangelii Gaudium* comes alive among ordinary people living ordinary lives. They are people who continue the faith of Jesus as he intended, people who belong in other Christian churches but still living his teaching, and people who live his faith away from the Church that he built.

He does not distinguish people on the basis of their religion. He brings them all to his kingdom. It does not matter whether you are a Christian, Jew, Muslim, Buddhist, Taoist, including atheist. He loves them all.

Pope Francis, be forewarned that there are those who twist your pronouncements to fit their personal agenda. Take the case of our country's Reproductive Health (RH) Law. The Supreme Court (SC) has finally approved it last April 8, 2014. Before this, though, the SC had issued Temporary Restraining Order to stop its implementation. Some corners have resorted to stretching the interpretation of your own words to convince the highest court of the land to declare the law constitutional. One of these glib lobbyists is a Mary Racelis, a research scientist of the Institute of Philippine Culture. She published her commentary in the *Philippine Daily Inquirer*, a leading newspaper, conveniently quoting you to persuade the magistrates to favor the law: "We appeal to those still uncertain justices to study Francis' *Evangelii Gaudium*, the 'Joy of the Gospel,' sometimes called the 'Magna Carta for Church Reform.' In it, Francis urges every bishop to internalize the 'desire to listen to everyone and not simply to those who would tell him what he wants to hear.' Further, the Church must be 'in contact with the homes and the lives of its people' and 'practice the art of listening, which is more than hearing' and work on 'above all—allowing the flock to strike out new paths'…

"Any justices still apprehensive that a pro-RH vote may contradict their Catholic roots can take heart in Francis' reform mission."

Pope Francis, the tentacles of secularism have already reached out deep and wide among the people. Your role of spreading the teaching of Jesus as he intended, is shrugged off as having of little consequence; in fact, your very words have been cleverly manipulated to accommodate the wishes of the evil one.

But all is not lost. The Supreme Court struck out eight provisions of the law anathema to the teaching of the Church even as they allowed the other provisions, though in essence making it a lame-duck law.

I don't know, Pope Francis; in times like this, I find solace and refuge in the writings of great poets so as not to lose myself in the sea of indifference and just raise my hands in surrender and give up.

I am reminded of the Lebanese poet, Khalil Gibran, who published the book, *The Prophet*.

In the book, the poet tells of a wise old man who brings justice and love to a small place. He has stayed in the place for a long time and was yearning to return to his home. The story goes that "Almustafa, the chosen and the beloved, who was a dawn into his own day, had waited twelve years in the city of Orphalese... One day, he climbed the hill without the city walls and looked seawards; and beheld his ship coming with the mist...

"And when he entered into the city to leave, all came to meet him, and they were crying out to him as if with one voice... Then said Almitra, the Sheerest, 'Speak to us of love...'

> 'Love gives naught but itself and takes naught from itself. Love possesses not nor would it be possessed; for love is sufficient unto love. When you love, you should not say, *God is in my heart* but rather, *I am in the heart of God*. And think not you can direct the course of love, for love, if it finds you worthy, directs your course......
>
> 'Love has no other desire but to fulfill itself. But if you love and must needs have desires, let this be your desires: to melt and be like running brook that sings its melody to the night, to

know the pain of too much tenderness, to be wounded by your own understanding of love; and to bleed willingly and joyfully, to wake at dawn with a winged heart and give thanks for another day of loving.

'To rest at the noon hour and meditate love's ecstasy, to return home at eventide with gratitude, and then to sleep with a prayer for the beloved in your heart and a song of praise upon your lips…' "

This then is the love Jesus has for us, and much, much more… the love he wants to give us. This love asks of us to walk with him… to walk with God.

Sr. Teresita Castillo, the visionary, dressed in black, at the right of the priest

Mama Mary in Lipa

The people are praying that the VATICAN will finally approve the apparition of MARY MEDIATRIX OF ALL GRACE

Pope Francis, you have large shoulders and sturdy legs. You look as tall, big, and determined as St. Peter who evangelized the first Christians. You are both big men because Jesus needs big men to carry his love and share it with the world.

The other night, as I settled in to end the day, I recalled an article I wrote for ST PAULS *Homelife* Magazine. We visited America just after terrorism was brought to its shores in a magnitude no one could ever imagine. Even then secularism reared its ugly head.

Thank God for Little Joys

We are now days into our vacation here in the US. Our last visit was three years ago just before the attack on the twin towers. That fateful day brought a lot of changes in this land of milk and honey and one can sense right away the difference. The entry check at customs now includes photo-shoot and instant fingerprinting. The interviews are more thorough though they continue to be courteous. The lines have become longer because of the new procedures enforced. Plastic containers are handed down to each passenger as you get to the first electronic watch dog. Your things pass through the x-ray machine which includes every metal the machines can sense. Then they ask you to walk through an arch-way with all the lights blinking and a metal detector waiting to blast as soon as they sense anything metallic in your body. That's when things really become interesting. You are taken out of the line and body-checked. You are asked to spread-eagle your arms while another handheld detector goes through you. Not satisfied, they ask you courteously to take off your blazer, your shoes, and your belt. Another officer picks them up for a visit once again to that darn x-ray machine. Not happy with nothing to show for all those searches, they list down your name and everything else they need before letting you go.

The Americans love the security check. It gives them a sense of freedom, freedom from fear to do what they please. But they will never be able to live down the threat of Osama Bin Laden right after 9/11, *"America will never be the same again. The Americans will find that they will be living in constant fear from now on,"* he boldly announced. And that fear is never more seen than in the way they put people to security checks in the airports.

Finally, you feel alive again. But it is a cautious feeling. America has changed. The feeling that America is invincible is not there anymore. 9/11 has changed all that.

But still life outside the airport is great. Once again the wonder of progress greets. The highways are not only wider but it seems new ones keep sprouting. More commercial centers are popping left and right and endless rows of well-located stores are waiting for the dollar burning in your pocket, to get into the register machines of the Nordstrom's and the Foleys and the Macys and all the factory outlets waiting along the highways.

The taste of French fries and burgers in McDonalds seems different. The fries are huge and they serve them in sizes you cannot finish. In the US, there are no regular fries, everything is served big. My grandson Diego will have a feast with their serving. Back home, he always double his orders, double chicken nuggets, double large fries, double Sprite. He just doubles them because their sizes leave him craving for more. Not in America. I double-dare him to double his orders here!

The one thing I love in my visit here is a trip to my favorite French restaurant, Jack-in-the-Box (fast food *ito*, guys!). Oh! But their spicy chicken really tastes nice. There's nothing that tastes like that in Manila. The veggies that go with the sandwich cracks in your bite, how fresh can you get!

And their serving will last you up to the next meal. The only other fast food center where they serve coffee that I love as in McDonalds is here in Jack-in-the-Box.

Some of you may think, *"Ang babaw naman ng kaligayahan mo."* But you know what? These are the small things that we enjoy day in and day out and never gave it a second thought.

When I was younger, I dream of what the rich and the famous do. Play golf at St. Andrews, place a bet at the roulette tables in Monte Carlo, make that drive in my Alfa Romeo across the mountains of Switzerland, and smell the mountain air we can only dream about. One needs money to do all these things. Yet, now that I have enough to afford these things, they don't seem that important anymore.

Now, I find being able to make an hour's walk without losing my breath more exhilarating, finishing a nice book invigorating, and making my regular appointment with Jesus in the morning Mass making my day. My taste has mellowed. I used to think that having a glass of wine with my meal makes me cultured. I pretend that Winston Churchill and I are sitting across each other on the veranda having coffee and me savoring a feeling of class. I have given up that wishful thinking. They were never really a part of me anyway.

Don't get me wrong. I don't mean to belittle those who go through life enjoying these things. But now I realize that I want to be as simple and as less pretentious as my wife. She finds everyone a close friend even as she meets each person only for the first time, where the flowering of her roses and the greening of her lawns are the pleasures of her days, where the smile of a child is an encouragement to share, and the many joys that she has, the little things that makes her life so full and satisfying completing her day.

While in my younger days traveling was an expensive way for us to know more of the world, today, the nuances of travel has change.

Travel is no longer limited to the well-to-do and the intellectuals who receive grants to do such explorations. For travel is no longer limited to actual, physical eyeballing of the things you want to see. A good book has the power to bring you to the most exotic places imaginable. Even as I write, my grandson Diego just entered the website of Niagara Falls and he is having a grand time viewing the still and moving pictures of the magnificent shots of the fall. He is lucky because in this particular link, he got himself connected to an audio-video guided tour of the Niagara. I can tell you that he learned more on that ten-minute video than I did when my family and I actually went to see the site a few years back.

And so let's not have the excuse that knowledge through travel may be limiting to those without funds because technology has caught up with us and travel can now be done through the cyber world. As far as I am concerned the world has shrunk and only those who see excuses as an achievement are content to doing nothing else.

And so for whatever it is worth, I now find the small things meaningful, the lowliest person interesting, and an ordinary day a day of bliss. And once again, thank God for small things!

Pope Francis, the small things are getting away from us. They are losing their meaning because the Christian values we share are under siege. The enemy, secularism, knocks insistently at the door!

You have always walked with God and in my heart you are the leader who will show us the way and stay the onslaught of secularism. In my many crises in the past when the devil seemed to be winning the minds of the people, Mama Mary always comes to our succor.

There is a growing movement in our country which begun in 1948. The apparition in spite of the Vatican's negative reception to the unfolding events, continues to grow. The Confraternity of Mary Mediatrix of All Grace was founded by Rev. Fr. Melvin P. Castro, based in the Bishop's residence in Tarlac City, Philippines. Membership to the confraternity is expanding by leaps and bounds.

Authentic documents trace the events that recall the apparition of our Mother. A young postulant, Teresita Castillo, in Mt. Carmel

Church in Lipa, Batangas was visited by Mama Mary. She introduced herself as Our Lady Mediatrix of All Grace.

When the young postulant was interviewed by Bishop Alfredo Versoza and his Auxiliary, Bishop Alfredo Maria Obviar, she was asked the question, "Why is the title of our Lady, Mediatrix of All Grace, shouldn't she carry the title 'of All Graces' meaning plural and not, 'of All Grace,' which is singular?" This question emanates from her title of the liturgical feast instituted by Pope Benedict XV in January 21, 1921 where she was proclaimed Mediatrix of All Graces.

Of course, the young postulant simply said, it was the title given by our Lady. The bishops requested that when the Mother comes again to talk to her, to please request for an explanation, which the young postulant did.

When she came back to report to the bishops, the explanation is so clear in its simplicity. Our Lady said, "The title of 'All Grace' refers to my Son, he is the One of All Grace. He gave me the title Our Lady of All Grace so I can carry my Son with me all the time."

Bishop Ramon Arguelles, current Bishop of Batangas, added this explanation: "Since grace is defined as a participation in the divine nature, it is theologically correct to refer to the source, the divinity itself, as 'All Grace.' Mary, a finite being, is full of the grace she received, as a glass is full of the water poured into it. Since the fullness of the divinity is in Jesus, Mary is therefore the Mediatrix of Jesus, the Mediatrix of All Grace."

The bishop once more asked, "What does our Lady want of us?"

Dr. Francisco Villanueva Jr., in his book, *The Wonders of Lipa* detailed the instruction of our Mother to Teresita:

On Friday, November 12, 1948, after Mass, the sister was called to the place of the Apparition and there on the vine was Mary, Mediatrix of All Grace. Her hands joined on her breast in an attitude of prayer. She looked tenderly but sadly on her little one and on the Community that followed.

Then she said: *"People believe not my words. Pray my child, pray much because of persecution. Pray for priests. What I asked here is exactly what I asked at Fatima. Tell this to the people. They don't believe in me nor do they give what I ask. Tell the sisters that I ask them to pray and help spread my devotion and to make penances to those who don't believe. When people come to pray and ask for graces, let them ask directly to me and not through you. These things may now be revealed. This is my last apparition in this spot."*

Blessing her little one and the Community assembled in the sacred place, Mary, Mediatrix of All Grace, vanished.

The Mother said, "The people must follow the prescription of St. Louis de Monfort to do 33 days devotion to her, Our Lady of All Grace, and on the 34th day, we will be totally consecrated to Jesus through Mary, individually and not as a group.

Why is the Mother asking for this consecration?

Even during that time, year 1948, Jesus knows that secularism is coming in the future. That early, God knows that should we consecrate ourselves to Jesus through Mary, and this ugly enemy of the Church will not come to pass.

However, the Vatican curtailed all belief in the apparition of Our Lady of Mediatrix of All Grace. The young postulant was dismissed from the congregation; the bishops were removed from the diocese to make sure none of the vestiges of the apparition will be remembered by the people. And yet, to no one's surprise, pilgrimages to our Lady did not stop. They continue to be robust these days.

The Catholic Bishops' Conference of the Philippines has placed its imprimatur on this apparition with prayers for recognition from the Vatican. As I write, our parishioners are undergoing the 33 days preparation. We know that the strongest weapon we can use to combat secularism is our faith and prayers to the Lord and our Mother.

Our Mother has deemed that it is time that the world, beginning with the people of the Philippines, totally consecrates us individually to Jesus through Mary following the formula prescribed by St. Louis de Monfort. The Lord Jesus Christ wants personal consecration as different from the consecration he asked for Russia. In Matthew 11:25—"at that time Jesus said in reply, 'I give praise to you, Father, Lord of heaven and earth, for although you have hidden these things from the wise and the learned you have revealed them to the childlike. ' "

Unknown to me, my friend John was in Lipa during one of the events that transpired in there. He was barely ten years old then.

He and his mother were living with his uncle whose wife was a devout Catholic. As far as John can remember, his aunt (in-law) has not missed joining any of the processions held in honor of St. Anthony of the Singalong Parish, Our Lady of Remedios of Malate Church, and Sto. Sepulchro in Paco, Manila. All of these churches were within less than ten kilometers where John's uncle resided.

When the aunt heard about the "happenings" in Lipa, Batangas, she hastily organized a pilgrimage to Lipa among their family members. The agitation of the party was lost to John and to his cousin, the eldest of his uncle's children who is ten years old like him. It seems odd but the ten-year-olds then were not as "knowledgeable and aware" as the ten-year-olds of the present day.

John's party arrived in Lipa early enough to locate themselves at the head of the growing crowd. Directly in front of them was a window at the second floor of the dormitory where a postulant was reported to have been receiving messages from the Holy Mother.

After the Mass, the recitation of the Holy Rosary started. In the middle of the decade, someone in the crowd agitatedly exclaimed, "... ang rosas, ang rosas!" Virtual bedlam ensued as people jostled. Not long after, order was restored but the crowd would not quiet down. From the din, John could only make out, "Milagro, milagro, being blurted out repeatedly.

In the rented van on the way back to Manila, John was a puzzled audience to the animated exchanges among his co-passengers. "Mayroon ba kayong nakitang milagro? (Have you witnessed a miracle)?" someone asked.

"Aside from the mob-like commotion, nothing," replied another.

"Parang may pinag-aagawan ang mga tao (It appeared to me that they were fighting for something)."

Then John butted in, "*Ako nakita ko kung ano ang kanilang pinag-aagawan* (I saw what the people were fighting for). *Mukhang mga flower petals!*"

His puzzled aunt retorted, "*Baka naman mga dahon mula sa mga puno ang nakita mo!* (You must have seen leaves being blown loose from the trees)!"

John replied with sureness in his voice, "*Hindi po.* (No, Ma'am), I saw the petals coming from the space some distance from the room where the postulant was said to be in. *Parang* magic (It's like magic)!"

"Showers of rose petals" was the common enough news even at the start of the reported miracles in Lipa City. A few individuals claimed that they were able to obtain such petals during their pilgrimage to the site. Further, the petals allegedly have the imprint of the Holy Mother's image.

The flower rose and the color blue are closely associated with the Holy Virgin Mary. When she appeared at Lourdes, she had a blue sash around her waist. The language of flowers suggests that roses stand for love and beauty—significant attributes of the Holy Virgin. Respected in the Catholic Church, the rose was used for ceremonial purposes. In fact, it is reported that the original rosaries were made of rosebuds and dried rose petals formed into a string of beads that were extremely fragrant. In olden times, dried rose petals were used to fill mattresses, which is where we get the expression, "sleeping on a bed of roses."

Yet, when we look at the many apparitions of the Blessed Mother, several things are in common: water, roses, and children. In Guadalupe, water and roses were the significant signs of our Mother. So, too, in Lourdes where the baths continue to bring miracles to the believers and, of course in Fatima the children were significantly present together with roses and water.

And there is more to come.

The Awesome Pope

John couldn't help relating another experience he had, this time directly with the Sto. Niño.

Again, his uncle's wife, upon hearing the "miraculous black-and-white picture," gathered the household members for another pilgrimage to nearby Sampaloc district in Manila. Here in a very modest house in a crowded neighborhood, a picture of the Sto. Niño—the Holy Child—was reported to become animated right before the eyes of the crowd.

When John's group arrived at the site, the living room, where the picture was located, was almost filled with people. At one end of the room was a table covered with a white embroidered cloth. On top was a crucifix against which the black-and-white picture was propped up. It was a simple 5 x 7-inch print and not framed. It was simply leaning against the cross with no visible support of any kind. A whiff of a breeze would have been enough to blow away the picture, a reason that there was no electric fan installed in the room, someone explained.

Not long after, *Aling* Idad, an elderly woman, obviously the owner of the house, stood before the crowd whom she invited to join in the recitation of the Holy Rosary. She also made the long-awaited announcement which attracted people to flock into her house. She claimed that the picture on the altar is miraculous. A "believer who prays in front of the altar may ask the Sto. Niño, the Child Jesus, to grant her petition."

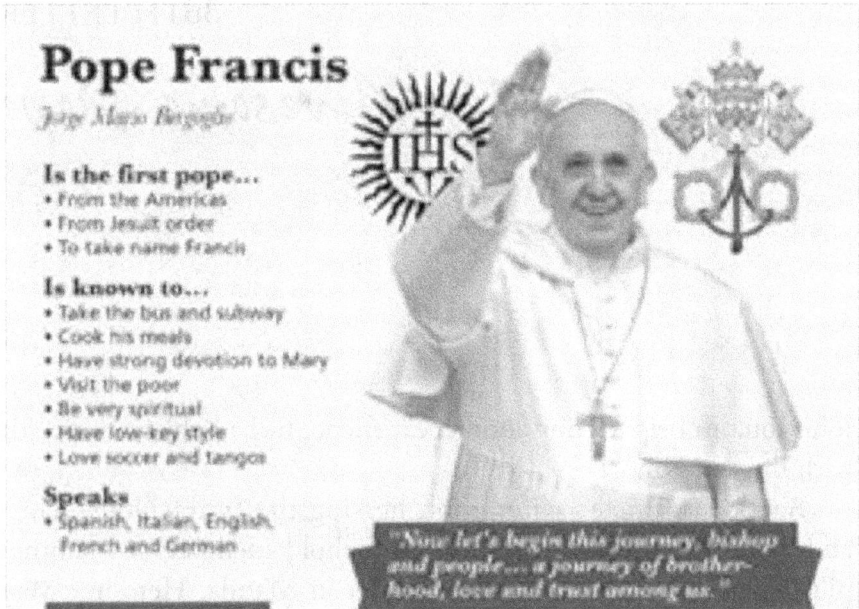

Pope Francis

Jorge Mario Bergoglio

Is the first pope...
- From the Americas
- From Jesuit order
- To take name Francis

Is known to...
- Take the bus and subway
- Cook his meals
- Have strong devotion to Mary
- Visit the poor
- Be very spiritual
- Have low-key style
- Love soccer and tangos

Speaks
- Spanish, Italian, English, French and German

"Now let's begin this journey, bishop and people... a journey of brotherhood, love and trust among us."

As reported by Pew Research Center

She added, "The picture will give you a subtle hint—yes or no. But you will have to pray from your heart extra hard."

On the way back home, there was an air of disappointment in the conversation among his aunt and the other "pilgrims." *"Mayroon ba kayong nakitang kakaiba sa bahay ni Aling Idad?* (Have you witnessed anything odd in the house of Aling Idad)?"

Aside from the remark—*"Parang may konting paggalaw noong litrato* (The picture seemed to move a little), they were unanimous with their *"Wala!* (Nothing)!"

John was about to butt in but decided against saying anything. His Nanay has always admonished him not to join in an adult conversation—*"usapan ng matatanda."*

The significant impact of what he witnessed when the Holy Rosary was being recited in Aling Idad's house was completely lost to the seven-year old John, until much later.

Heeding the advice of Aling Idad, John, with uncluttered and simple-minded innocence prayed, *"Habaan po ninyo sana ang buhay ng Nanay ko.* (Please give my Mom long life)."

A few seconds later, John noticed that the picture started to move, initially tentatively, then as if someone was manipulating it, it began to roll unto itself. (Think of an architect or a draftsman rolling his manuscript then inserting it into a hard blue tube for filing away.) After the picture was completely rolled, it laid like a tube in front of the crucifix where earlier it was standing as a sheet.

Then in a very short while, the rolled picture started to unroll, again by itself, until it once again became a flat sheet of ordinary picture leaning against the crucifix!

John's attention was plastered on what he saw.

Moments later, the picture, this time in its usual sheet form, again started to move. Then the upper edge was moving towards the opposite end until the picture assumed the position of a folded paper. Then slowly the two joined edges begun to separate until the picture has become a sheet once again.

He prayed for a long life for his Nanay. His Nanay passed on 60 long years later.

"Rudy, how could my companions have missed the movements of the picture? Aling Idad's place was well lighted and we were not even five feet away from the makeshift altar where the picture was," John told me.

Then with a visibly worried look, he continued, "Were those real miracles I was privileged to witness, my close encounters with the heavenly? Or were they devices used by the devil for his purpose?"

"John, I believe that what you experienced was similar to mine during our recent pilgrimage to Lourdes in France. I know you remember my encounter with our Mother in her baths. It kept me thinking for days. I found the answer when we were in Fatima. It was Pope Benedict XVI and St. John Paul II who gave me the insights as I read it in the book of Sister Lucia, one of the children in the apparition of Fatima. Pope Benedict XVI and St. John Paul II simply defined the meaning of private revelation and gave credence to personal encounters with the Lord."

Pope Francis, you always walk with God. You are the leader that God gave us. And if it is the first time for us to walk with God, please let us walk with you.

We want to walk with God from now on. Here is a song that Mario Lanza sang in the movie, *The Prince*. The lyrics are full of meaning and described the Prince pleading to God to guide him as he assumes the kingship of their kingdom.

I'll walk with God

I'll walk with God from this day on.
His helping hand, I'll lean upon.

This is my prayer, my humble plea.
May the Lord be ever with me.

There is no death, though eyes grow dim.
There is no fear when I'm near to him.
I'll lean on him forever
and he'll forsake me never.
He will not fail me
as long as my faith is strong,
whatever road I may walk along.

I'll walk with God, I'll take his hand,
I'll talk with God, He'll understand.
I'll pray to him, each day and every day
and he'll hear the words that I say.

I will never walk alone.
If you guide me to your eternal throne,
even as you prod me gently with your rod,
when I walk with you, my God.

We will walk with God, braced with his inexhaustible mercy... "How good to come back to him whenever we are lost. God never tires of forgiving us; we are the ones who get tired of seeking his mercy. The Eucharist, although it is the fullness of sacramental life, is not a prize for the perfect but a powerful medicine and nourishment for the weak."

Pope Francis, as I was putting the final touches of this page, a report came out in the front page of the largest broadsheet in our country.

The Pew Research Center, a highly respected research institution in America, did a poll among Americans to measure Pope Francis' first year performance on a number of issues. The poll was conducted from February 14-23, 2014 among 1,821 adults. The result was measured with margin of error of 3% plus or minus and 6% for subgroup of 351 Catholics. The following data is generally in favor of the Pope, considering the negative projection of the Catholic Church to the general public in the light of scandals that have been haunting the Church for several years now.

71% of respondents see the Pope representing major change by 2050 in the following areas:
1. 6 of every 10 Americans expect the lifting on the prohibition of birth control
2. 50% of respondents would allow priests to marry
3. 40% of respondents want the Church to ordain women as priests
4. 50% of Americans expect the Church to recognize same-sex marriage

The Pope is seen doing well on the following priority issues:
1. 81% see the Pope doing well in spreading the Catholic faith
2. 76% see the Pope addressing the need and concern of the poor
3. 62% see the Pope doing well in overhauling the Vatican bureaucracy
4. 54% see the Pope doing good in correcting the problem of sex abuse scandal

5. 40% of respondents are seen praying more often
6. 25% of respondents say that American Catholics have increased enthusiasm for their faith
7. 22% of respondents say that the number of church attendance did not increase. However, Rev. Thomas Reese, a senior analyst at the *National Catholic* Reporter, said that since church attendance has been declining since the 1950s, this is a victory.

Sr. Mary Ann Walsh, Director of Media Relations for the American Conference of Catholic Bishops, reported anecdotal evidence of fuller church attendance, increase in church donations, increase in number of people going back to confession.

VIVA POPE FRANCIS!

The War We Must Win

I saw an old movie last night.

Set in the muddy trenches of World War I and filmed in period black-and-white, the movie has a plot that revolves around leaders of contrasting personalities and how each responds to a crisis.

For almost a year the Germans continue to frustrate the French Army's attempt to capture a hill again and again. The politicians want the war to end. Media is at the back of the generals to capture the hill once and for all. The chief of staff is a manipulative leader who dangles the glory of promotion and fame to his regimental commander. He knows that it is an impossible task but they have to please the politicians and the media.

The soldiers of the battalion ordered to take the hill are exhausted, hungry, and practically nearing the end of their courage. Their battalion size is cut to half by the rain of bullets coming from the German machine gun. They fight like wounded bulls. When the bugle sounds, the captain is the first to advance. His foot is first to leave the trenches. When the call to fall back is heard, his back protects his retreating men.

The order is given again. Attack at all cost, no quarter given to the enemies. The men know the order is futile. There is no replacement and their canteen is almost dry. Worst, they are counting their bullets. Still, when their captain blows the whistle, they are there with him. Understandably, a portion of the force refuses to attack. It is a stupid order. They are being sacrificed for the glory of their regimental commander. Again the attack fails.

But this time there is hell to pay. The regimental commander wants to save face. His men fail and they suffer for it. There is an order for a court martial. The captain is ordered to pick three men to face the trial, a trial that will end in an execution. The captain refuses. He challenges his superior to give his men a chance. He will defend them.

The trial is rigged. It is a Kangaroo court. The men have no chance at all. In his final act of frustration, the captain offers his life for his men. There is no way the officer corps will accept his offer. It will be an indictment of their stupidity.

The men are placed before the firing squad. Before the order to shoot is given, one of the prisoners asks to speak. He shouts, "Do not grieve for us; grieve for those who allowed this mockery of justice to happen, for today they killed freedom."

"Fire!" is the last word that everyone hears.

What is the message of this story? Not all are meant to be leaders, more so, the kind of leader in our story. He is someone who faces danger to shield his men, a leader who inspires, but, above all, a leader willing to die for his men.

Leaders are only as strong as the people he leads. When people are weak and refuse to lift a finger to help, it is best to let that group, or battalion, or corporation to collapse. Close it and build from its ashes.

Leadership is service, a sacrifice. Like the director in a movie, when the reviews are good, the actors and actresses bask in the glory of its triumph. The film director? Who cares, that's what he's expected to do. Ah! But when the movie fails in the box office, the director is the only one blamed.

Is that fair? If we all agree that we share equal responsibility in making any organization succeed, then we should offer the same, if not more, sacrifices as that of the leader. For that is what leadership is all about.

Behind the concept of leadership is motivation. The leader starts with himself. If he is not motivated to conquer the challenge at hand, in all likelihood his people will be weak. A motivated subordinate does

(Photo taken from Lee Drew)

World War I: Battlefield Action

not see a boss at his back because what he sees is a leader who trusts him and gives him empowerment. What a subordinate does on his own time, like tending roses on weekends without anyone urging him to do so, is the measure of what a truly motivated subordinate is all about. He does it without threats, exhortation, or cajolery from anyone.

The leader is no different from his people. He knows it. The people's motivation derives from him. He knows that motivation is a positive process of the mind which cannot be bought with money or promise of promotion.

In the words of Peter Drucker, the management guru,

> Leadership is responsibility. All the effective leaders I have encountered... both those I worked with and those I merely watched... knew four simple things: a leader is someone who has followers; popularity is not leadership, results are; leaders are

highly visible, they set examples; leadership is not rank, privilege, titles, or money, it is responsibility.

When I was in my final high school years, our excellent history teacher… himself a badly wounded war veteran… told each of us to pick several of a whole spate of history books on World War I and write a major essay on our selections. When we then discussed these essays in class, one of my fellow students said, "Every one of these books says that the Great War was a war of total military incompetence. Why was it?"

Our great teacher did not hesitate and shot right back, "Because not enough generals were killed; they stayed way behind the lines and let others do the fighting and dying."

Effective leaders delegate, but they do not delegate the one thing that will set the standards. They do it.

The story you read is fictional. But it became the paper discussed in one of the classes of Peter Drucker, a renowned management guru. The conclusion which the class arrived at on the issue of military incompetence of the French army was: "because not enough generals were killed; they stayed way behind the lines and let others do the fighting and dying."

The story penetrates the very essence of the price of leadership. Effective leadership takes a lot of sacrifices. In war, the troops gain courage when they see their commanders dying with them in the field of battle. The price of glory is leaders dying for their men.

As children of God, we find out how to determine the best way to heaven. It is difficult to grasp even as the Church is not lacking in leadership in the face of obstacles thrown by the devil. Luke 12:56-58 says, "You hypocrites! You know how to interpret the appearance of the earth and the sky; why do you not know how to interpret the present time? Why do you not judge for yourselves what is right? If you are to go with your opponent before a magistrate, make an effort to settle the matter on the way; otherwise your opponent will turn you over to the judge, and the judge hand you over to the constable, and the constable throw you into prison."

The kingdom of heaven is within you. Let everyone then wisely receive the admonitions of the Master that he may not lose the season of the mercy of the Savior, which is now being dealt out, as long as the human race is spared. ... What is more fragile than a vessel of glass? And yet it is kept, and lasts for ages. For though the chances of a fall are feared for the vessel of glass, yet there is no fear of fever or old age for it. We then are more fragile and more infirm; because all the chances which are incessant in human things, we doubtless through our frailness are in daily dread of; and if these chances come not, yet time goes on; a man avoids this stroke, can he avoid his end? He avoids accidents which happen from without; can that which is born within be driven away? (*New Advent Catholic Encyclopedia*).

Let us see how this fragility happens in ordinary life and how a church leader shows the right way.

Jesus Christ's death paid for our sins

The author praying the Rosary at Fatima

The War for Heaven

Pope Francis, in a recent *Huffington Post* article, author Rea Nola Martin accepts the label "cafeteria Catholic" (what Luis Cardinal Tagle calls "practicing atheist") with confidence and pride. However, Fr. Brandon Vogt encourages her to leave the cafeteria and discover the heavenly banquet. Let us follow the writings of Fr. Brandon and his "dialogue" with Ms. Martin:

> The phrase "cafeteria Catholic" refers to a baptized Catholic who doesn't embrace everything that the Church teaches—someone who picks and chooses, *a la carte* (hence "cafeteria"), from among the Church's moral rules, rubrics, and spiritual norms.

Many "cafeteria Catholics" are the products of bad catechesis. They disobey certain Church teachings because they're simply not aware of them. Others reject difficult rules because they've never heard them presented in a coherent, persuasive way, seeing them more as restrictive as keys to flourishing. But this doesn't describe Rea Nola Martin. If we're to believe her account in the *Huffington Post*, she's well aware of what the Church teaches and why. She has "studied the mystics and read the *Summa* by Thomas Aquinas just for fun." She has "read

the entire Bible more than once and the Gnostic gospels, too."
This, according to her, explains the primary reason why she's a "cafeteria
Catholic": *because of Jesus.*

Martin: Although I have studied and admired many a spiritual
master, Christ is my go-to. He's the one whom I look
to for spiritual guidance, inspiration, counsel, and
redemption. He's the inner voice I check-in with all
day long. That's why I'm a cafeteria Catholic.

Fr. Brandon: No serious Catholic would disagree with her first
three sentences. Christ is the beginning and end of
everything that the Church believes. However, it's
not immediately clear how one jumps from valuing
Christ to ignoring what his Church teaches, since
the two are a package deal (Jesus said to his apostles,
"Whoever hears you hears me."). Martin spends the
rest of her article defending that leap. Unfortunately,
her reasons are so packed with misunderstandings
and confused assumptions, it would be impossible to
engage every point within this short post. I'll attempt
only to tackle her most pertinent comments.

Martin: If there's one thing Christ taught me, it's to challenge
the status quo.

Fr. Brandon: Perhaps in her comprehensive journey through the
Bible, Martin missed Jesus' teachings on salvation,
charity, prayer, enemy, love, marriage, sacrifice,
church discipline, community, evangelization, and
discipleship, and that explains why the one thing
Jesus taught her is anti-establishment activism. And
it also might explain what comes next.

Martin: To that point, Christ redressed the corruptive socio-political norms of his own religion. He befriended the disenfranchised, worked on the Sabbath, and upended the tables of the money changers. Christ was a cafeteria Jew.

Fr. Brandon: Her point seems to be, "Hey, Jesus ignored some religious teachings, so why can't I?!" Before following that logic, however, we should keep two important facts in mind. First, Jesus is the Son of God; Martin is not. As the Second Person of the Trinity, Jesus had the unique authority to fulfill, extend, or revamp any part of his own divine law. It's his prerogative, and until Martin becomes the Fourth Person of the Holy Quadrinity, it is one she doesn't share. Also, Jesus was less a "cafeteria Jew" than a Jewish culinarian. He didn't pick and choose what food to eat; he cooked the food, and chose which to serve. By placing him on the wrong side of the serving counter, Martin reduces Jesus to just one more religious patron among others. After her weak defense of Christ as "a cafeteria Jew," Martin then gets to the meat of her article. She lists four Catholic teachings which she is happy to pass in the cafeteria line. Let's examine each one.

Martin: I find it impossible to swallow the Catholic Church's stance on women as unqualified or inappropriate for the deaconate or priesthood. Back in the day, women were suppressed and uneducated. Now they're not. In fact, the latest statistics in the United States show that women are more educated than men. Notwithstanding the superior education, I challenge a single parish to stay open without the women whose hard work and spirituality enable the communities to exist. And with the dwindling male priesthood, how will the Church possibly continue without opening its priesthood to over 50 percent of its population? And if they continue to dismiss them, how many women of succeeding generations will stay?

Fr. Brandon: There's much to embrace here. For example, no Catholic would doubt the indispensable role that women have played and continue to play within the Church. Nobody is suggesting that women stop working at parishes, dioceses, ministries, etc. The opening paragraphs of Pope John Paul's *Letter to Women* offer a litany of praise and thanks for women, and he devoted another apostolic letter, *Mulieris Dignitatum*, to their dignity and vocation. However, this section contains some major misunderstandings. The most serious is that education is the primary qualifier for the priesthood, as if the Church delineates candidates by IQ level. While it's true that priestly candidates must endure a rigorous formation program, priests are not judged and accepted by intellect alone. A good priest is not one that simply "knows a lot of stuff." A good priest images Jesus Christ, acting in his person—including his gender—to help parishioners encounter the true High Priest. It's also ironic that after earlier claiming "Christ is my go-to [whom] I look to for spiritual guidance," Martin rejects his lead on exclusively ordaining male disciples. That makes her less a "cafeteria Catholic" and more a "cafeteria follower of Christ." The Church can always do more to ennoble women and promote their great dignity, but that doesn't require ordaining them to the priesthood any more than ennobling men requires them getting pregnant.

Martin: I also find it impossible to accept the position of the Catholic Church on gays and lesbians, that gays and lesbians are not only undeserving of the dignity of marriage, but of relationships period. That sticks in my throat. By accident of my birth and gender orientation, I am granted a life of dignity and acceptance, while others are not? This kind of bias presupposes that homosexuality is a choice, which contemporary evidence shows that it clearly is not. Anyone who knows gay people (most of us) understands that. I'm pretty sure that Christ would pass on this item, too.

Fr. Brandon: While Martin claims to "find it impossible to accept the position of the Catholic Church on gays and lesbians," it's not clear that she actually understands that position. In other words, she's rejecting a straw man that I and other Catholics would swiftly reject, too. For instance, Martin insinuates that the Catholic Church teaches that gays and lesbians are "undeserving of... relationships period." If this were true, I would just as vigorously protest. But it's not. Perhaps in her comprehensive reading, Martin missed the *Catechism*'s definitive section on homosexuality (*CCC* 2357-2359), but it does not condemn "relationships period" among people with same-sex attraction. In fact, it explicitly encourages chaste, life-giving friendships.

Martin also suggests that the Church doesn't grant homosexual people "a life of dignity or choice," a strange claim since, again, the *Catechism* expressly notes "[Homosexuals] must be accepted with respect, compassion, and sensitivity. Every sign of unjust discrimination in their regard should be avoided" (*CCC* 2358). The Catholic Church remains the greatest defender of the dignity of all people, regardless of gender, age, religion, or sexual orientation. Finally and most seriously, Martin doesn't distinguish between same-sex attraction and same-sex activity. For instance, she suggests "homosexuality" is not a choice, which may be true if she's referring to same-sex attraction—the *Catechism* is quick to admit that the "psychological genesis [of homosexuality] remains largely unexplained"—but certainly false if she's referring to same-sex activity. Yet even if she was right, and it was conclusively shown that same-sex attraction is genetically determined, that fact would be independent of whether same-sex actions are morally acceptable. Most of us are genetically predisposed to all sorts of immoral activities, but that doesn't determine the intrinsic morality *of those activities*. Even if a man is genetically predisposed to gluttony, we wouldn't praise him eating ten hamburgers in one sitting.

Martin: I reject the Church's stance on divorced members of their own religion who wish to receive the Eucharist. Isn't the Eucharist the point? Isn't it the transformative food that strengthens the spirit? How can it be denied to parishioners just because they didn't have the connections or the money to secure an annulment and I did? To my knowledge, there were no second-class citizens in Christ's following.

Fr. Brandon: Again, there's much to applaud here. Martin is right that the "Eucharist is the point." The *Catechism* describes it as "the source and summit of the Christian life" (*CCC* 1324). It's undoubtedly the "transformative food that strengthens the spirit." She's also right that nobody should be excluded from communion simply because he/she doesn't have enough money or connections. The Church regularly sings hymns based on Isaiah 55: "All you who are thirsty, come to the water! you who have no money, come, buy grain and eat," Finally, it's true that "there were no second-class citizens in Christ's following." But behind all those agreeable facts hide two serious confusions.

First, Martin assumes that divorced Catholics are not able to receive communion. This is simply not true. The Church only withholds communion from those who have civilly divorced without an annulment and then have chosen to civilly remarry. This follows from Jesus' clear command: "Whoever divorces his wife and marries another commits adultery against her; and if she divorces her husband and marries another, she commits adultery" (Mk 10:11-12). Since adultery is a mortal sin, and those living in mortal sin are not spiritually prepared to receive Christ in communion, they should refrain. Surely, Martin agrees with her "go-to" source on this topic.

Second, the annulment process does not depend exclusively—or at all—on connections or money. This is a wild assertion, and since Martin offers no evidence for her claim, we should reserve paying it serious attention.

Martin: I think statistics will bear me out when I say that population control is one of (if not the) greatest global dilemmas facing humanity today and for the foreseeable future with respect to food, water, disease, living space, and ecological repercussions. So, even if I didn't believe (which I do) that family planning is the only way to stay sane (I'm one of eight), I would still find it impossible to accept the Church's stance on birth control based on the above ethics.

Fr. Brandon: In Martin's final point, she questions the Church's rejection of artificial birth control. Her main argument is that since overpopulation is one of the greatest threats today, this rejection seems "impossible" and unethical. Yet while Martin is right that we're facing a serious population crisis, it's not overpopulation—it's under population. As the Population Research Institute shows, the global population will peak in about thirty years but will then rapidly decline (since global birth rates have reached unprecedented lows.) Overpopulation is a myth and therefore no good reason to accept artificial birth control.

Martin: Okay that's my list. (I could add married clergy, but that would exceed the word count.) What's yours? If you think you are not a cafeteria Catholic, consider Pope Francis' recent references to capitalism. Are you a capitalist? And what about war? Notwithstanding abject evil, are you in favor of killing people to protect the economic interests of your population? Such wars have been waged with and without our knowledge. Even the "holy" Crusades were acknowledged as a moral debacle centuries later. The bottom line is: these are all complex issues deserving deep thought and consideration. To be a cafeteria Catholic is a good thing if it means that you are putting your conscience first. As long as your conscience is in good shape and your ego is in check, it works. After all, history has proven that individuals, not institutions, lead the parade of evolutionary progress. Customs rooted in society must change; only truth is eternal.

Fr. Brandon: Martin can't help adding a couple more jabs in her closing remarks. For example, she demands married clergy, apparently unaware that the Catholic Church already has millions of married clergy (deacons, Eastern rite priests, former Anglican priests, etc.). She sums up her entire position with these words: "To be a cafeteria Catholic is a good thing if it means that you are putting your conscience first. As long as your conscience is in good shape and your ego is in check, it works."

The question, of course, is how do you know if your conscience is in good shape? By what objective rule is it measured? For Martin, the answer seems to be, "I measure my conscience by my own beliefs," the equivalent of painting a bull's-eye around your already-embedded arrow. I hope one day Martin will discover the emptiness of "cafeteria Catholicism," eschewing it instead for the entire banquet that Jesus offers through his Church. The former might satisfy her appetite temporarily, but only the latter will fill her soul. (*Fr. Brandon Vogt is the Content Director at Word on Fire Catholic Ministries.*)

Let me add a few words.

The theme of this book addresses the very context of secularism. This is the new enemy of the Church. It comes in many forms. Ms. Martin articulated one, as a proclaimed "cafeteria Catholic." Reading behind the lines of her arguments, she insists on even using the Jesus Christ a "cafeteria Jew" from her perspective. Of course, she did not spare Pope Francis. In essence she is saying the Pope is also a "cafeteria Catholic."

The two stories you read are studies in contrast. On one hand, the heroes of World War I are saying that we are willing to die for you but we need you to die with us, too. Make the same sacrifice that you are asking from us. On the other hand, Ms. Martin is saying that the rule of the Catholic Church is difficult to follow. I am not willing to sacrifice and she justifies her choice by saying that this is what Jesus wants.

There was a time when I used to write for *HomeLife* Magazine published by ST PAULS Publishing. An article which I wrote became the front cover of the magazine during Lent in 2006.

The Passion of The Christ—DISTURBING

Towards the end of the movie is a drop of water. It is the drop of water that says it all. New life is born. And from his pit Satan howls. He knows. Jesus is here to stay. *The Passion of The Christ* is meant to be like that, to give birth to new life.

Our deliverance came in amazing miracles. Adam and Eve lost the kingdom in the garden of Eden. God gave us a chance to recover the garden with Noah spearheading the drive for salvation. God washed the earth for forty days and forty nights. When he finally stopped the deluge the sun came out with a leaf in the dove's bill signaling a new beginning for mankind.

Man wasted that. The forty years of travel in the desert when God save us from the Egyptians were replaced instead with disobedience by dishonoring our covenant with God. And when we were finally in the Promised Land we followed the dictum of the Law but not its substance. We prayed in the temple and cursed outside as soon as our backs were turned from the tabernacle. Still God persisted. Instead of punishing us which we rightly deserved, God sent his Son to save us, to die for us. With Christ's death Satan thought that he won the fight between good and evil. He was wrong. That one drop of water representing Jesus Christ's blood gave us new hope.

My wife, Leth, captured in one word the effect that the movie had on us: disturbing. *The Passion of The Christ* unsettled me. A Filipino friend said, "It is a miracle movie." An American friend commented and saw it from another perspective. He did not find anything significant about the movie. "I was disappointed," he said. "After all those big brouhaha they ended up with nothing."

He saw nothing but horror.

I said, "If you watched it with the usual slant to entertain, you are right. As a horror movie, there were better movies shown. The series on Dracula will win hands down."

How odd. Two cultures saw it from different perspectives.

But *The Passion of The Christ* is not meant to entertain. If there is anything that the movie wanted, it is to remind people that the predictions in the Book of Revelation are now more accurate than ever. Man is going back to his old ways, openly defying, challenging God's ways. Of course, there will be hell to pay.

I now know why the Catholic Bishops' Conference, while encouraging the parishioners to watch *The Passion of The Christ*, asked the people to watch it with open minds and not hate the Jews. Mark, one of the evangelists saw it best in his gospel.

> Now on the occasion of the feast he used to release to them one prisoner whom they requested. A man called Barabbas was then in prison along with the rebels who had committed murder in a rebellion. The crowd came forward and began to ask him to do for them as he was accustomed. Pilate answered, "Do you want me to release to you the king of the Jews?" For he knew that it was out of envy that the chief priests had handed him over.
>
> But the chief priests stirred up the crowd to have him release Barabbas for them instead. Pilate again said to them in reply, "Then what [do you want] me to do with [the man you call] the king of the Jews?" They shouted again, "Crucify him." Pilate said to them, "Why? What evil has he done?" They only shouted the louder, "Crucify him." So Pilate, wishing to satisfy the crowd, released Barabbas to them and, after he had Jesus scourged, handed him over to be crucified.

And the Jews, the chosen people, sealed their fate forever.

You cannot help but hate the Jews for doing what they did. They were inflamed with so much hatred for a man that did them no wrong. The years that followed the death of Christ were the beginning of the decline of a nation so loved by God that he gave them the land of promise, to enjoy the milk and honey that flow from its bosoms. The people that God loved so much, the people to whom he made a covenant to love and protect, was the same people that crucified his beloved Son. It is no wonder that generations after generations, the Jews were the people that roamed the earth with no place of their own.

So much was written about their holocaust. But their suffering as a people was in fact a glorious day, a victory. Finally, the sympathy of nations recovering from the devastation of a big war granted them the one thing they can never have, a piece of land. And yet, their find created another upheaval that today continue to sow fear and hatred among the Jews and the Muslim world.

It is an unusual movie, this *The Passion of The Christ*, where people as one, stepped out of the theater, silent. In deep thought, they were engrossed with themselves. There was this feeling of guilt that for every pounding of the nail on the cross, each stroke was made heavier by the brunt of our sins. There were no usual comments of how good the actor was, or how well it was directed, or how entertaining the whole picture was, because all that I heard was silence, a deafening silence, as people slowly thronged out to the nearest exit.

Personally, after all the years of praying the Rosary, especially the Sorrowful Mysteries, I came to understand better what the passion really means and why Jesus died for me. He said, "I am the way and the truth and the light. No one comes to the Father except through me" (Jn 14:6).

The movie made me realized the real suffering of Jesus. I felt that every hit, every drop of blood that splattered, every wound inflicted by the Romans soldiers is the stroke of every sin that I committed. And yet Jesus was above it all. "Father, forgive them, they know not what they do" (Lk 23:34).

It is a lesson of understanding why I am a Catholic, a believer, that what God did as a man is the only way he can bring me back to the side of his Father. That without his suffering, I will never have the chance to leave my sins and be free from the clutches of evil.

My wife said, "We really are soul mates." The movie had the same effect on me… disturbing.

The Book of Wisdom 18:14-16; 19:6-9, captures in essence the message of the movie:

> For when peaceful stillness encompassed everything and the night in its swift course was half spent, your all-powerful word from heaven's royal throne leapt into the doomed land, a fierce warrior bearing the sharp sword of your inexorable decree, and alighted, and filled every place with death, and touched heaven, while standing upon the earth.
>
> For all creation, in its several kinds, was being made over anew, serving your commands, that your children might be preserved unharmed. The cloud overshadowed their camp; and out of what had been water, dry land was seen emerging: Out of the Red Sea an unimpeded road, and a grassy plain out of the mighty flood. Over this crossed the whole nation sheltered by your hand, and they beheld stupendous wonders. For they ranged about like horses, and leapt like lambs, praising you, Lord, their deliverer.

This work that Mel Gibson created is a classic, a movie that you want to see over and over. This explanation from a theological sense shows clearly that Jesus Christ's supreme sacrifice is *the price of heaven*.

My friend John, standing extreme right, on the way home… greeted by thousands of yellow ribbons hanging on trees lining the road… the whole darn barn cheering!

Green, Green, Grass
of Home

Dear Pope Francis, as I was about to bring the manuscript to my publisher when I received an e-mail from my friend John:

Dear Rudy,
I had my First Communion when I was eight years old.

If memory serves, there were more than 20 of us communicants at the Espiritu Santo Church along the corner of Avenida Rizal and Tayuman in Manila. All were visibly impatient and fidgety in their seats in anticipation of the distribution of the Eucharist. Then, before the time of the Extraordinary Minister of Holy Communion (EMHC), it was the priest himself who served the host to communicants who knelt around the altar. For your information, I was once an EMHC at the St. Anthony Parish Church in our locality. One Sunday, after Holy Mass, our parish priest approached me and invited me to his office where he announced my "appointment" as such. Oddly, he did not ask for my acceptance, but immediately emphasized that the identification of prospective EMHCs are made through the priest's discernment. I would have asked, why me? Four Saturdays of seminar followed at the Arzobizpado in Intramuros.

Excuse me for that digressions.

Two weeks earlier, the good Sr. Delia momentarily took over from our regular student-tutor from Espiritu Santo to walk us through the Holy Communion protocol. A portion of her message stuck to me, and, I guess, also to the other eight-year-olds. She said the moment we take into our mouths the Holy Eucharist we will feel an almost indescribable feeling of elation, almost a free-flying sensation—in today's parlance, an emotional high. "You would have sprouted wings."

To most eight-year-olds, that statement can only be taken literally, especially coming from a Catholic nun "who will not tell a lie."

But even then, much earlier, Sr. Delia told us a wonderful story:

There was once a mother who introduced to her own son a hunchback boy as his playmate. She was very careful to emphasize to her son not to refer to the boy's deformity as this has always been a very sensitive matter to him. She admonished her son to play with the handicapped boy as a friend as if he is perfectly normal. However, only after a few minutes of playing, she was very much dismayed to hear her son ask his playmate, "I know what is on your back. Do you?"

The handicapped boy was visibly embarrassed, but before he could utter a word, the son answered his own question for him, and said, "That mound holds your wings. Someday God will break it open, and you will fly away like an angel."

Of course, no wings were forthcoming to any of us. But the good sister told the truth about that extra special sensation. I can never forget how I felt then. Never mind if it was all from our imagination triggered by a potent suggestion from a Godly person. Never mind if my hunger pain was trying to crowd out the "heavenly" feeling. During the time, a communicant was supposed to fast, including avoiding a sip of water, hours before Holy Communion.

All these years I have search to recapture that heavenly feeling.

I had put so much thought about how and when I can tell you about what I really and honestly felt about religion because that heavenly feeling which I have been longing for continues to be elusive.

As you may know, my hesitancy was prodded by my acute awareness of and deference to your—and someone else's—devotion to the Roman Catholic religion. Just then you announced to me that you were starting to write a new book—your seventh, but was still undecided on a central plot. In the end, you made up your mind to feature my own John character as the principal figure in the story. For me, this was perfect timing.

As I wrote you, I no longer subscribe to organized religion, in view of my unhappy encounters with representatives of the Catholic Church with their acts and deportments which I firmly believed were serious and outright contradictions of what I was told and read about the faith. I was severely disillusioned!

Here I was reminded of the same situation from a Dutch boss in an earlier employment, which he wrote me about. Recently, he stopped going to his church—a Baptist—but made sure that he continue with his tithes "for the benefit of those who still do."

Once during one of our numerous travels together, we saw by the sidewalk (along the same street where Cebu City's Sto. Niño Cathedral is located); an elderly male beggar sprawled on sections of what were once carton boxes, this time his makeshift bed.

According to the sidewalk vendors, the poor man has been in the same spot for some years. It is not difficult to imagine how a typical mendicant like him looked like. But this poor man was different. He had a gaping hole where his right nostril should be. His skin on his face was starting to peel off, and the rest of the surface had this uncharacteristic sheen not unlike that of a *lechon*. His begging hand was badly gnarled! It was obvious that he was an unfortunate victim of Hansen's disease, commonly known as leprosy! No wonder, he was being ignored by passersby including the locals and tourist visitors of the nearby church.

But not my Boss, the Dutchman!

We approached the beggar. I interpreted for my boss. We were going to take him to a hospital for medical attention. My boss bodily carried him to the taxi cab that I hailed. Inside at the back seat, the man lay across our laps—his head on the Dutch's and his feet also showing the ravages of his disease—on mine! The stench was worse than that in Tabuan, a nearby town in Cebu City noted for its wide variety of dried fish.

I cannot help but recall the story of Mother Teresa of Calcutta who, one day while walking in one of the poorest districts in Mumbai, chanced upon a beggar sprawled in the gutter. Mother Teresa nursed the man and had him brought to the nearest hospital with the help of kind bystanders. Nurses were busy in the hospital. She did not leave the leprous man but washed his gaping wounds whose smell was noxious to a hospital security guard who remarked, "I will not do that for a million dollars."

To which Mother Teresa replied, "Neither will I," meaning, she is willing to do it for free, for love.

Let me continue.

We were refused admittance by the first private hospital we got into. Instead, we were referred to a public hospital which maintains a leprosarium. Here the Dutch arranged for the admission of the beggar, left some cash with the hospital concierge, with the message to call him in Manila for additional funding. Before we proceeded to our destination, he gave the beggar "pocket money."

Doesn't this remind you of the parable of the Good Samaritan?

In another event in Davao City, the Dutch and I steeled ourselves to have our first attempt at the much-talked-about durian fruit, which reputedly "smells like hell but tastes like heaven." He bought a whole fruit for each of us. We collected our best efforts to ignore and not to be discouraged by the fruit's characteristic smell. When the vendor handed to us the yellowish flesh of durian, I noticed a handful of boys who clearly needed a bath and definitely not in their Sunday's best around us, gawking as if waiting for something.

As quickly as we put a piece of durian in our mouths, we spat out the morsel. What happened next embarrassed me as a native, at the same time must have appalled my boss! The poor boys bested and jostled against each other in order to grab for the durian which we just rejected even before the pieces hit the ground. Obviously, the boys had anticipated our not-too-subtle "rejection" of the fruit which has remained unaffordable to them.

They have witnessed the monumental failures of a number of intrepid souls who have gone before us.

My boss quickly made an ocular "census" of the boys around at that time, which numbered about 20 in all. He called them and bought for each the much-sought-after "king of fruit" so called.

But the experience, emotional and heartrending as it was, did not bring back the old heavenly feeling. I had merely a temporary high… that was all that it was!

My disappointment with wayward priests continued to gnaw at me. I believe when Jesus in Matthew 23:13 said, "Woe to you, scribes and Pharisees, you hypocrites. You lock the kingdom of heaven before human beings.. You do not enter yourselves, nor do you allow entrance to those trying to enter."

He was expressing his thoughts about institutionalized, legalistic religion as a major obstacle to genuine and honest faith. True, Jesus' outburst was grating to the people around him who claimed to be religious yet whose decorum in their daily lives did not coincide with their outside projections. He warned, "Not everyone who says to me, 'Lord, Lord,' will enter the kingdom of heaven, but only the one who does the will of my Father in heaven" (Mt 7:21).

I believe that this was a timely reminder that we cannot always judge who is and who is not a Christian. I began to nurture the belief that organized religion has become a stumbling block or a Berlin wall rather than a widely opened welcoming portal into God's presence.

I am afraid that the Church which I once knew has degenerated into religion without the true Spirit. Many people I know go to church, not out of piety, but because they have to be seen by their neighbors and friends. Some have to catch up with the latest gossip. The younger set have to meet their beloved, while some have a new branded Sunday's best to show off!

They have mutated into mechanical Christians. I distinctly remember one Sunday, in the middle of a Mass, I deliberately set aside my good manners, glowered at the Mother Butler's, an all-female church lay group, seated immediately behind me in their blue-and-white attires and shushed them. A few minutes earlier, I threw them my sharpest dagger-looks, but still they continued conversing among each other in loud tones enough to distract the other churchgoers seated nearby. And they were talking about last night's TV soap opera episode!

It was reported that Gandhi once said, "I like your Christ, but I do not like your Christians. Yout Christians are so unlike Christ."

I recall what a certain personality commented, "Christianity is doing what Christ did. That is why we are called Christians."

Rudy, as one of my closest friends, I was very much distressed to read about your anxiety and worry that my attitude towards organized religion is a prelude to secularism. However, I take this as a brotherly tap on my shoulder to remind me that God is ever present in our daily life.

You will notice that in his parables Jesus constantly used the analogy of life. He said that the kingdom of heaven can be compared to sowing seeds on the ground; to a vine sprouting branches; to a faith which begins as small as a mustard seed. His liberal use of parables is evidence of Jesus' concern with daily life. In John 17:15—"I do not ask that you take them out of the world, but that you keep them from the evil one."

Jesus clearly expressed his concern with daily life not only as the subject of his parables but with the manner that he used them. But, of course, Jesus with his true-to-life parables did not intend to hold scriptures hostage to the capriciousness of contemporary life. Rather, he cites the contemporary context as an entry point to exploring and understanding true faith.

After living in the good part of my seventy-plus years, I have personally witnessed, heard from personalities themselves, and read about how people lose and find their own religion. People undergo a seemingly unending process. For some, the seeds of faith sown in them as early as when they were even barely able to walk, grew into oak-like trees due to the fertile ground into which the kernels were planted. For others the faith that they grew up with loses its meaning and significance as they reach their adolescence. Still a number of people who never even gave a fleeting thought about the spiritual, would develop a compelling urge to explore religion.

Rudy, you wrote earlier about the very much identifiable stages of spiritual development that people go through. I am not sure where I can be found in these stages when I declare—"I am spiritual, but not religious." which may be the same as saying—"I no longer subscribe to organized religion."

I declared this to you in all boldness because I am quite confident that you are not judgmental and narrow-minded. You realize that spiritual development is a process.

I guess we all have our own individual spiritual mountains to climb. Often there are stumbling blocks—people and events that threaten to impede the progress of our spiritual life. I'd like to imagine that until I had several of my sad and unfortunate encounters with personalities and occurrences several years ago; I was almost in the middle of my mountain.

I am fully aware that there are many paths along the mountain which one may choose from. One rough path may be strewn with boulders and rocks and lush with trees and similar outcroppings. Another may be smooth but steep. Indeed, it is too tempting to decide to take the latter because of the lack of obstacles present in the former.

However, the climber will soon realize that the rocks, boulders, and vegetation, which he initially considered as stumbling blocks, provide him firm foothold and hand rails that will prop him higher. But he needs some time and an inordinate amount of exhausting efforts to be able to negotiate the obstacles. On the other hand with the smooth path, he will find himself often sliding down, thus cancelling a few feet from the progress which he makes each time.

Which path to choose?

I'd like to share with you what can be called "clergy jokes" which I once read. I believe, they can be taken as an enumeration, hopefully in an entertainment mode, of the "personalities and events" that I wrote about in the earlier part of this letter:

> A distraught woman went to see the parish priest and asked him if he would say final prayers during the funeral of her dog which died. "I cannot do that, Ma'am, he said. "Why don't you try the Protestant minister?"
>
> "OK," she said, "but please, may I seek your advice? How much must I pay for his services—is ten thousand pesos good enough?"
>
> "Hold on," he said, "why didn't you tell me that your dog was Catholic?"

✤ ✤ ✤ ✤ ✤

> A rabbi and a priest were discussing their professions. "Do you ever get ambitious?" asked the priest.
>
> "Well," said the rabbi, "I suppose that I could always move to a larger congregation. What about you?"
>
> "Well, I suppose I could become a cardinal," the priest replied.
>
> "And then?" the rabbi pursued.
>
> "Well, theoretically it is possible that I could become a Pope."
>
> "And then?" asked the rabbi.
>
> "Isn't that enough? Do you want me to become God?" said the priest.
>
> "Well," replied the rabbi in a soft voice, "one of our boys made it!"

Meantime, my spiritual mountain beckons. Alas, years afterward, that wonderful "feeling" has remained elusive to me. My continuing study, the good deeds I do, the love I share with my family and friends, even the lightness of spirit I nurse did not bring back the heavenly feeling I felt when the Holy Eucharist touched my tongue the first time…

…Until that "session" which you arranged with Fr. Joe.

Before we parted after several minutes of enlightening conversation, I requested the kindly priest to bless me. After asking me to kneel down before him, he cupped his hands over my head and intoned—*"I bless you in the name of the Father and of the Son and of the Holy Spirit."*

Immediately, there was that wonderful magical "feeling" again!

Thanks a million, Rudy!

Pope Francis, as they say, when heaven let raindrops fall, it comes in torrent. Before I could even leave for my appointment with my publisher, another message through my mobile phone came:

> Rudy,
>
> Thank you very much for your concern, I have gratefully experienced and have been a recipient of God's perfect timing. He did not merely answer my prayers, he granted most of them. Someday you and Del (a classmate in high school) may find me seated abreast both of you at Christ the King Church.
>
> Thank you a million.

> John,
>
> Thank you, make it soon.
>
> Rudy

Isang Pihit Lang, Sa Kanan

$\mathcal{A}$ few days after I finished this manuscript, I had this sense that the book is not complete. I hesitated sending it to ST PAULS Publishing. There was this empty feeling that something was missing.

One Sunday morning, I wasn't feeling well so I switch on the TV to EWTN. I caught the priest about to begin his homily. His opening words were, "Let me invite everyone who belong to other faiths to come and join the Catholic Church."

I strengthened up on my chair interested. "But I am especially inviting Catholics who left the fold because of mistakes I may have made or some other priests, or parishioners who may have wronged you."

He paused as if trying to choose the next words, "I am truly sorry."

"Please do not let my mistake, our mistakes keep you away. Do not let a person change your life forever."

"Please forgive me."

That was the homily.

After the Mass, I opened the Bible and searched for the readings. The homily was related to:

Rom 13:8-10
Owe nothing to anyone, except to love one another; for the one who loves another has fulfilled the law. The commandments, "You shall not commit adultery; you shall not kill; you shall not

steal; you shall not covet," and whatever other commandment there may be, are summed up in this saying, [namely] "You shall love your neighbor as yourself." Love does no evil to the neighbor; hence, love is the fulfillment of the law.

I knew what was missing. I have not been very clear with message of the book. I called my friend John and requested him to help write the epilogue (not that he has not done so much already).

What he wrote was full of anguish, heart-crushing words, yet forgiving, chiseled with such eloquence that made me a bit guilty that somehow I may have forced him to reveal the secret which he kept in his heart for so long. Here it is:

> Illegitimate…
> *Bastardo…*
> *Anak sa labas…*
> *Putok sa buho…!*

Pejoratives all! But the most biting was: *"Hindi ko nga alam kung saan nanggaling ang batang yan!* (I really do not know where that boy came from)!" Thus remarked by no less than a high-ranked non-Catholic Christian church leader referring to a five-year-old while seated in the *"Obispo's"* dining room. He was an uncle of the boy's mother. To the boy in his innocence, the thoughtless and unkind utterance would otherwise be totally insignificant. But when he espied that his mother furtively threw him a worried look, he knew that it was a missive meant to deride. It was then when he felt its painful stab!

Now I know. No wonder, my older playmates would boisterously shout at me, *"Walang tatay! Walang tatay!"* each time I beat them in our backyard games! Clearly, they were innocently parroting what they must have heard what their elders had to say about me.

Like Hester Prynne, the adulteress in Nathaniel Hawthorne's *Scarlet Letter*, I imagined emblazoned across my chest was *"Walang tatay!"* for all to see!

The good part of my youth had been one of pretending and imagining! One time, my elementary school teacher prodded the students to tell a short story about their fathers' occupation. As an aid, she flashed sheets of Manila paper each with illustration of a man at work. One by one, my classmates proudly recited their short accounts. Then the picture of a carpenter came. When no one raised his hand, I did mine and stood up. Haltingly I started, "My father is a carpenter..." while trying to be as believable as I could!

The session went on. Then on the third (fourth?) sheet when no one "claimed" the picture of an ambulant ice vendor, I once again stood up and staked my own, "My Tatay is a *sorbetero*..." There were laughter, unsuccessfully stifled, in the classroom. *"Dalawa ang Tatay mo?"* A seatmate exclaimed.

My Nanay's meager wage could hardly afford my basic necessities. Very much less the reversible jackets which were in vogue among the male teeners then. There was this hand-me-down jacket from an elder cousin, which I imagined was specially tailored for me by Windsor's, the tailor of choice, by many more fortunate students. I had to triple fold its sleeves to reveal my hands. My mother had stitched to the shoulder the right sleeve which has started to separate. My Jacinto rubber shoes had to be lined with separate layers of newspaper to plug the now gaping hole on its sole. I tried to convince myself those were Converse-Chuck Taylors, the Rolls Royce, of sneakers in 1950s.

More than a year ago, my high school friend, the three-time awardee of the prestigious Catholic Mass Media Awards for his authored true-to-life Bible-centered books, Rudy, proposed to write about my life story in his seventh book. In direct contrast to my much-unfounded efforts to hide my paternal situation in my younger years, I readily agreed.

I feel that I owe it to the "bastards, *putok sa buho*, illegitimates" to assure them that it is never too late to have a second happy childhood. I wish that they will open themselves, as I did, to the divine guidance which will lead them to the right relationships, and that they, too, will experience the perfect timing of coincidences. The latter is God's way of staying incognito. But in reality, it is his handiwork of providential intervention in human events.

Merriam-Webster Dictionary defines homestretch as "the part of a racetrack between the last turn and the finish line"; "the final stage." This is where the expectant racing enthusiasts' huff and puff where they stood, psychically willing their respective horse bets to lengthen and multiply the animals' strides for the dash to the finish line. Excitement will be at fever pitch. The riders stand on their stirrups but their body hunched down on the horses' neck to diminish the resistance of the onrushing wind, giving it all they've got to beat the rest.

At almost 76 years of age, I find myself on the homestretch. I successfully hurdled the ruts and puddles and sharp turns of the track; survived the crowding and nudges and similar foul tactics of my "co-racers" as we sped along; as the underdog endured the taunting of the grandstand spectators who are cheering for the odds-on favorite. At last I made the last turn. The straight part of the race track looms ahead promising an "easier ride." Or so I thought.

The Apostle Paul wrote in Philippians 3:12-16, "It is not that I have already taken hold of it or have already attained perfect maturity, but I continue my pursuit in hope that I may possess it, since I have indeed been taken possession of by Christ [Jesus]. Brothers, I for my part do not consider myself to have taken possession. Just one thing: forgetting what lies behind but straining forward to what lies ahead. I continue my pursuit toward the goal, the prize of God's upward calling, in Christ Jesus. Let us, then, who are "perfectly mature" adopt this attitude. And if you have a different attitude, this, too, God will reveal to you. Only, with regard to what we have attained, continue on the same course.

I realize that most definitely, the homestretch, deceitfully looking easy riding, is a place where one must concentrate all that is left of his energies and singular resolve to push for the finish line.

The thoughtful loving care of my children rendered to me a comfortable life. They provide me with material things which were but dreamed of and wished for during my younger years. Nanay was right, or might I say prophetic, every time she assuaged my childish frustration over not being able to obtain what I wanted that would be beyond her means: *"Hayaan mo, John, paglaki mo magkakaroon ka rin niyan. Mag-aral kang mabuti. May awa ang Diyos* (Be assured, John, you can have those items when you grow up. Just make good with your schooling. God's grace will see to that)."

Sadly, even then as now, I have this gnawing feeling of a vacuum in my persona.

I still remember this wonderful, heavenly feeling when, for the very first time at Holy Communion, the officiating priest (at the Espiritu Santo Church at the corner of Rizal Avenue and Tayuman Street in Manila), laid on my tongue the holy wafer. I felt it melt away in my mouth. Later, I tried with all my might to squeeze from my gland as much saliva as I could to be able to swallow the few solid pieces of the bread. The day before our First Communion, our religious instructor was emphatic with her instructions to see to it that we swallow every bit of the Communion bread. And that we should not spit out a drop of our saliva until after we take something solid or liquid into our mouth.

The after-Communion flighty sensation stayed with me each time. However, as I grew up, with the realities of life and people around me, I noticed the degree of this sensation diminished, slowly at first, then disappeared altogether.

The cruel remark of the "Obispo"; my embarrassment during my wedding day caused by the thoughtless and very unchristian acts of a parish priest; the sight of another parish priest with his fiesta-like dining table laden with pork and meats on a Good Friday; the whisper to a church volunteer of another one to allow special accommodation to someone with the offer of a generous sum; the blatant indiscretion of a well-known church leader, and a few more. I believe that these realities have sterilized my mind and emotions to the terrible extent that I started to doubt the integrity of organized religion and its people.

One afternoon, that elusive "airy, floating-like" feeling, although ever slightly, crept up on me. My friend, Rudy, twisted my arms sufficiently enough to get me meet Fr. Joe, his spiritual adviser. After almost 30 minutes, I requested the good Spanish father to grant me his blessings. While kneeling down, Fr. Joe cupped his left hand on my head, and made the sign of the cross with his right. Was that my imagination of having been lifted up?

Still, despite this, I find convenient excuses to Rudy's repeated request to bring me to a similar encounter with his godly spiritual adviser. I can only ask him to be extra patient with me. I just couldn't tell him that I am almost there.

Once I espied a small boy wearing a T-shirt on which was prominently printed, "Please have patience with me. God isn't finished with me yet." But I assure him that I am becoming spiritually alive again. Thanks to his (and "Lisa's") efforts and prayers. A religious author once wrote, "To be spiritually alive means to be growing and changing; not to settle down among a series of systemized beliefs and duties, but to endure and go on enduring the strains, conflicts, and difficulties incident to development."

Another one commented, "It is only through struggling with the pain of our own crises, tragedies, sins, depressions, and problems that our greatness as human beings is realized. Our crises are anvils on which our growth is forged."

Once there was the story of a youngster who was energetically pedaling his bike upwards on an incline of the road. Shortly, he was pleased to give way to a passing passenger jeep. His intention was to grab hold of the vehicle's *estribo* or loading platform and then be ferried by the jeep. And without exerting any effort, he may be dragged by the vehicle over the steep incline. Alas, the vehicle was running too fast to give him the chance to have a handhold. Laboriously, he continued pedaling. Then he espied another passenger jeep. He had the same intention, but this time as the vehicle ran in front of him, the passengers at the back directly in front of the estribo extended their arms to the young biker. He grabbed at the arms. The vehicle pulled the thankful biker over the incline.

I can be that young biker. The arms held towards me are from my "advocates," Nanay, my shepherds, Rudy and "Lisa" who will not tire guiding me back to the fold.

I have been very fortunate to meet the right kind of people in my more than 75 years. I believe that there is the Divine Director who provides each one the prods and cues towards the right relationships.

There was his bigheartedness in causing me to have special relationship with the following individuals:

My Nanay—she for the whole of 39 years, before an unforgiving and pharisaical society, fortified herself against unkind remarks for being a single mother, and steeled herself in cold, lonely nights, braved through almost menial jobs to enable her to selflessly nurture and guide me until her death at age 67.

"Lisa"—although I was not the lucky recipient of her valentine-heart, she, with my own deep-blossomed emotions of a teenager, taught me that my *Scarlet Letter* can be sufficiently obscured, albeit momentarily, to embolden me to have most pleasurable and memorable 30-minute walks with her to her home. (Presently, I am very happy to hear from Rudy, that he and the lady extend to me their Christian-hearts). She "substantiated" to me the adage, "You know it's love when all you want is that person to be happy, even if you are not part of their happiness."

Sally, Nene, Bot—former caring office mate, selflessly loving sweetheart and life partner *non-pariel*. She who gave me four wonderful children and forever eradicated the stigma of my own scarlet letter. The boldest and most trusting St. Scholastica-St. Paul's educated woman for vetting on a Cecilio Apostol Elementary School-Arellano (Public School) graduate whom she favored instead of Ateneo blues and La Salle greens.

Carol—my present wife. She unashamedly and decisively "crossed borders" to tell me of her love that one dismal day after having lost Bot sometime back and losing my job the week before! She who bore me an intelligent son who passed with high marks all his entrance exams at the Ateneo, UST, and UP where he is now enrolled.

Divine intervention is unmistakable to people meeting towards committed relationships, and who are drawn together to teach each other lessons. The latter all but prepare each individual for another new and similar relationship. We all have our own profound almost magical relationships provided for by the Divine Creator. All that has to be done is to simply look—be thankful.

I was this boy. When I was young, I was also outside of the Church. How I long to come in!

Rudy's *Letters to Pope Francis* will open the eyes of every reader to the magnanimity of God's boundless love, if only one puts his unqualified trust in him. The book will remind everyone that we, as frail merely created humans, can only fill our jugs with plain water. It is up to God to convert this water into wine.

With God's grace they will not be disappointed.

Please continue praying for me. "Just one more turn to the right and I am inside with you in Jesus Christ's Church."

GOD BLESS US ALL!!

I now pick up John's narrative.

John, your youthful experiences, living at the time when cultural imperfections dictate condemnation of "sinners" by the very people who should have given their understanding and love, left trauma in your mind. Living with people who are "poor in spirit" and literally living in poverty was a sure-fire prescription for turning against the workers of the Lord. It seems that even the gods in Olympus were against you.

Understandably, anyone in your situation would fight to maintain dignity and honor to the point where, looking for someone to blame, short of blaming God, he blames his wayward workers. In the process, he blames the whole church.

Without passing judgment on anyone, not on you, not for a million years, when the whole Church is blamed for the mistake of a few, then that someone has reached the primordial seventh deadly sin, which is the sin of pride. St. Thomas Aquinas described it: "Pride is the excessive belief in one's own abilities that interferes with the individual's recognition of the grace of God. It has been called the sin where all other sins arise." He added, "The root of pride is found to consist in man not being, in some way, subject to God and his rules."

Pope Francis, as I put the last period in my letters to you, please know that we keep in our heart your teachings that reflect on *the wounds of Christ*. Sometimes we are tempted to be that kind of Christian who keep the Lord's wounds at arms length. Yet, Jesus wants us to touch human misery, to touch the suffering flesh of others. He hopes that we will stop looking for those personal or communal niches which shelter us from the maelstrom of human misfortune and instead enter into the reality of other people's lives and know the power of tenderness.

Still, we keep in mind your *way of beauty*—where every form of catechesis would do well to attend to *way of beauty*. Proclaiming Christ means showing that to believe and follow him is not only something right and true, but also something beautiful, capable of filling life with new splendor and profound joy, even in the midst of difficulties. Every expression of true beauty can thus be acknowledged as path leading to the encounter with the Lord Jesus.

OTHER BOOKS BY THE AUTHOR